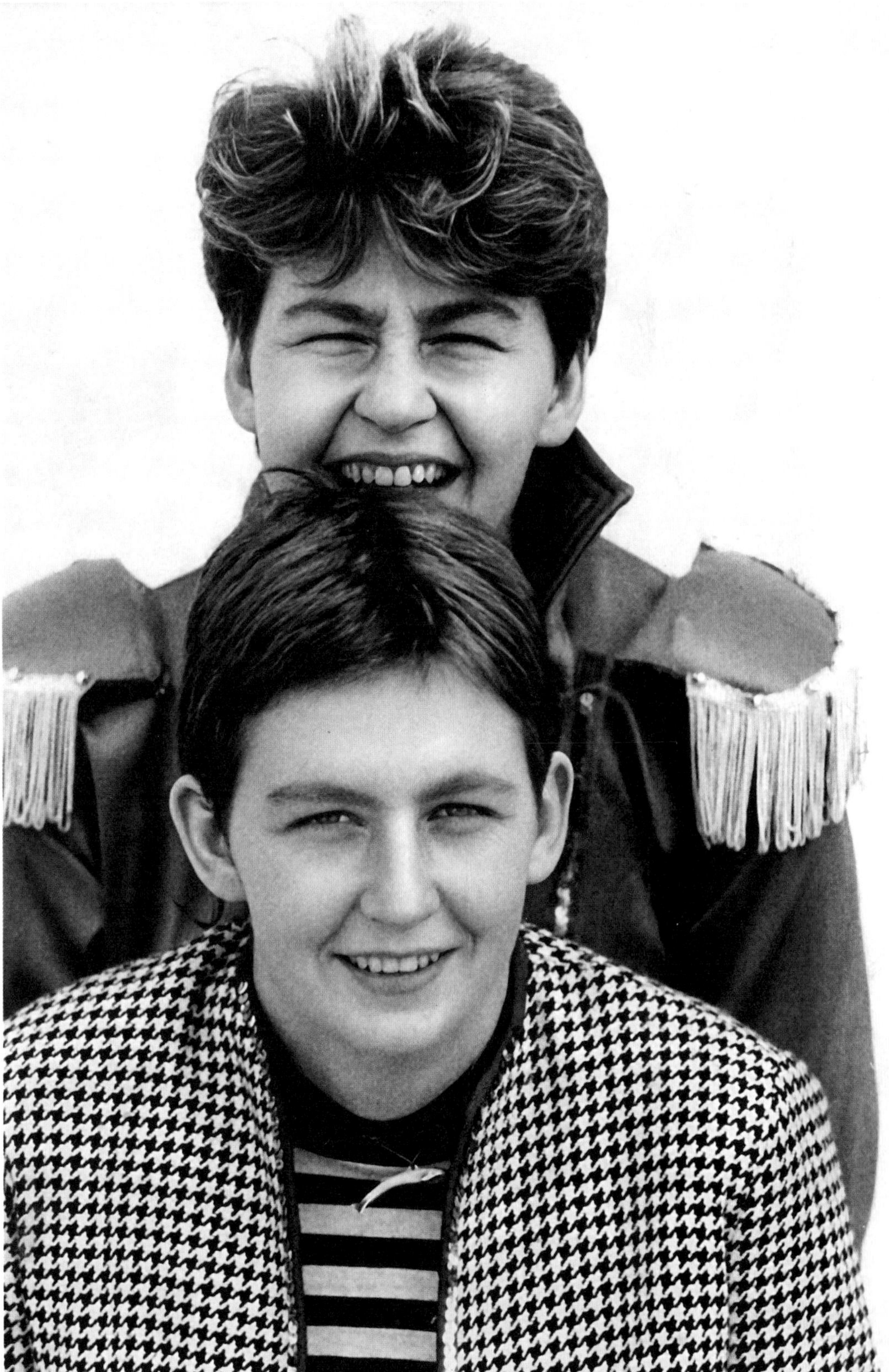

Untouchable
GIRLS

Untouchable GIRLS

The Topp Twins' Story

Jools and Lynda Topp

ALLEN&UNWIN
SYDNEY·MELBOURNE·AUCKLAND·LONDON

AUTHORS' NOTE

You will hear from both of us in this book. To help you out, Jools writes in the black text and Lynda writes in the grey text.

First published in 2023

Text © Julie and Lynda Topp, 2023

Image credits: cover photographs as credited on the back cover; p. 2 Jocelyn Carlin / New Zealand Students Arts Council; p. 6 photographer unknown / used with permission of Are Media; p. 9 Sally Tagg. All other images as credited throughout. Every effort has been made to trace the owners of copyright material. If you have any information concerning copyright material in this book, please contact the publisher at the address below.

All rights reserved. No part of this book may be reproduced or transmitted in any form or by any means, electronic or mechanical, including photocopying, recording or by any information storage and retrieval system, without prior permission in writing from the publisher.

Allen & Unwin
Level 2, 10 College Hill, Freemans Bay
Auckland 1011, New Zealand
Phone: (64 9) 377 3800
Email: auckland@allenandunwin.com
Web: www.allenandunwin.co.nz

83 Alexander Street
Crows Nest NSW 2065, Australia
Phone: (61 2) 8425 0100

A catalogue record for this book is available from the National Library of New Zealand.

ISBN 978 1 99100 638 7

Design by Katrina Duncan
Set in Silva Text
Printed in China by 1010 Printing Limited

1 3 5 7 9 10 8 6 4 2

MIX
Paper | Supporting responsible forestry
FSC® C016973

To Mum and Dad

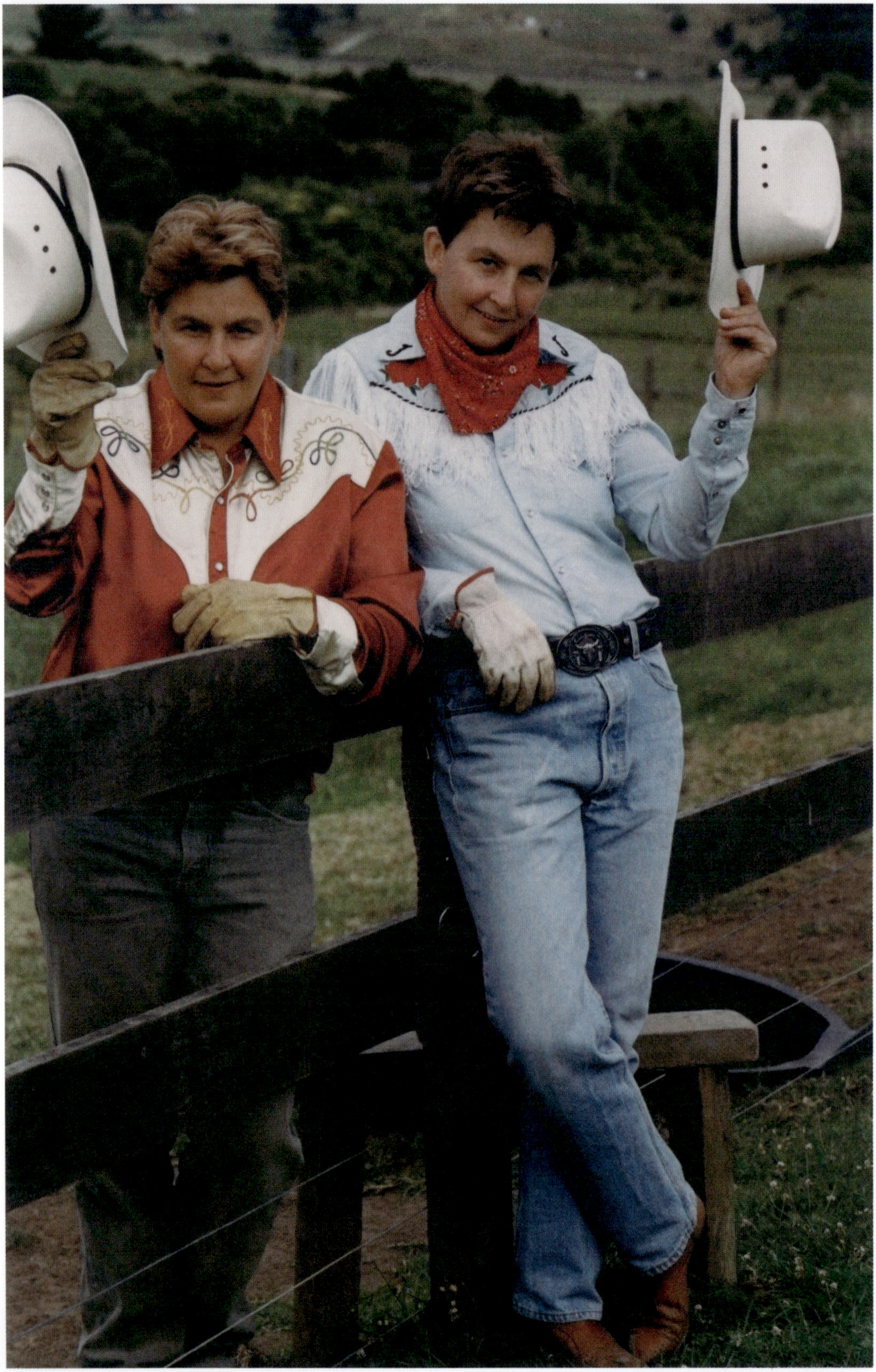

Contents

	Preface	11
1.	Country Girls	13
2.	Stewed Tamarillos	27
3.	Brother Bruce	39
4.	School Days	51
5.	Jools on a Slippery Slope	63
6.	Joining the Army	71
7.	Dunedin: The Topp Twins are Born	87
8.	Auckland: The Place to Be	95
9.	1981: Part of History	105
10.	Outlaws in the Bush	119
11.	Busking and Busted	125
12.	The Art of Political Protest	135
13.	The Gingham Sisters	147
14.	The End of the Rainbow	159
15.	Australia and the World	167
16.	The Gypsy Caravan Tour	177
17.	Arani Enters Our Lives	185
18.	Feathers, Leathers, Boas and G-strings	189
19.	'You Boys Sure Are Funny'	201
20.	Camp Mother, Camp Leader and the Kens	209
21.	The Edinburgh Fringe Festival	225
22.	Mary and Donna	233
23.	When Cancer Comes Calling	243
24.	Untouchable Girls	251
25.	Wedding Belles	261

26.	Topp Country	267
27.	Horses are My Life	277
28.	Two Dames Lose their Beloved Dad	283
29.	Lockdown	291
30.	Sneaky Little Creep	297
31.	Topp Class: The Topp Twins Tribute Show	305

Epilogue	311
Topp Twins Awards and Honours	315
Acknowledgements	319

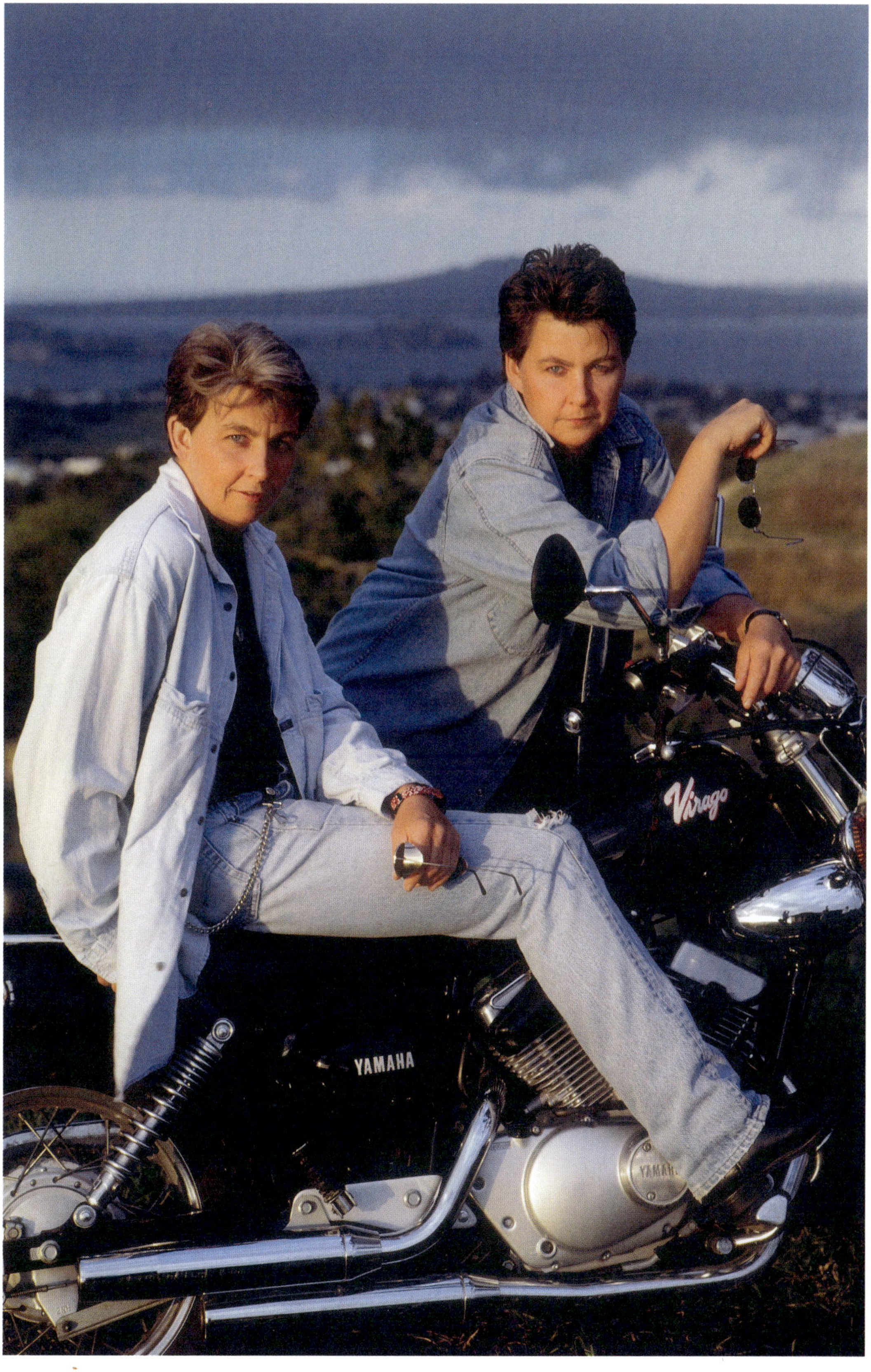

Virago
YAMAHA

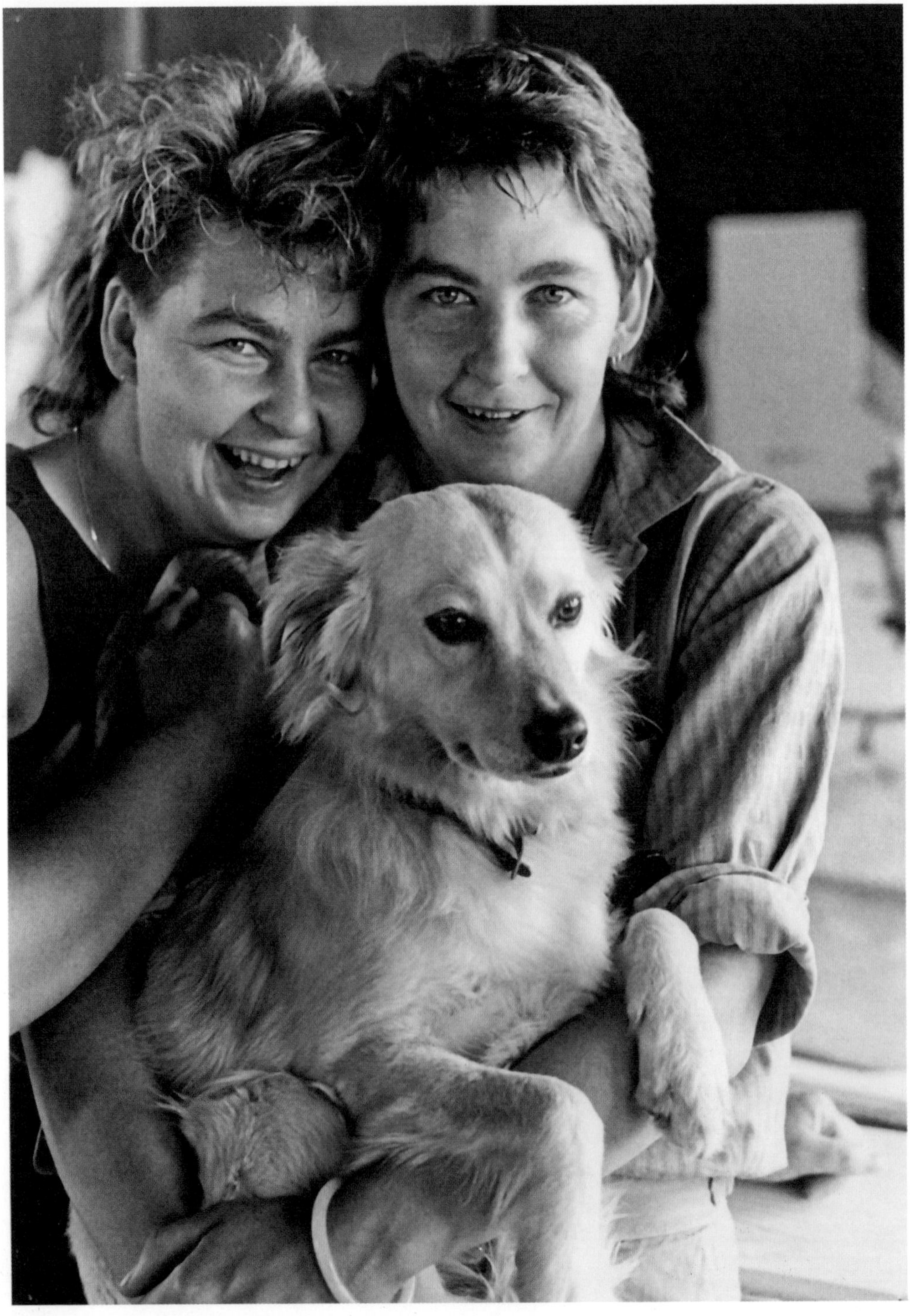

Preface

I'm in a hospital gown — two of my least favourite things.

Hospitals because I have cancer, and gowns because I'd rather be in a pair of old jeans and a checked shirt. Anyway, I'm lying on a hard table about to have my first session of radiation treatment, and I can't help but think of the song Lynda wrote to champion New Zealand's nuclear-free movement back in the day.

The song's chorus said it all: *I only hope that we don't die from radiation burns*. I almost laugh out loud thinking that the very thing we dreaded could now possibly save my life.

My sister must have known something — she's bald now and sick with cancer too. I guess it's a twin thing. Am I angry? Not at all, because what a life we've lived.

On 14 May 1958, at approximately 10 p.m. at the Huntly Maternity Hospital, Baby Topp, weighing 5 pounds 6 ounces, was born to Jean and Peter. Doctors had been expecting a 10-pound baby and immediately whisked her away, thinking there was something wrong.

Opposite: Lynda (left) and Jools with their beloved dog River. STUFF LIMITED

I'm trying to remember what it was like to share a womb. The thing that stands out is that it was hot — bloody hot. I remember Lynda's foot close to my face — maybe that's why I decided to leave first: I paved the way and made a tunnel for her to follow.

When I came out I was all wrinkled, my face was scrunched up and I was tiny. The doctor took one look at me and panicked. Meanwhile Lynda, unbeknown to the frantic doctor, was having a lovely time. She had a womb with a view, and space now to stretch out. She often jokes that she had a cigarette and a martini, rolling around in that great expanse for another five minutes before popping out and weighing in at 5 pounds 3. The doctor realised that the 10-pound baby Mum was expecting was actually two 5-pound babies. The Topp twins had arrived.

So let me tell you what that meant for me, Julie, as I was named. I was born with my friend — my darling baby sister, my mate, someone who has always had my back and who has always made me feel strong and confident in this journey called Life.

This story is both mine and my sister's. At times we have had different personal experiences, but mostly for 65 years we have shared the same saddle and traversed trails together.

We hope you enjoy the ride.

1

Country Girls

Mum and Dad met in 1953 at a Christmas Eve dance in the Waerenga community hall. 'Out the back of Te Kauwhata' was how Dad would explain it to people who didn't know where the place was. After a year of courting, they were married. Brother Bruce was born on Christmas Eve a year later, and we arrived two and a half years after that.

Dad and his brother, Uncle Tom, farmed a small Southdown sheep stud, but Dad had always wanted to work on a big sheep station, so when we were six months old he loaded us and everything we owned into an old flatbed truck and we headed off to greener pastures.

Dad had got a job as the head stockman on a big sheep and beef station in Tolaga Bay on the East Cape. As the wife of the head stockman, Mum was expected to cook for the shepherds. It was hard work, looking after three kids under five, preparing meals every night for the family and the shepherds in a house with no electricity and just a coal range to cook on. She recalls the shearing gang feeling sorry for her and having a whip-around to give her money to buy something for us kids.

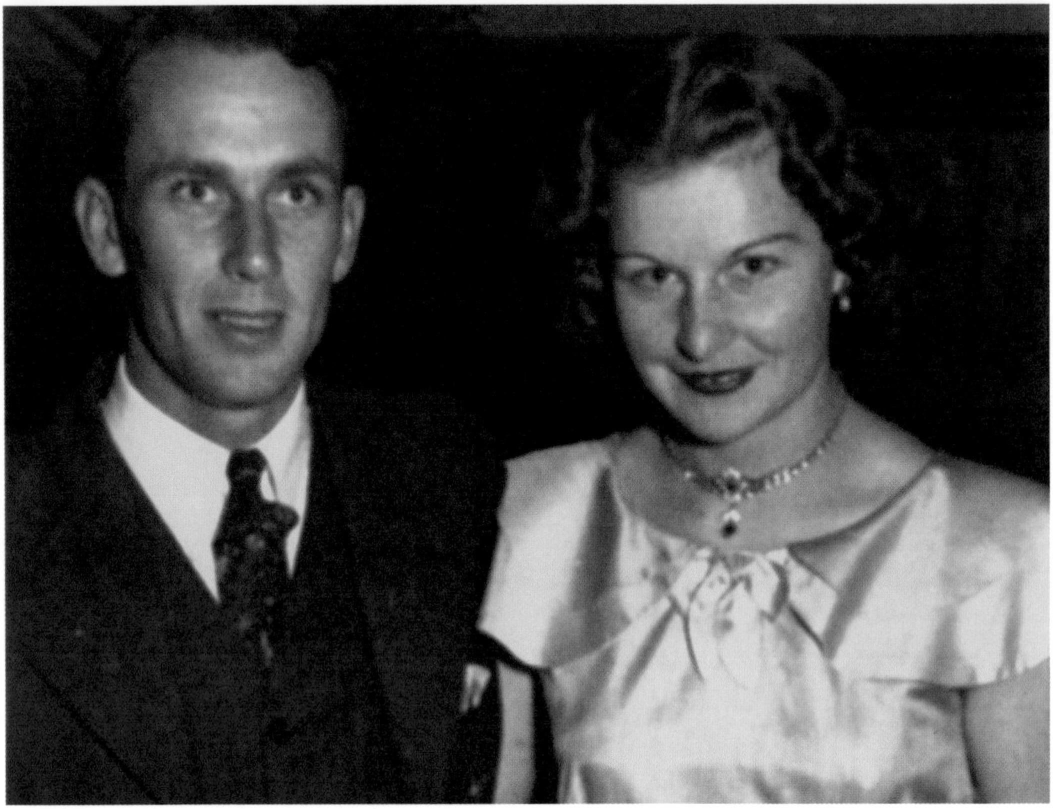

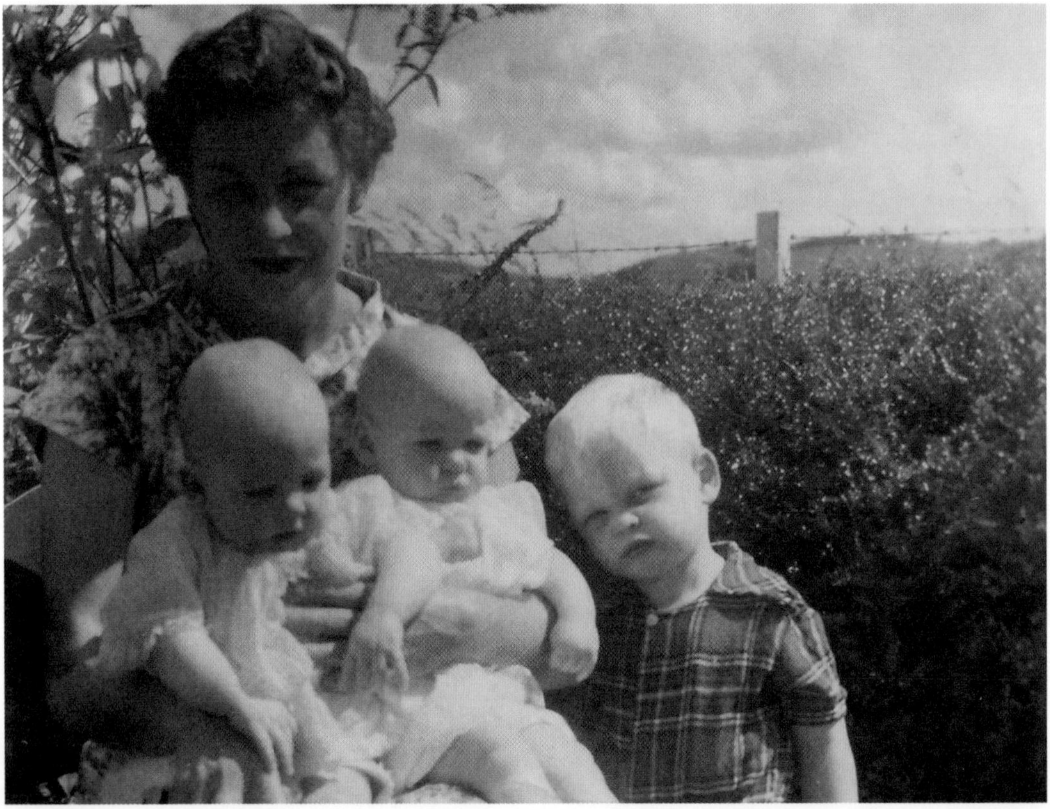

Our next move was to a big sheep station in Waimiha, south of Te Kūiti, where we lived in an old wooden farmhouse in the middle of nowhere. Mum described it as a lonely, isolated place, with a desolate view. The house was dark and dank and we didn't stay there long. Soon it was back up north to where Dad leased a farm block off the port of Whangārei. It had been set up as a dairy unit, so Mum and Dad bought a small herd of Friesian-cross cows and settled into their new way of life.

Sadly, this was to be short-lived as the port company took the land back for development. The herd was sold, and Dad got a job as a stock agent with Wrightson's. We headed back down south, to Havelock North.

Still in the back of Dad's mind was the dream of being a high-country shepherd, so when he was offered a huntaway pup he jumped at the chance. We were living in a small two-bedroom house in town at the time and Dad made a bed of sacks in the lean-to at the back door for him. Jools and I named him Sam and thought he was the most adorable thing we'd ever seen. Mum, on the other hand, didn't seem as pleased: three young children and now a puppy, with Dad out all day long visiting farms.

The following week Sam went missing. We rushed inside to tell Mum that Sam was nowhere to be found, and just then the phone rang. Mum picked it up. She was very apologetic to the caller, then hung up, gathered us kids together and we headed out the door. Jools and I insisted we take our trikes and off we went.

Sam was having a lovely time splashing around in the school swimming pool with all the kids. He was hauled out and handed to Mum. Back at home, Mum decided to put Sam under the house.

Opposite from top: The twins' parents, Peter and Jean, in their courting days; Jean with the twins and their big brother Bruce at the farm in Waerenga.
TOPP COLLECTION

It was one of those houses that had boards all the way around and she thought he would be safely locked away until Dad came home.

The little gate leading under the house did not have a very secure lock, so Mum pushed the old lawnmower in front of it and got Jools and me to sit on it. We spent a few hours there performing our Very Important Job of guarding Sam. Little did we know that Sam was meanwhile digging out the other side of the house and was soon heading back into town.

> Every time Sam went missing, we would head into town on our trikes asking people if they had seen him. We realised quite quickly that people thought we were as cute as bugs' ears.

This was obviously the very early start of the Topp Twins' public touring. Every time Sam went missing, we would head into town on our trikes asking people if they had seen him. We realised quite quickly that people thought we were as cute as bugs' ears, being only three at the time and being identical twins. A stop at the old lady's place on the corner would always net us a biscuit and a glass of milk, then it was on to the doctor's waiting room where the receptionist would load us up with lollies from a bottomless jar. After a brief stop at the local butcher for two cheerios (small red sausages), we'd be on our way to the old folks' home for morning tea.

Sam turned out to be an amazing escape artist. We found him on the veranda of the local pub drinking beer from a glass, stealing

Opposite from top: Santa meets Lynda and Jools in Havelock North; Lynda (left) and Jools in the only dresses they were happy to wear (because they had dogs on them). TOPP COLLECTION

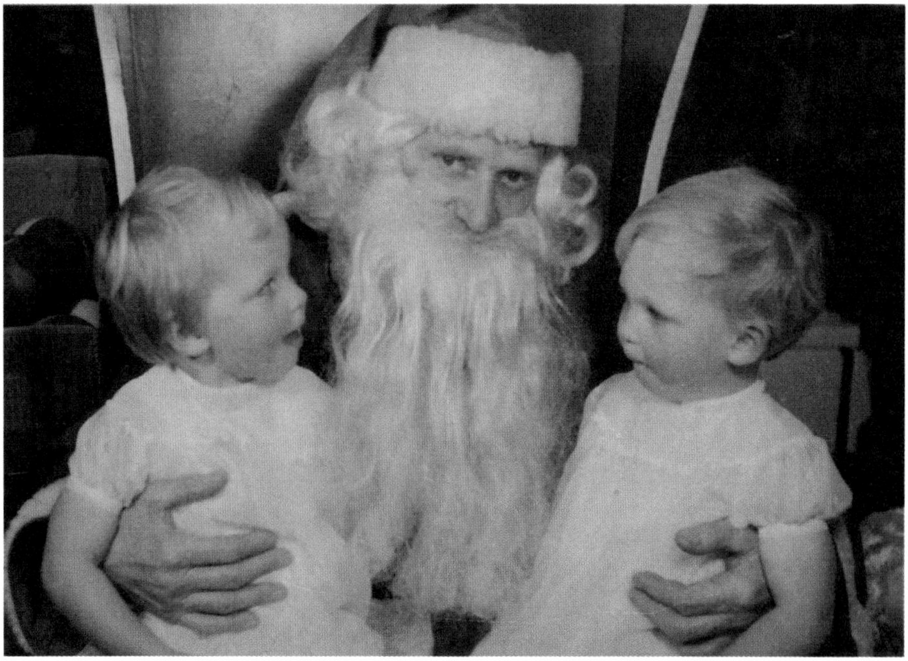

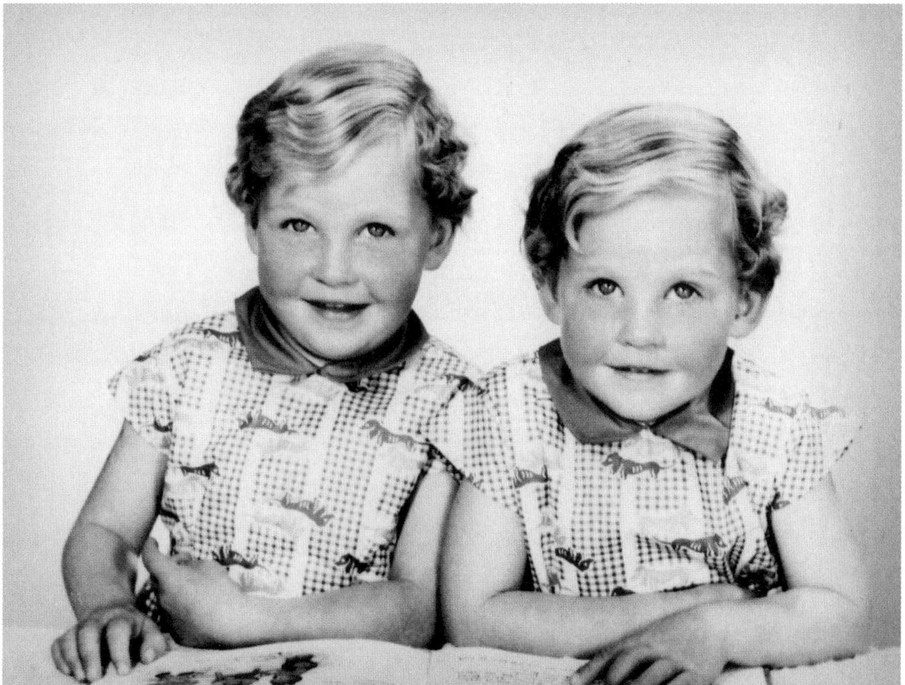

and burying a whole fruit loaf in the church garden, running off with the cricket ball from a local game, and joining the kids in the school cross-country run.

We thought Sam was the most incredible dog and loved him to bits, so it was a sad day when Dad decided to give him to a young shepherd he had met on one of his stock agent visits. He sat us down and told us it wasn't fair to keep Sam in town — he needed an active life working on a farm. We gave Sam a big final hug, then Dad loaded him into the car and drove away. We cried all day and all night.

We both hated wearing dresses and kept pinching our brother's trousers.

The next day Mum decided to take us into Hastings to cheer us up a bit and to do some shopping. She had never got her driver's licence so we walked into town to catch the bus to the big city of Hastings. Mum would always dress us in matching outfits and today we had on our pink and white dresses with smocking on the top. Mum thought they were beautiful on us; we thought they were weird even at an early age.

We got on the bus with Mum holding a hand each. It was exciting peering out the window, so high up and looking down on the cars. We had cream buns with a dollop of raspberry jam at the local tearooms, and then Mum bought us a new pair of trousers each. We both hated wearing dresses and kept pinching our brother's trousers.

On our way back to catch the bus, Jools and I spotted a wooden revolving door into a classic men's clothing store — you know, the ones that had sliding ladders and beautiful wooden countertops. We were hell-bent on going through that door while Mum, now loaded up with shopping bags, was trying to catch the last bus home. She tried to stop us and we both starting screaming and then held our breath.

Mum had by then dropped all her shopping and was smacking me to try to get me to breathe again. A local policeman saw the commotion and rushed over to see what was happening. Initially he thought Mum was belting us and he was coming to our aid, but he soon realised we were both holding our breath so he grabbed Jools and starting smacking her. You can't actually hold your breath for too long when you're three, so eventually we started breathing again, probably to stop the smacking frenzy.

We were taken to the police station, where Jools and I were registered as breath-holders. Then the officer bundled us all into a police car and drove us back to Havelock North. All in all, it was a great day out for us — we'd had so many adventures we'd hardly thought about our beloved Sam.

After Dad's stock agent stint we were back up north for a new farming adventure in the Waikato. Dad couldn't seem to stay away from dairying and was trying his hand at sharemilking on a small farm in Gordonton, which is where we started our schooling.

On our first day of school we were excited but a little reluctant when Mum put us on the bus. As we stepped out at the front gate of Gordonton School we saw Miss Williamson riding her big old grey horse through the gates. It was love at first sight. Our first teacher rode to school every morning and the school provided a small paddock for her horse during the day. We were smitten and spent morning break, lunchtime and after school patting him and feeding him apples and Vegemite sandwiches.

From top: Lynda and Jools, both wearing Bruce's trousers. Lynda is toting a toy gun and Jools holds a pocketknife; Lynda (left) and Jools with their mum in Gordonton, circa 1961. This image was used on the cover of the 2005 album *Flowergirls & Cowgirls*.
TOPP COLLECTION

The next two years were a great time for us, running around the farm helping feed calves and helping Mum in the garden. The school offered us the basics of reading, writing and arithmetic. On reflection, the mornings were filled with academic work and the afternoons with sport and outdoors activities. Both Jools and I became masters at the game of marbles, and Mum sewed us little drawstring bags where we kept our most prized cat's-eye marbles and our beloved bonkers.

> The next two years were a great time for us, running around the farm helping feed calves and helping Mum in the garden.

Each day crates of milk were delivered to the school, and mid-morning we would all line up to receive our half-pint bottle, which was downed by every kid in a matter of seconds. I remember there was a bottle left over one day and the teacher asked if anyone would like an extra one. Jools put her hand up straight away and finished off that extra milk with gusto, wiping her chin with a swipe of her sleeve and heading back into the classroom for storytime on the mat before lunch.

About halfway through the story, Jools projectile-vomited her pint of milk all over the kids directly in front of her. Mrs Young, our second-year teacher, came to her rescue, stripping her down to her singlet and rompers, washing her clothes and her face, and sitting Jools next to her while she finished the story. I remember feeling great love for Mrs Young. My first crush, I believe.

Mum and Dad were doing well with the dairying and we moved to a bigger farm, not far away in Taupiri. We still attended Gordonton School. After pestering Mum we were eventually allowed to help in the milking shed. We asked Dad if we could get a pony. He said no, because of the sharemilking, but if we ever bought a farm of our own we might.

Every weekend was spent playing outside. I remember Jools and I fashioned ourselves coats out of a couple of old chook-feed sacks and pretended to be cowgirls riding out in the wild west.

It was Jools who came up with the idea of stick horses. We grabbed a saw out of Dad's tool shed and headed down to the bottom of the farm where there was a nice stand of mānuka. We cut two branches, each with a fork at one end. We then raced up to the barn and added binder-twine reins to each of the forks and off we rode into the sunset.

> Jools and I fashioned ourselves coats out of a couple of old chook-feed sacks and pretended to be cowgirls riding out in the wild west.

Dad played along. Around four o'clock he would yell out to both of us to get on our horses and bring the cows up to the cowshed. The first time he said it we raced down the hallway, out the back door to where our sticks were tied up to the hitching post we had made, and galloped off as if we were in a Hollywood western. Life was good for a couple of seven-year-olds.

Then there were the dreaded Sunday mornings.

Mum had decided that we should go to Sunday school. Mr Ballantyne, the Sunday-school teacher, would pick us up and take us to the local Presbyterian church just down the road. It meant we had to wash our faces, brush our hair and get out of our beloved farm clothes and into dresses, white socks and flash shoes.

Sunday school consisted of colouring in pictures of Jesus, singing hymns and learning prayers. The singing bit we liked — the main problem we had with Sunday school was that it messed up our weekend outdoor activities. It was an inconvenience. There were little exams we had to sit to see if we had learnt the word of God. If you passed you got a sticker, and after 10 stickers you got a postcard. It took Jools and me a long time to get postcards but when we finally did, we rushed home to show Mum. It was a picture of Jesus praying and at the top in fancy lettering it said: 'Ask and you shall be given.'

We hung our postcards above our beds, got into our old clothes, then marched into the kitchen and asked Mum for two gingernuts, two pieces of shortbread and a thermos of tea, as we were heading down to the back of the farm on our horses to check the boundary fence. Mum said we couldn't have biscuits because we would be having lunch soon. 'But Jesus says "Ask and you shall be given",' we replied. Mum was not convinced, so we headed out the door to check the boundary fence without biscuits.

The following Sunday, Mum sat us down and said we were now old enough to decide whether we wanted to go to Sunday school or not. There was a lot of whooping and hollering as we dashed outside to play.

The one thing we kept up from our stint at Sunday school was singing the hymns we'd learnt, and when Uncle Alan and Auntie Evelyn (Mum's sister) came to visit, they asked if we would like to sing at our cousin's twenty-first. We were seven years old.

Mum helped us learn 'Walking in the Sunshine', bought us boaters and canes and taught us a simple dance routine.

Celebrations started around 5 p.m. at the local hall in Papakura. Everyone had a big feed and looked forward to dancing to the band later in the night.

For a couple of country kids who were usually in bed by 7 p.m. it was all a bit much, and by 7.30 Lynda and I were both fast asleep in the back seat of our big old yellow DeSoto car. Dad called it a

GORDONTON
1966
S 1 & 2

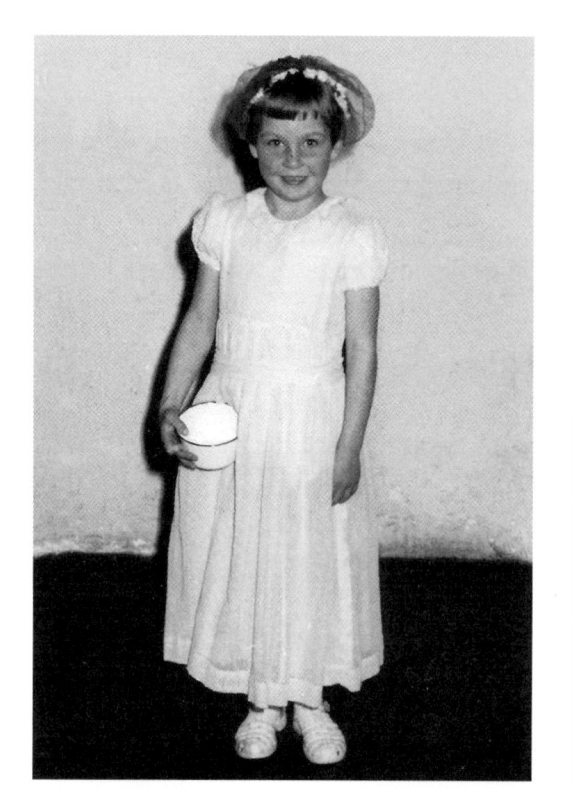

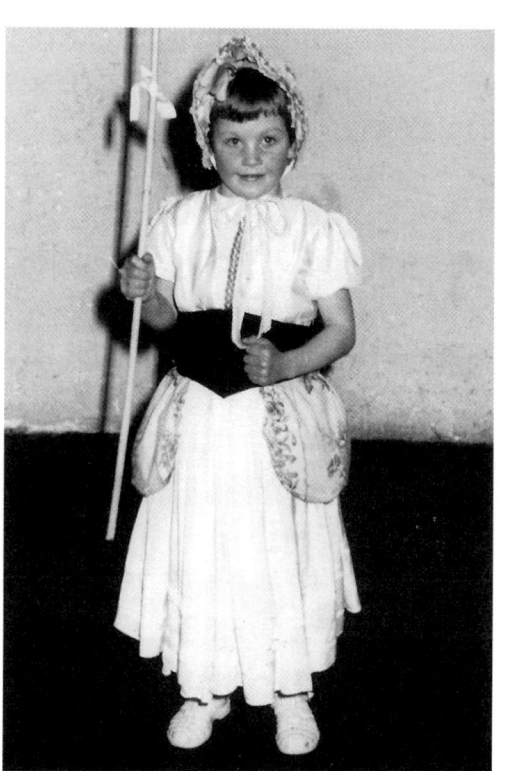

big American Yank tank. It had big pointy wings at the back and lights that looked like torpedos. It was very wide and there was enough space in the back for both of us to lie down for a decent bit of shut-eye.

Here was our big break and we were both dead to the world. But Mum was not going to let this chance go by, so she woke us up and got us ready for our first-ever gig.

We wiped the sleep out of our eyes, stepped out on that stage and sang our hearts out. Uncle Alan played the ukulele as we swung our canes and waved our hats in the air like real pros. We wowed the hell out of everyone. They clapped and cheered and told Mum we were just too damned cute for words.

We walked offstage with big grins on our faces, and two minutes later we were fast asleep again in the back seat of the car.

That night we both caught the performing bug. It would be another 12 years before we did our first paid gig, in Wellington with a theatre group called Red Mole at the famous Carmen's Balcony nightclub.

Opposite from top: Lynda (left) as Little Miss Muffet and Jools as Bo Peep at a school fancy dress party; The twins' class photo at Gordonton School in 1966, when they were eight years old. Lynda is on the far left of the second row from the front, and Jools is fifth from left in the row above her.
TOPP COLLECTION

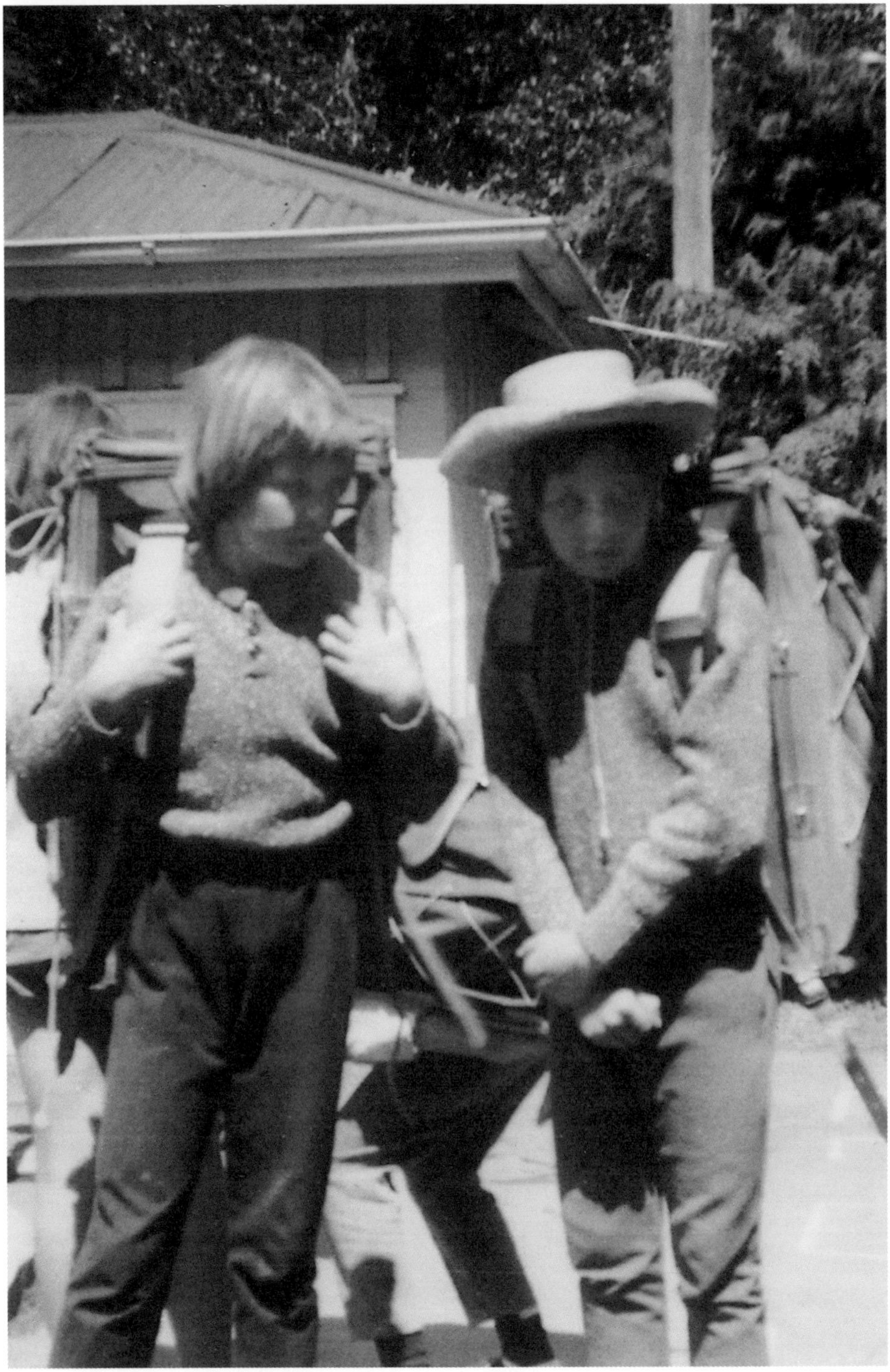

2

Stewed Tamarillos

Mum and Dad worked hard as sharemilkers and finally must have made enough money because we were off to a new place, and this one would belong to the Topp family. The rest of our childhood and teenage years were spent on the dairy farm in Slater Road, Ruawaro, 14 kilometres west of Huntly.

The house was a big brick one with three bedrooms, a large lounge with a fireplace, and a modern kitchen. The dining room had windows that pushed open to the garden to allow the wonderful smells of whatever was flowering at the time to waft in.

Bruce had his own bedroom, while Jools and I shared a room with twin beds and lime-green candlewick bedspreads. Mum and Dad's room had built-in wardrobes. There was a brick woodshed attached to the house, with a secret little cupboard in the back that came out beside the fireplace in the lounge. It was Jools' and my job to stack new wood in that little cupboard each night in winter, and sometimes we would climb through and surprise Mum.

Opposite: Lynda (left) and Jools getting ready for school camp.
TOPP COLLECTION

The farm consisted of 108 acres with a milking shed, a barn, a well-established garden and a wonderful old orchard full of plums, pears, tamarillos, redcurrants and nectarines. A concrete driveway led to a concrete pad right outside the front door where Dad parked his big American car. By then he had traded in the yellow DeSoto and bought a 1967 Plymouth Belvedere, automatic with mother-of-pearl buttons on the dashboard. Jools and I both got our driver's licences in that car.

Farm life was a series of wonderful smells — freshly mowed lawns, flowers in Mum's beautiful garden, the farm dogs, the cowshed's distinctive aroma, the washing just in off the line after being in the sun all day, Mum's baking straight from the oven.

My childhood memories are held together by the smell of all these things, and I am reminded of them if I catch a whiff anytime in the wind, anywhere in the world.

We both loved life on the farm. Our parents were always there for us, and after school and at weekends we couldn't wait to be out working on the farm with Dad. Milking the cows, feeding out hay, digging thistles or riding the horses — it was all a joyous thing, even if we were tired and grubby a lot of the time.

Dad (Peter) had grown up just outside Gisborne, with two sisters (Pat and Marie) and five brothers (Burt, Colin, Tom, Jim and David). Every now and then one of them would come to visit, or we would pack up the car and head off to see them in winter, when the cows were not being milked. We loved seeing our many cousins.

Opposite: Dad at the Rotongaro Rural Sports Day. TOPP COLLECTION

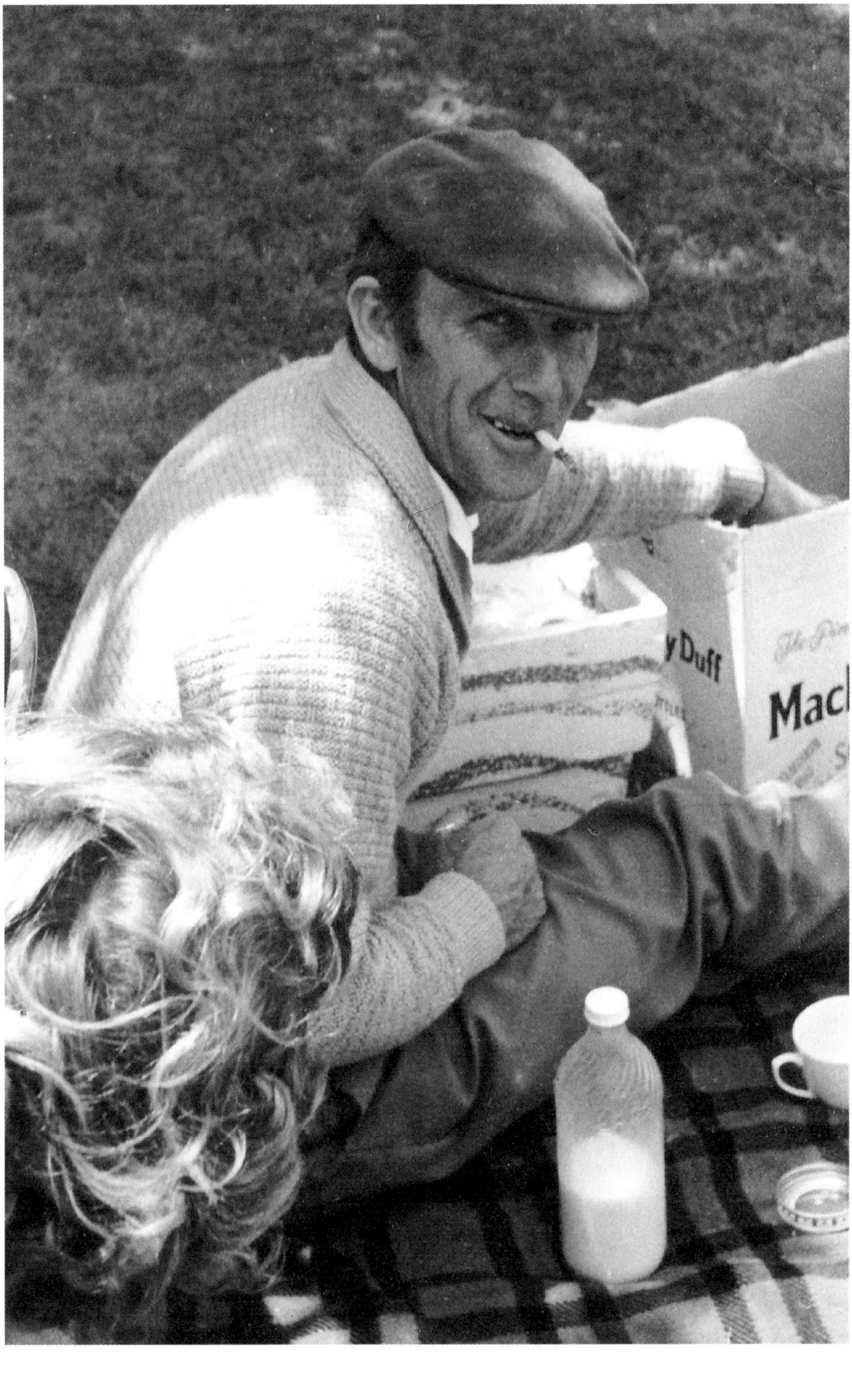
y Duff
Mack

Dad never really played with us, and if he spoke to us it was usually a directive: 'Go let those dogs off', 'Go catch the horses' — jobs that needed doing. The cool thing was that he made us feel confident. We knew that he knew that if he asked something of us, we'd get the job done. He'd been teaching us how to do these things all our short lives, and then allowing us to work things out for ourselves.

I remember the first time we made hay at Ruawaro.

Dad cut the grass with an old mower on the back of our David Brown tractor. I had overheard him talking to Mum about having enough money to hire the baler but not enough to have the hay raked into rows. So the five of us — Mum, Dad and us kids — got out there and turned every goddamn blade of grass twice with pitchforks, setting it in rows for the baler to rake up. We laboured away for two long days. Mum made delicious bacon and egg pie and gingernuts, which we washed down with homemade lemon barley water. The weather was perfect for making hay.

So the five of us got out there and turned every goddamn blade of grass twice with pitchforks.

The baler arrived and started work. Everything was going well, then, just as the last bale squirted out the back of the machine, you could feel a tiny drop of rain.

We all looked at one another — we needed to get that hay in the shed pronto before rain ruined it. We loaded up the old trailer, and before we'd even unloaded it, neighbours arrived from everywhere with stationwagons, trailers and trucks. With their help we got that hay in the barn in about 20 minutes, beating the rain by five.

Dad looked like he was going to cry with relief — he was so grateful to our neighbours for their help. There was a cold beer for everyone — even us kids shared in a long-neck bottle of Waikato Draught with a dash of lemonade. Mum said it was called a shandy and I remember it being the most beautiful and refreshing drink I'd ever tasted.

One of the jobs we loved was helping Dad milk the cows. The shed was an old walk-through type with four bays and the cows happily walked in and stood to be milked. The yard was open so there was always a cow chewing her cud right next to your ear waiting her turn. There were 70-odd cows in the herd and Dad knew the names of every one. Biggie, Rat, Rabbit and Louise were some of the names I remember.

Life was good. We always had food on the table, and a big old American car.

Dad was true to his word and we got our first pony at Ruawaro. His name was Nobby and he'd had his tail docked to make him a cob — a hunter-type horse. Docking is a cruel practice from back in the day and is now outlawed. Cows used to have their tails docked too, but Dad said the cows wouldn't be able to swat the flies off their backs without tails, so he never did it, thank goodness.

Nobby had actually been lent to us by friends and he was the coolest horse. A whole lot of kids in the district learnt to ride on Nobby.

Dad said we weren't allowed to ride without him being there, and we had to ride for a whole year without a saddle. After a few weeks of this we started sneaking out and riding Nobby together, with an old halter we made from plaited baling twine. Dad must have known but he never said anything. We sure got a good seat riding bareback.

Nobby was in his twenties when he came to us, and he knew every trick in the book. If you rode him too far away from the horse paddock he would only ever walk. All encouragement to get him to trot or canter failed miserably, so of course you'd soon turn for

From top: Jools (left) and Lynda learning to ride; Peter taught the twins to respect horses and became a keen polo player himself. TOPP COLLECTION

home and *boom* — off he'd go, straight into a canter back to his paddock. If we rode him for what he thought was too long he would head for the low-hanging branches of the pine trees and just keep going till we were knocked off or had to bail.

We rode that pony nearly every day for a whole year. Then one afternoon we came home from school and rushed out to see our beloved Nobby but we couldn't find him anywhere. Dad leaned over the gate and told us they had given Nobby back so he could teach some other little kids to ride.

We rode that pony nearly every day for a whole year. Then one afternoon we came home from school and rushed out to see our beloved Nobby but we couldn't find him anywhere.

We were inconsolable — how could they give our beloved Nobby away? We both cried and cried, until Dad told us to go and look in the paddock around the back of the barn.

We stopped crying immediately and took off like a shot. There in the paddock stood Springy, a 16.3-hand thoroughbred ex-steeplechaser. I remember Dad saying, 'I decided you needed a bit of a challenge for your second horse.' (Understatement of the year!)

Jools and I used an old 44-gallon drum to get up on Springy, and unlike Nobby he would go like the wind. We took turns riding him, as he didn't really like having two people on him. We found this out when he promptly bucked us off the first time we tried.

Dad had been offered an old Morris commercial truck, and for some reason the deal included a young filly. When Kerry arrived, Jools fell in love with her and Springy became my horse. Oh what joy — now we could ride together all over the farm.

One day we rode up to the neighbours' place and called in for a cuppa. Wayne and Marilyn Holmes managed a big farm, and we soon discovered Wayne's collection of old 78 records and a wind-up gramophone. Marylin said we could play some records and the first one I picked up was 'My Pinto Pony and I' by Australian yodeller June Holms.

When we got home we told Mum about our amazing discovery and asked if we could take our guitar with us next time.

I cranked the handle and placed the big old needle onto the first ridge in the 78. Then I went into a 'yodel coma', as I later called it. I just thought, I have *got* to learn how to do that. I was absolutely mesmerised by the sound. We spent a good hour listening to those 78s and found two more great yodellers, Australian Shirley Thoms and American Patsy Montana.

When we got home we told Mum about our amazing discovery at the neighbours' place and asked if we could take our guitar with us next time. Mum said it would be too hard to carry the guitar on horseback, and what if we dropped it? So we'd ride like maniacs to the Holmes' place, wind up the gramophone, listen intently to the song and try to keep it in our heads while we rode like the wind back home.

Inevitably, by the time we got home we'd pretty much lost the tune. We became very good riders and horsewomen, but it took a long time to learn how to yodel. Everywhere I went on my horse I would practise my yodel, far from civilisation. Jools said I sounded like a strangled cat for a long time but I persevered.

I probably practised for about six years before I first yodelled in public. I was about 15 and we were at a party in Huntly. Suffice to say it brought the place to a standstill. Jools had no great desire to learn to yodel, but when I started doing it in our shows in our twenties she started singing a yodel harmony. She can only do it if I'm yodelling. If she tries to do it by herself, she's the one who sounds like a strangled cat.

Our mum Jean had five siblings: George, Jack, Lorna, Evelyn and Bill. The Dalziel family were farmers of Scottish heritage and the kids went to school in Waerenga. They lost their beautiful mother when Mum was quite young, and Aunty Lorna looked after Mum and Uncle Bill, who were the youngest. It must have been tough on them all, and Mum vowed from an early age that if she had children, she would try to be the best mum she could be, and she was.

Mum showed her love for us in so many ways. She knitted jumpers and cardigans for us, ran the whole household, maintained a beautiful garden and was full of wise words. When we were about eight years old Mum told us we should never hate anybody. You could dislike someone, but hating would hurt you more than anyone. Another brilliant Jean Topp line was 'Tell the truth faster — it will get you out of trouble quicker.'

A lot of the love she gave us came in the form of home cooking — gingernuts, peanut brownies, banana cake, roast dinners, apple and blackberry pie, and just about everything else out of the Edmonds cookbook. Our favourite was stewed tamarillos. What a childhood delicacy.

From top: Mum as a young girl in the rooftop playground of the Farmers department store in Auckland; Mum doing the cancan at a show put on by the local Women's Division of Federated Farmers at the Ruawaro hall. TOPP COLLECTION

Stewed tamarillos

Pour boiling water over 8 tamarillos so that the skin peels off easily. Cut into halves lengthwise and add half a cup of sugar.

Pop them in a pot, just cover with water and heat till they boil and the liquid goes a bit frothy. Turn off the heat and let them cool.

Put them in the fridge.

Get a small Agee jar and crush in two Weet-Bix biscuits. Spoon in some tamarillos and juice.

Pour cream straight from 'the spotties' (that's what Mum called the cows) all over it.

That's what we took to school for lunch but it hardly ever made it to school — we nearly always ate it on the bus.

One day Mum told us from now on we could decide for ourselves whether we wanted to wear matching clothes (which we had until then). Pretty much every day after that, it didn't matter who got up first, we would both end up wearing the same clothes. We'd be having breakfast and *boom* — we'd realise we were wearing matching outfits. It was kinda weird, but I guess that's twins for ya.

Mum belonged to the Women's Division of Federated Farmers and once a month she would be picked up to meet with all the other ladies at the local hall. I remember her taking cuttings from the garden to swap, and making cakes for morning tea. Every year they would put on a show and the whole community would go. The one I remember best was a western theme, and it was amazing to see all these middle-aged women dressed up as cowboys with five o'clock shadows smudged on their chins.

Mum was dressed as a cancan girl at the bar. She looked amazing, and when she got off her barstool and launched into a classic cancan the whole hall went wild. We somehow knew that at the end of the cancan the dancers would flick their skirts right over their heads, and all us kids rushed to the front of the stage to see this final flourish. Sure enough, Mum flicked her skirt to the sky and there, sewn onto her frilly knickers, was a painted eye, and underneath it the words 'I'm watching you!' It brought the house down — Jools and I were proud as punch.

Mum had done competition ballroom dancing as a young woman and she was never short of a partner at the local dances at the Ruawaro hall. Dad was always up for a waltz but he wasn't much of a dancer otherwise. Mr Zweirs would always ask Mum for a dance when a foxtrot or a rumba rhythm started. They would sweep around the dance floor and all the ladies from the supper room would come out to watch. The two-man band knew every song ever written.

Mum spoke to one of the band members about how we loved to sing, and how Jools and I would pretend to be performers at a fancy resort, doing 'shows' with hairbrushes for microphones and a tennis racket for our guitar. He suggested that a ukulele might be a good start for us. So on one of Mum and Dad's infrequent trips to Hamilton she bought us a ukulele.

Well, our lives changed at that point. This was no toy ukulele — this was a beautiful Hawaiian-style instrument, big-bodied and with a tone like a summer breeze. Oh my god, the joy we both felt when she handed us that box . . . We strummed and placed our fingers to try to make a chord straight away, and within an hour we were singing our hearts out.

Jools was a natural, and even though she only knew a few chords she could play anything. 'Blackboard of my Heart', 'Walking in the Sunshine', 'Pearly Shells' — I don't know how we knew all these old songs. We never had a song book — it's like we were born with those songs in us.

3

Brother Bruce

When Jools and I were babies, Bruce used to walk beside Mum, with one hand firmly gripping the handle of our pram, and declare to all and sundry that the two babies inside were 'my twinnies'. He was a loving, devoted older brother who took that role very seriously. Mum would tuck him into a chair with pillows so he could bottle-feed one of us while she dealt with the other.

Bruce's early teenage years consisted of music and gardening, and of course helping on the farm. He could play the piano by ear and sing harmony, and every spare moment he had would be spent listening to, cleaning and/or cataloguing his extensive record collection. Mum had bought him a portable record player with the speaker in the lid. It was a beautiful cream and teal colour and would be a real collector's item today. He would buy an album, play it, record it onto a cassette, then put the album into a sealed bag and place it in a big wooden chest he had in his room.

Jools and I were forbidden to touch his record collection and we never did. Bruce actually still has all those albums in 2023 — well over 2000 of them, many of which have only been played once.

One day Bruce was nowhere to be found. A search was instigated, and Jools and I found him in the wardrobe in his bedroom,

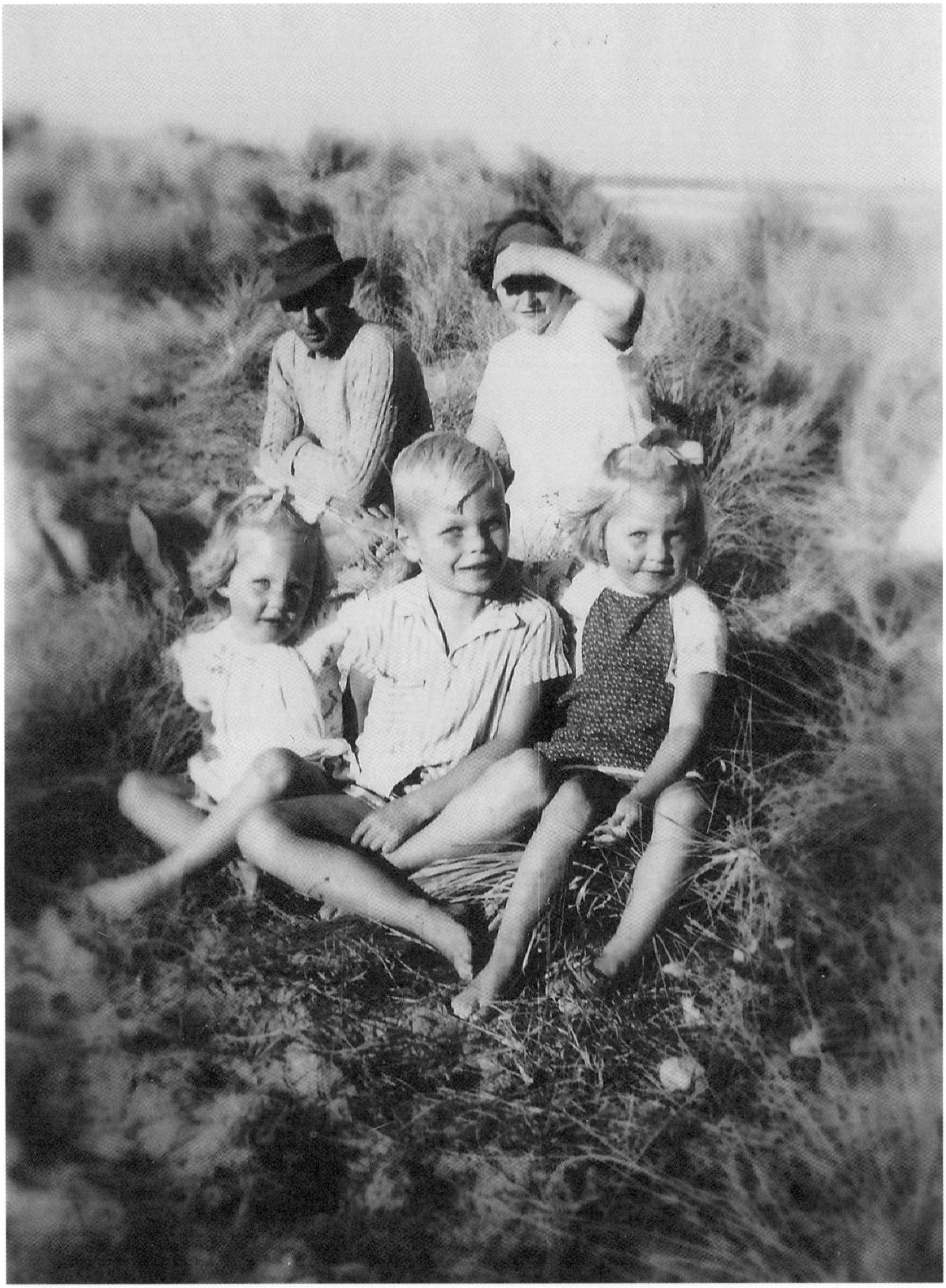

sitting on a small chair with his portable record player on his knee. With the headphones on he was listening to Elton John cranked up *loud*. When Mum asked him why, he said he was trying to get Elton John's music as loud as possible, with no outside sound intruding.

Unfortunately this quest led to the demise of Bruce's beloved portable record player. He had been outside with Dad, helping clean the car, and when Dad tried to start the motor they heard the double-clicking sound of a flat battery. Dad told Bruce to get the spare battery, and together they attached it with jumper leads. After a couple of turns the Belvedere roared into life.

Bruce must have thought about this for a while and it gave him an idea. Somehow he managed to swap out the six D-size batteries that ran his record player for the spare car battery. He turned it on and the beautiful teal record player blew up in a puff of smoke, a loud bang its dying sound.

Bruce loved to garden with Mum, and from quite young he would help her weed and plant new flowers. As he got older he started landscaping new garden beds and created a rockery garden all by himself.

At the age of 14 he entered the My Favourite Arrangement competition at the Rotongaro Rural Sports Day, which was the equivalent of an A&P show. My Favourite Arrangement was decided by public vote on the day and the entries were anonymous. The winner's name was announced late afternoon.

Opposite: The Topp family enjoying a rare day at the beach in Hawke's Bay, circa 1961. TOPP COLLECTION

When Bruce's name was read out, there was this look of shock and surprise among the other competitors, mostly country ladies. Mum was so proud of him. Jools and I, who had been jumping our horses in the show ring, had raced over for the announcement. We thought it was absolutely amazing — the youngest-ever entrant and the only male in the history of the show had taken out the top prize!

When Bruce's name was read out, there was this look of shock and surprise among the other competitors, mostly country ladies. Mum was so proud of him.

Bruce went on to get an apprenticeship with Berin Spiro, one of the top florists in New Zealand at the time, and was the first ever to score 100 per cent in his junior florist exams. He eventually became an executive board member of Interflora, with the portfolio of Educating and Training, and later became president of Interflora Pacific, travelling the world in that role.

Our brother also played a big part in enabling us to become entertainers. He got a job with the Bremmers, who owned a big station up the road from us. They also owned Bremworth Carpets and were keen to employ locals on their farm. Bruce spent hours mowing lawns and gardening at the big house, which supposedly had a ballroom dance floor upstairs. He used some of his earnings to buy us our first guitar, and with it came a book called *Play in a Day*, which is exactly what Jools did. She learnt how to play the guitar the day we got it and never looked at another instruction book.

Left: The Topp siblings with their cousins Felicity (centre) and Mason (front). TOPP COLLECTION

Above: Lynda (left) and Jools with Bruce in 1999. ARANI CUTHBERT

Fun time on the farm now centred on horses, and when we were about 10 years old Dad decided he wanted to play polo. He joined the Taupiri Polo Club and every weekend during summer we would load the horses onto the old Bedford truck and head off to polo matches all around the North Island. Jools and I were Dad's grooms — we would saddle the horses, bandage their legs, plait their tails and warm them up before the game. Dad only ever played in the B grade but he was the envy of all the A-grade players for his two willing grooms.

Eventually a few of the A-grade players asked if we would groom for them in the big match of the day. It's hard work being a groom — you're always there at the truck looking after horses while the player gets all the glory — but we loved every minute of it. Some of those players went on to play for New Zealand.

On one of his visits to the country Prince Charles (now King Charles) played a game at the Auckland Polo Club. A string of polo ponies was put together for him from some of those A-grade players, and as I had ridden most of those horses I was asked to groom for Prince Charles on the day. I briefly met Charlie when I handed him his next horse after each chukka.

Years later, when Charles brought Camilla to New Zealand for the first time, we were asked to perform for them at SkyCity. Camp Mother and Camp Leader performed four songs and duly did our comedy routine at a packed charity fundraiser.

In accordance with royal protocol we had briefly met the couple before the event. While we were lined up waiting outside the lift, along with Kiri Te Kanawa and others, Kiri asked if Jools and I were going to behave ourselves and we promptly told her 'No!' At that moment the lift opened and the royal couple stepped out. As we were introduced, Prince Charles said, 'I've heard a lot about you, and we are looking forward to your performance.' Then they disappeared into a sea of black ties and evening gowns.

From top: Lynda riding Tosca; Willing grooms Lynda (left) and Jools with Dad's polo ponies Rebel, Tosca and Kerry. TOPP COLLECTION

There is no glamour backstage at a royal command performance. Camp Mother and Camp Leader made their way through the bowels of the SkyCity kitchen, dodging waiters hauling dirty plates across to massive plastic bins and dropping cutlery into barrels of hot soapy water.

We waited side stage as spectacular desserts designed by Peter Gordon were delivered to tables, then suddenly our names were announced and we were on. We had been given strict instructions not to use foul language or offend the royal couple in any way. I wondered as we stepped into the bright lights whether Camp Leader would adhere to those rules. She had been known to be unpredictable . . .

We had been given strict instructions not to use foul language or offend the royal couple in any way.

In the event it was all pretty seemly. Camp Mother managed to throw in a few titty lifts, and we taught the entire audience the pelvic yodel, telling them they could practise in their own home or castle.

Our last song was dedicated to Camilla to celebrate her first visit to New Zealand. It wasn't one of our songs but a beautiful tune written by Eddie Low, who had given us permission to sing it. 'Songs of Home' is a song of great love for New Zealand, in a combination of English and te reo Māori. We told Camilla a copy of our CD containing that song would be gifted to her.

Opposite: Lynda and Jools meet Prince Charles and Camilla in 2012.
COURTESY OF SKYCITY ENTERTAINMENT GROUP LTD

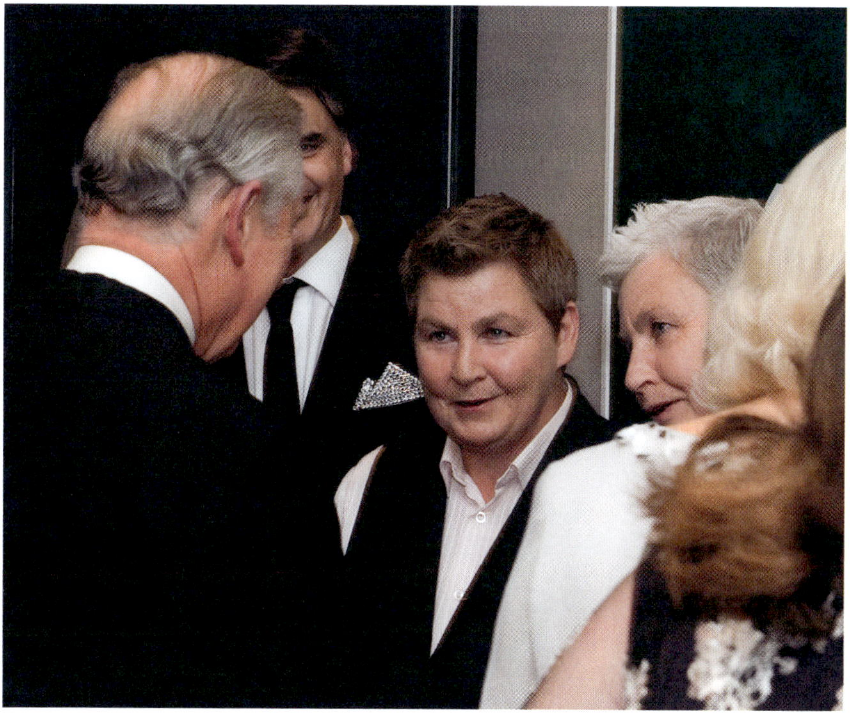

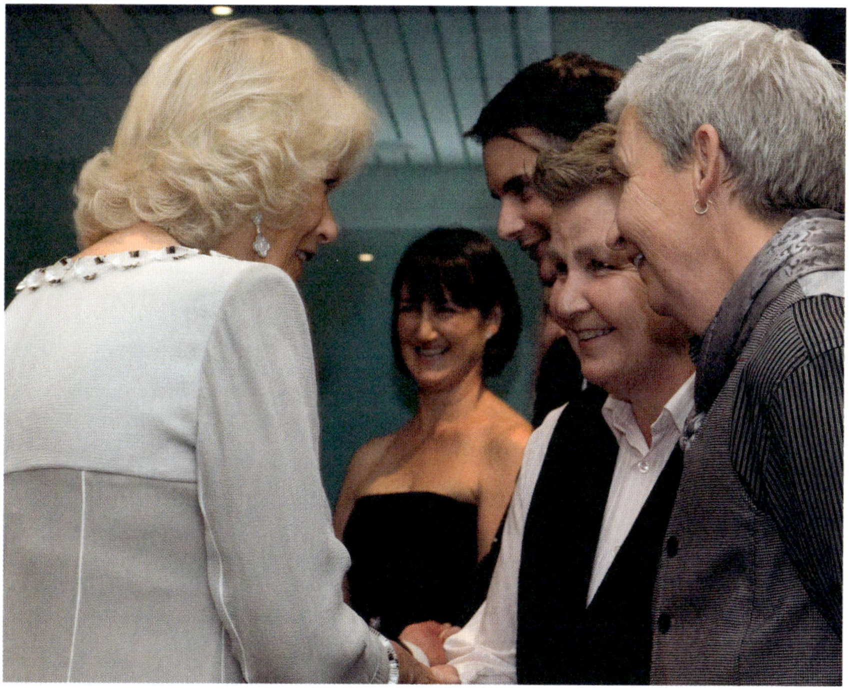

We said our goodbyes and headed back out through the kitchen and entrance lobby. As we waited for the lift, two suited security guards wearing earpieces came running towards us. Alarmed, we began explaining that we were just heading to our room to get changed, but then one of them told us the prince had requested us at his table.

Jools, who was still in character as Camp Leader, told him we didn't have time to meet the prince, but Camp Mother told her it would be rude not to at least shake his hand, so we were escorted into the throng of celebrities, CEOs, politicians and socialites.

My twin sister had just stayed absolutely in character, despite addressing the future King of England, and he clearly enjoyed the exchange.

John Key, the then prime minister, was deep in conversation with the prince when we arrived, so we waited patiently, standing around a bit awkwardly with the security guards. Pretty soon Prince Charles saw us out of the corner of his eye and stepped forward with an outstretched hand. 'I did enjoy your performance,' he said in his very English accent. 'I'm sure you toned it down a bit on our behalf. Do you by chance have any DVDs we could watch?' Camp Leader puffed her chest out and replied, 'Yep, we do. I'll get our people to talk to your people and we'll get it sorted.'

Both the prince and I smiled. My twin sister had just stayed absolutely in character, despite addressing the future King of England, and he clearly enjoyed the exchange.

I then leaned in and told him I had met him many years earlier at a polo match in Auckland. His face lit up and he said he remembered it well, as he had taken a tumble off his horse in the third chukka. He proceeded to tell me the names of the other players on his team and how wonderful the ponies had been. Quite impressive memory skills, I thought.

Then we engaged in some small-talk about their trip. He said they would have loved to see a bit more of the countryside, visit some farms and so on, but they had to do the obligatory rounds. I told him he should put his foot down next time he was here, and he replied, 'Well, we would love to, but your government is paying for the trip!'

Then he was gone, whisked away by a team to the next round of introductions.

About six months later we received a letter with a fancy royal seal on the envelope. It read:

Dear Topp Twins

My boys and I enjoyed watching your DVDs, and we wish you all the best with your career.

Charles

Lynda proudly showing off her Wellington to Huntly Relay T-shirt, 1975.
TOPP COLLECTION

4

School Days

Ruawaro is a Māori word that means 'two coals' or coalmine. Luckily there was not enough coal to dig up so it was mostly farming around us.

Ruawaro School was a country school with big macrocarpa trees at the front gate, two classrooms, a netball/tennis court and a big paddock out the back that was used for everything from rugby to Calf Club Days and playing fields for our made-up games. There were 29 kids when we started, but at one stage while we were there it got down to 11 so we knew everyone pretty well.

Brian Watkins was our teacher and he looked like an older version of Elvis Presley. He had a great head of hair that was smothered in Brylcreem, some of which always seemed to end up in his ears. He was kind and loved to read us stories — every kid would get out of their seat and crowd around his desk to hear the latest chapter of whatever book he was reading us.

Miss Burgess taught the younger kids. She was an imposing woman who was rather terrifying and unpredictable. We learnt through her at a very early age to question authority. Miss B was a great believer in corporal punishment and Lynda and I both received 'six of the best' on each hand with the school's giant leather strap.

Our classes stopped at 2.30 p.m. each day and we all had to clean the classrooms before the bell rang for home time. One day I was on cleaning duty in Miss Burgess's classroom. I was sweeping up and found a whole lot of beads on the wooden floor that the primers had been playing with. I gathered them all up and asked Miss B what I should do with them. She pointed to some boxes of craft material and off I went to deposit them.

> Scunge Rag was played with great gusto during any break in the school day. If you were tagged you became the Scunge, and your job was to offload that title as soon as possible.

On my way to the boxes I spied Miss Burgess's big flat-soled shoes, the ones she wore to ride her bike to school. For some reason — I just couldn't help myself — I quietly poured the beads into one of her shoes.

I finished my chores and wandered off to catch the bus home, thinking what a brilliant prankster I was. The next morning I was called to her classroom and all the beads were lined up on the chalk holder along the bottom of the big blackboard. The blood drained out of my face. Miss Burgess was not a happy camper and I was doomed. I was marched to the office and my corporal punishment was duly handed out. I cried all day, thinking how unfair and barbaric it was.

It was our cleaning duties that gave rise to a game known by the glorious name Scunge Rag. Whoever came up with the idea had been given the task of cleaning the bathrooms. He or she soon discovered that the rag used to clean the toilets could become a projectile to tag someone. Scunge Rag was played with great gusto during any break in the school day. If you were tagged you became the Scunge, and your job was to offload that title as soon as possible by flinging the dirty rag at some other poor unsuspecting student.

Usually there were about 12 kids on our little school bus but on one particular morning there were 12 kids and seven home-built trolleys. If there had been a crash, we would never have got out safely due to trolley overload.

It was all in aid of a trolley derby.

Lynda and I had designed a triangle trolley with three wheels. We thought it was a brilliant concept (heavily influenced by the fact that we could only find three wheels in the old shed filled with broken lawnmowers). It went really fast because it was quite light and short.

Everyone arrived at school with their trolleys and our new teacher, Mr Cosson, set up a trolley driver's licence course on the tennis court, then marked a track right around the school lawns for us to race on.

We spent days practising, pushing and riding our respective race cars . . . until there was an almighty crash one day and trolleys were banned.

Caveman's hockey was played with a cricket ball. Once the bell rang you had two minutes to find something to hit the ball with, but it wasn't allowed to be a hockey stick. This game proved way more dangerous than the trolleys and it too was banned when the teacher found one of the boys playing with an axe.

I don't really remember learning anything much in the classroom at Ruawaro. 'New maths' had just come into the school curriculum, replacing arithmetic, and even the teacher didn't understand it.

He just put the answer book on the big table in the middle of the room. You tried your best and checked the answers yourself.

―――

The best day of the year by far was Calf Club Day. Dad would pick out two pretty calves for us and we'd brush them, feed them and teach them to lead for weeks before the big day.

I remember one year Lynda won Best Led Calf, Best Turned Out and Best Dairy Type. Three red ribbons later she proudly did a circuit of the ring with the big purple and gold ribbon for Champion Calf. I don't know who was more excited, Lynda or Dad.

After the big day the calves would be turned out with the rest of the weaners and go on to become milking cows in the dairy herd. They were always pets, and loved a good scratch under their neck when they came into the shed for milking.

> The best day of the year by far was Calf Club Day. One year Lynda won Best Led Calf, Best Turned Out and Best Dairy Type.

Much later, when we lived in Auckland, I dreamt an entire song from start to finish. When I woke in the morning I immediately wrote it all down. 'Calf Club Day' became one of our most popular songs.

Opposite top: Calf Club Day at Ruawaro School. Jools (left) with calf Jenny and Lynda with Louise, who went on to win Champion Calf. TOPP COLLECTION

Opposite bottom: Jools (left) and Lynda posing with calves again — this time on a photoshoot at Te Henga (Bethells Beach) for their first EP, *Topp Twins Go Vinyl*. MARGIE PALMER

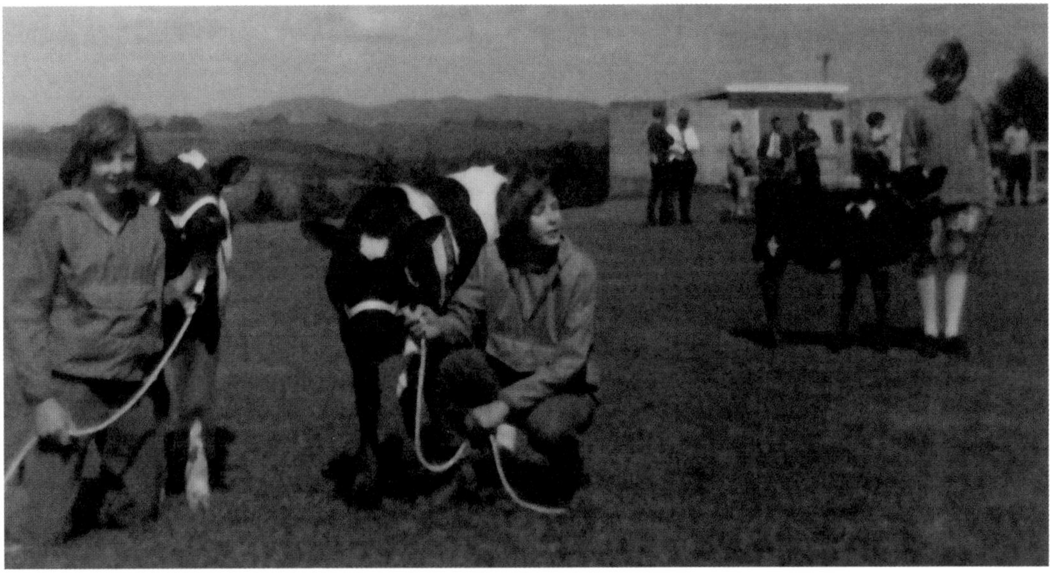

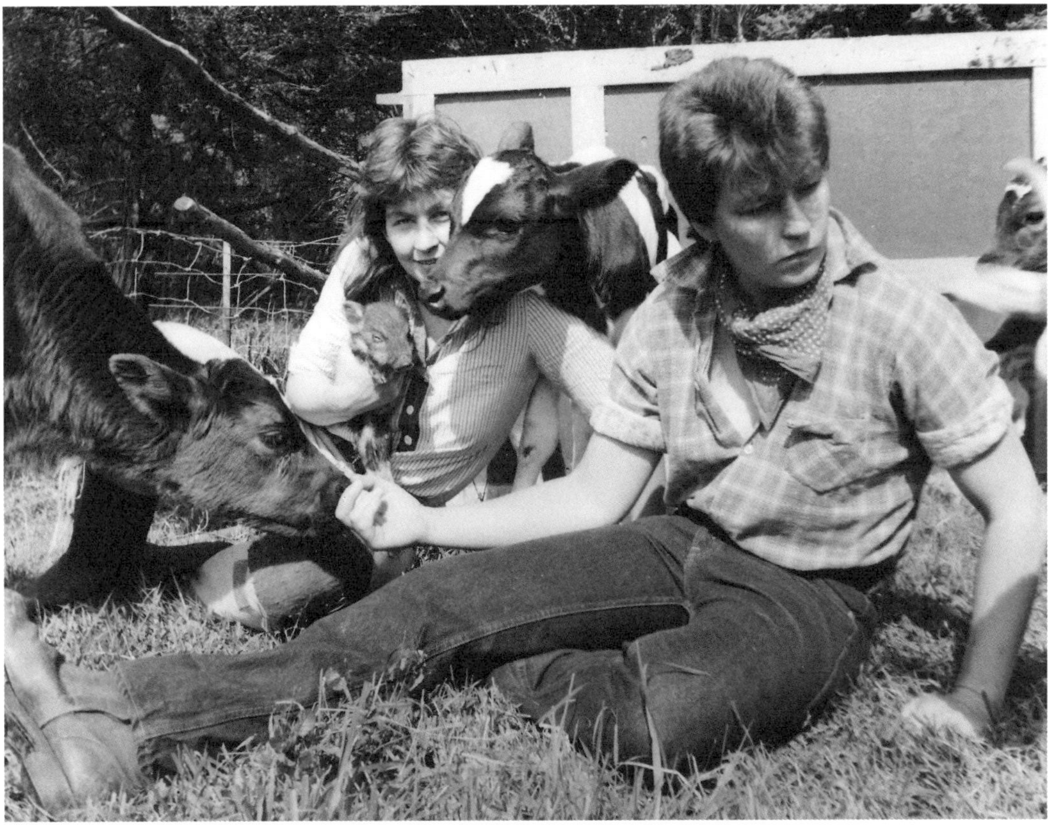

Calf Club Day

I woke up this morning remembering my past
Those days they sure went fast
Summer days and making hay
It feels like Calf Club Day
Feels like Calf Club Day

And memories are precious
But gold and silver have stolen that word
But gold and silver have stolen that word

They're cutting grass in the lower field
They're laughing and sweating
It's going to be a good yield
And I love it when it smells this way
It feels like Calf Club Day
It feels like Calf Club Day

Memories are precious
But gold and silver have stolen that word
But gold and silver have stolen that word

I see my calf, she's got big brown eyes
She's my best friend and I'm only five
And I love it when I feel this way
It feels like Calf Club Day
It feels like Calf Club Day

And memories are precious
But gold and silver have stolen that word
But gold and silver have stolen that word

It's Calf Club Day again
It's Calf Club Day again
It's Calf Club Day

SCHOOL DAYS

When we started at Huntly College we were surrounded by the Māori community, with Waahi Pā nearby. We used to see the Māori Queen, Dame Te Atairangikaahu, down at the local 4 Square store opposite the college, and were taught how to play 'the Māori strum' by some of the hottest guitar players in the kapa haka group down the back of the bus on the way home.

Huntly College had brilliant sports teams, a champion kapa haka group, some wild and whacky teachers, and an attitude.

Huntly College was cool. There were about 800 kids, so it was a bit of a contrast to Ruawaro School. It had brilliant sports teams, a champion kapa haka group, some wild and whacky teachers, and an attitude.

We were both pretty fit from farm work and ended up playing hockey and competing in the athletics team. At our very first college sports day we caught the attention of the athletics coach. I won the 100-metre and 200-metre races, and when they called for the girls' 400-metre and 800-metre races to begin, only Lynda and I lined up, so we knew it was going to be one hell of a competition over both distances.

I was always a bit faster than Lynda, so I pulled away in the last 50 metres to take out the 400 metres. We had time to catch our breath and then stood back at the starting line for the 800-metre middle-distance event.

I took off once again and led the whole way on the first lap. At the 600-metre mark I heard Lynda, who was right beside me, say, 'Let me go, Jools,' so I did. 'Way you go, Lynda,' I said, and suddenly she took off like a racehorse, screaming down the back straight. I couldn't have beaten her if I'd tried, and she won by a good 50 metres.

From that day on I ran the 400 and Lynda ran the 800 metres. Mum had said once that I was built for speed but Lynda had the stamina of an ox. Another one of Mum's memorable sayings was: 'If you put Lynda through a mincer, she'd come out whole.'

Funnily enough, the 1500-metre race was considered too long for girls, but I reckon if there had been a 1500-metre race that day, we would have had a crack at that one too. That same day I went on to win the javelin and long jump, and Lynda took out the high jump and discus.

From then on we seemed to spend a *lot* of our time training. Road running, resistance training, weight training, speed training — you name it, we were doing it. Arthur Lydiard, the great New Zealand marathon runner and athletics coach, was at the forefront of a new kind of training regime and our college coach, Brian Curle, was convinced it would give the whole team an edge.

We had a special training pass that excused us from classes when required, and it also came in handy if we didn't like a particular subject and decided we'd rather go run a few laps of that 400-metre track.

We ended up doing the commercial course in school — not because we chose it but because we were country gals. If you came from a farm you were automatically put into that course, whereas if you came from town you did the professional course, where you learnt French. We learnt shorthand typing and accounting, which bored the shit out of both of us.

Opposite from top: Lynda winning the high jump at a Huntly College sports day; The team photo for the 1975 Wellington to Huntly Relay. Lynda is seated in the front row, far right. TOPP COLLECTION

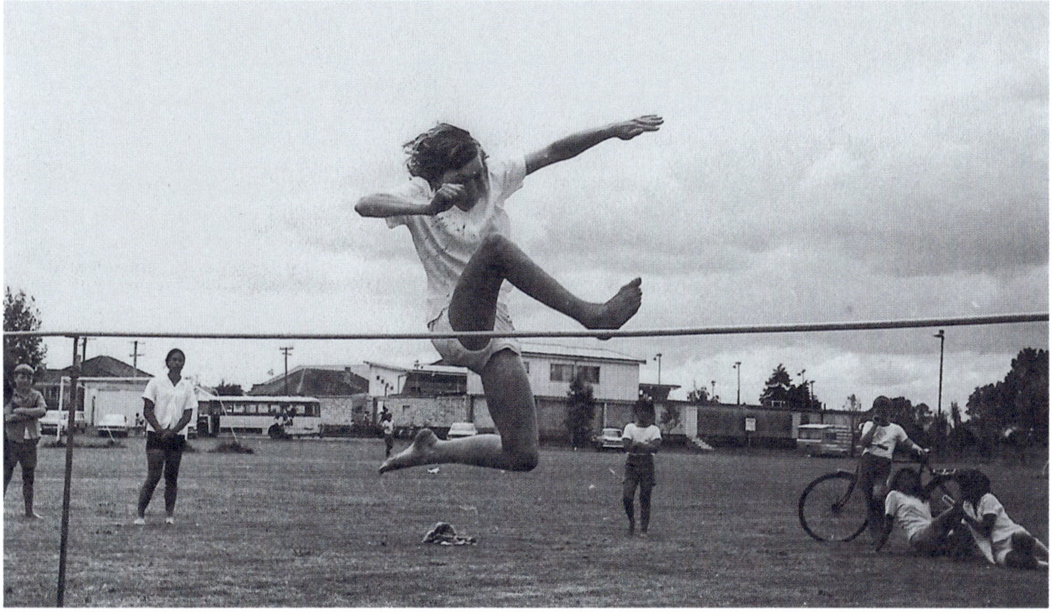

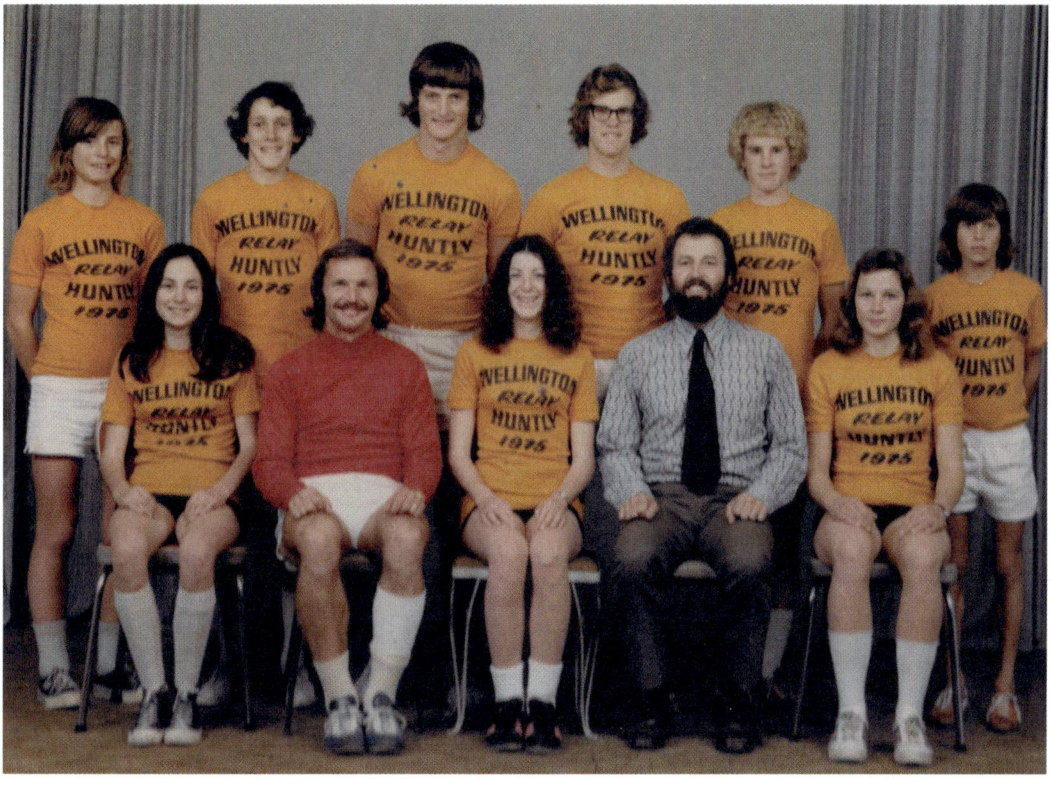

WELLINGTON
RELAY
HUNTLY
1975

Mrs Taylor, our teacher for these subjects, recognised early in the piece that we were not destined to become secretaries or accountants, so she allowed us to run around that 400-metre track for hundreds of miles.

Brian Curle threw everything at the team, and we collected many wins at the inter-school athletics meets at Porritt Stadium in Hamilton. Lynda went on to hold the record for Junior Girls 800 metres, excelled at high jump at the national finals and won Champion Sports Girl many times at the Huntly College prizegiving. I, on the other hand, won Best Sportsmanship trophy for being a good sport after losing the overall championship.

At least we both had a trophy to take home to show Mum and Dad.

Lynda was a member of the school relay team that ran from Wellington to Huntly to raise money for a school camp. They ran it in under 48 hours and made the six o'clock TV news that night. The school bought a few acres of land so they could have their very own place for students to learn the value of the great outdoors.

When we weren't training or doing schoolwork, we would be playing the guitar and hanging out with friends. They encouraged us to enter the Huntly College Talent Quest, so Bruce, Lynda and I, as The Topp Family, did a three-part harmony rendition of Bill Withers' 'Lean on Me'. We thought we sounded pretty good and got a great response from the audience, but then Bruce McKenzie stepped up with his electric guitar and blew us out of the water. We were happy with second place. We'd been a big hit with our friends.

It was a very sociable group and we enjoyed one another's company. Our mate Robyn Blair was especially helpful when it came to cooking and sewing classes. Home economics, it was called. Lynda and I had wanted to do the woodwork class instead but were told that was only for boys. Our teacher, Mrs Kerr, spent many hours trying to teach us the arts of sewing and baking but it just wasn't in us. So when it came time to make an A-line skirt for our final exam, Robyn stepped up and sewed ours for us. She did a really good job because she loved sewing, and we both got an A! Not bad when Lynda and I had both struggled to sew a handkerchief.

Mum made all our clothes, including dresses for the school dance. One year we wanted to wear miniskirts with knitted tank tops and knee-high boots. This was a very fashionable look and we wanted to look cool.

Mum was horrified and refused to let us, so we never went to the dance. No one would back down. A few years later Mum graciously apologised for not letting us go to the dance in the clothes we wanted to wear, which made us love her even more.

From top: Jools (left) and Lynda on their motorbike; Huntly girls (from left) Leonie, Lynda, Sue and Jools on a day at the beach in Tairua, 1974. TOPP COLLECTION

5

Jools on a Slippery Slope

After gaining School Certificate at 16, I was ready to bust out of college and get a job. No university for me — I was going to join the workforce and earn some money. I got a job at Barry Roberts Pharmacy in Huntly's main street. It was a flash establishment with a big mirrored wall and lots of luxurious things like soaps and perfumes and a whole wall of makeup.

I did a Shiseido course, learning how to apply the famous Japanese cosmetics, which stood me in good stead later when it came to stage makeup. It was a long way from milking cows, that's for sure, and I loved working there.

Lynda had gone back to college so it was the first time we'd been apart.

I became good friends with the rest of the staff, and moved in to Huntly, where Mrs Bell rented me a room in her house and cooked my meals. I made $32 a week when I first started. My rent and board was $12 and I thought I was a millionaire. I saved my money and bought a pair of big red platform shoes to go with my flared jeans, and my own little portable cassette player. I went partying with my mates, hanging out at the Huntly South Rugby League Club. I went out with Chris Peel, who played in the forwards and was a good Kiwi bloke. (Obviously the whole lesbian thing hadn't kicked in at this stage.)

Little did I know that this era in my life would change things forever.

When I first started work I was pretty naïve — a real farm girl and even a bit shy. But I loved having new friends and a new family of mates at the rugby league club. I remember one of the guys owned an old house that had been condemned and we all went down there one day and gutted the entire inside. The boys put in a big timber frame so it wouldn't fall over, chainsawed a hole in the wall to fit a beer tanker (towed in on a trailer), and it became Huntly's party house.

When I first started work I was pretty naïve — a real farm girl and even a bit shy.

The cops were happy because they always knew where the party was, and kept an eye out for any unruly behaviour. We knew all the local cops and respected them — some of their kids partied with us as well.

I remember one night when everyone was dancing and drinking. It got to the end of the night and we couldn't find Troj, one of our mates. Turned out he'd got a bit drunk and found an old carpet in the woodshed to sleep on. He rolled it out on the lawn, lay down and rolled himself up in the carpet to stay warm while he slept. He obviously hadn't realised the lawn had a slight slope to it, and by the time we found him he was stuck in his carpet roll at the bottom of the hill. He couldn't unwind himself because the carpet was too heavy.

After we stopped laughing we hauled him out and got him home. We all looked out for each other — that was part of living in a small town.

Right about this time there was a new party high — marijuana. 'Buddha sticks' were being brought into the country and we were sold on them. Our parents' drug had always been alcohol but we wanted to be different from our parents. We wanted to be cool.

I remember someone rolling a super-joint with about 10 Zig-Zag papers stuck together. It got passed around the room and you damn near needed a poultice on the back of your neck to draw on it. Unlike President Clinton, in Huntly we did inhale.

So now this farm gal was a party gal, experimenting with drugs. It didn't feel bad — it felt new and exciting.

But I was heading down a slippery slope . . . I knew that my chemist shop had some drugs we called uppers and downers. The Ministry of Health sometimes sent out reminders to chemists to be wary of young people playing around with drugs, and information on dosage guidelines, so I knew how many you could safely take.

I'm not proud of this, but I helped myself to some of these drugs and tried them out.

At this time Lynda had a weekend job at the local takeaway bar in town, the Clockwork Orange. One fateful night I headed to the Clockwork to get something to eat. I'd taken some of my pills to see what would happen and when I arrived I was out of it.

The Clockwork was the first takeaway bar in Huntly to have a microwave and you could order corn on the cob, served with lashings of butter. I ordered one from Lynda and waited patiently for it to cook. When it was ready Lynda handed it to me, saying, 'Your corn on the cob's ready.'

From top: Teenagers Jools (left) and Lynda, with their friend Sue Peel in the centre; Lynda in her college days.
TOPP COLLECTION

In my drugged state I heard this as 'The cops are here', so I jumped the counter and ran out the back of the shop. Somehow on the way I managed to land both feet in a bucket of water that had been used for mopping the floor. I fell over, dropped the little tin of pills I had in my pocket, and disappeared out the back door into the night.

It might have been hilarious, but the consequences were major. You see, the guys who owned the Clockwork Orange were both ex-cops, and the next day they found my little tin of pills. They were worried about me, so they told the local cops.

When a young constable walked into the chemist I thought nothing of it — l was ready to help him with whatever he'd come to buy. But he spoke to my boss, Barry Roberts, and when they called me out the back of the shop I knew I was in big trouble.

I tried to explain that I was just a young kid experimenting with all this new stuff and I'd meant no harm.

Barry Roberts said, 'Jools, I think you might have to be on permanent holiday' — meaning I was fired. The cop said, 'We'll have to tell your parents.' Oh no, I thought. I knew Mum would be so disappointed.

At the time, Mum and Bruce were running a florist shop in town. As we left the chemist I saw Mum in the distance coming out of a department store. I turned to the cop and said, 'I'll be back in a minute.' I took off and ran to Mum — I wanted to be the one to tell her what I'd done. Her line 'Tell the truth faster' echoed in my head.

When I reached Mum I was so out of breath I could hardly speak, but I managed to let her know that I had stolen a whole lot of drugs and the cops were coming but everything was okay. Well, I could see by the look on Mum's face that everything was *not* okay. The young policeman caught up with us and I was escorted inside the florist shop. Possible charges were: stealing from my employer, possession of stolen drugs, dealing in prescription drugs — and theft. I had never paid for my corn on the cob.

What happened next came out of a combination of forgiveness, trust, leniency and love. I was banished to the farm — sort of like home detention — and I had to milk the cows with Dad for six months. I was forbidden to see any of my Huntly friends, which was hard as all this was my fault, not theirs. But I also felt that I was lucky to get a chance to put things right and leave all the drug drama behind.

Mum and Bruce took me back to the farm that night and I was dreading how Dad would react to my life of crime. Luckily for me he was out at a meeting, so I crawled into bed and awaited my fate in the morning.

> Mum and Bruce took me back to the farm that night and I was dreading how Dad would react to my life of crime.

I woke and reluctantly made my way out to the kitchen to face the music. Dad looked out from behind his newspaper and calmly said, 'I knew you were heading for trouble, girl. Have something to eat and meet me at the cowshed.' Oh, how I wanted to hug him and tell him I loved him for not giving me a hard time, but Dad wasn't much of a hugger so I held myself back, grabbed a cup of tea and headed out into the early morning.

I quietly worked with Dad on the farm for the next six months. I learnt to love him even more, and I think he liked having me around.

Opposite: The twins' beautiful dad, who quietly got the young Jools back on the right track when she needed it. ARANI CUTHBERT

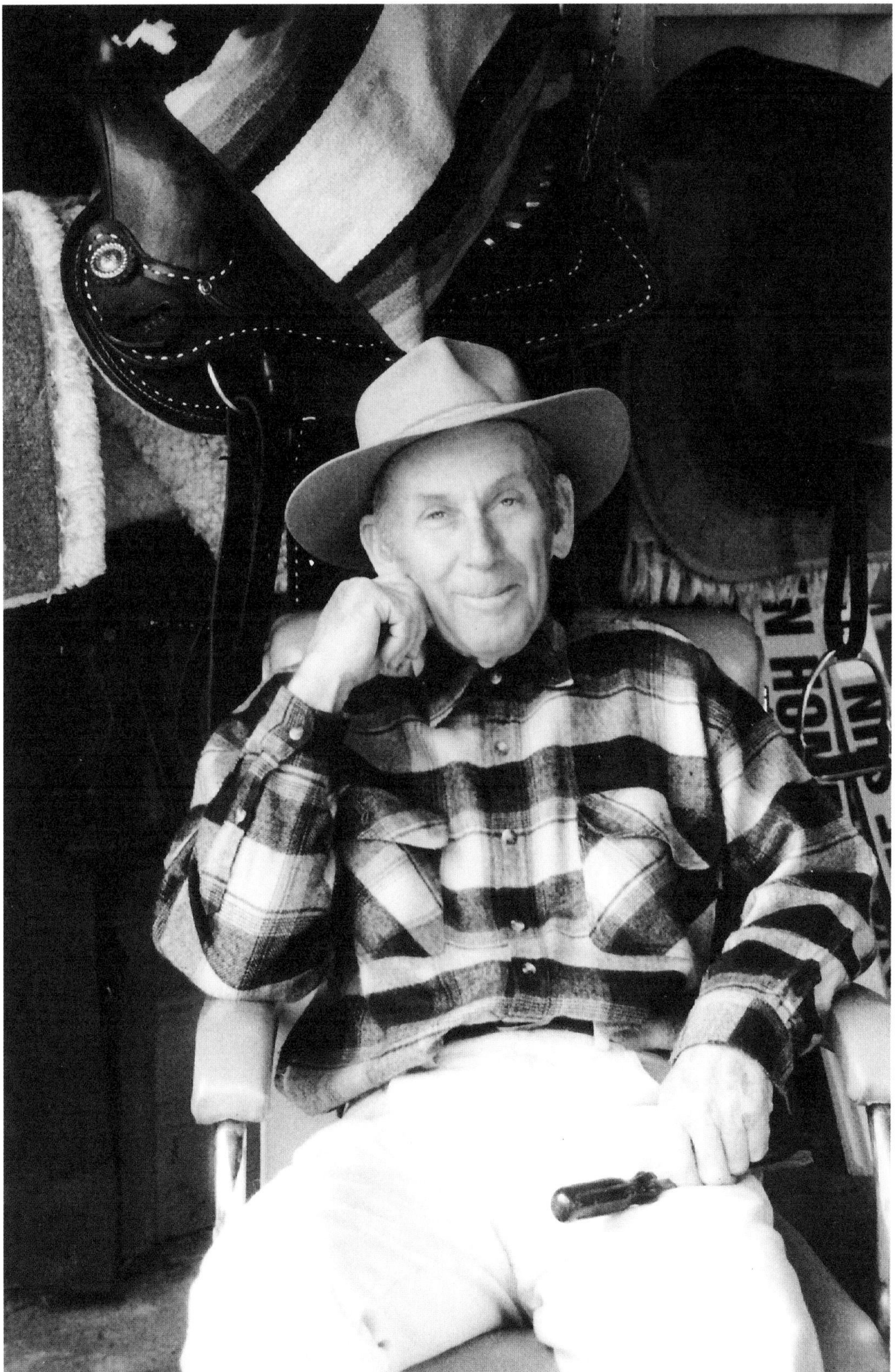

So thank you Barry Roberts, the local Huntly cop and Dad. You gave a naïve 16-year-old girl a second chance, and for that I shall always be grateful.

While all this was happening, Lynda was still attending Huntly College and she never once judged me for my criminal past — in fact she never even asked me why I had done such a stupid thing.

At the end of her college year Lynda applied to join the Territorial army, and Dad said to me, 'Why don't you join your sister?'

So in 1976 we both set off on another journey and a new life.

6

Joining the Army

Dad drove us to the railway station in Hamilton and we all stood around awkwardly, no one quite knowing what to say. Dad broke the silence. 'It'll be good for you girls to be in the army,' he said. Then he walked away, turned back to yell 'Be good!', hopped into his Plymouth Belvedere V8 and drove off.

Mum had said her goodbyes at home. She later said she'd have cried if she'd come to the station.

For the next few weeks Jools and I would be training to be soldiers. We slung our green army bags over our shoulders and headed in to catch the train to Christchurch. It sounded so exotic — the furthest we'd been before was Uncle Tom and Aunty Ethel's place out the back of Whangārei on school holidays, and a couple of trips to Hamilton.

The train pulled out of Hamilton station at around dusk and we slept most of the way to Wellington. We boarded the Cook Strait ferry the next day. We'd never been on a boat before and both of us got crook during the crossing. Then it was back on the train to Christchurch, where we were met by an army RL (Regulation Lorry).

There were several of us and it was late when we all piled into the back of the truck. The metal fold-down seats were hard as rock and cold as hell. A man in uniform barked instructions to us to hold on and not stand up at any time during the journey.

It was probably around 11.30 p.m. when we pulled into Burnham Military Camp, 30 kilometres west of Christchurch, where we were instructed to get out and form three lines in front of the barracks.

What followed over the next three months was what we have described as a pyjama party with guns.

We were 28 young women from all over New Zealand embarking on the last Women's Royal Army Corps (WRAC) basic training ever. The following year men's and women's basic training were integrated.

What followed over the next three months was what we have described as a pyjama party with guns. We learnt to march, salute, fire an M16 rifle, set up and use a Bren machine-gun, erect an RC-292 radio antenna, drive a truck, read a compass, and cross a river with a pack and rifle. Oh and of course how to stand up and fight for our country.

We also learnt countless other useful things like how to make a beret look cool.

Over three months, a bunch of women who hadn't known each other beforehand were moulded into a close, loyal, caring team. We helped each other look good on parade and made sure our buttons sparkled and our boots were shiny. We pulled an army Land Rover out of the Rakaia River with a rope and our bare hands.

From top: Army girls polishing their boots; Jools having a laugh with two fellow recruits.
TOPP COLLECTION

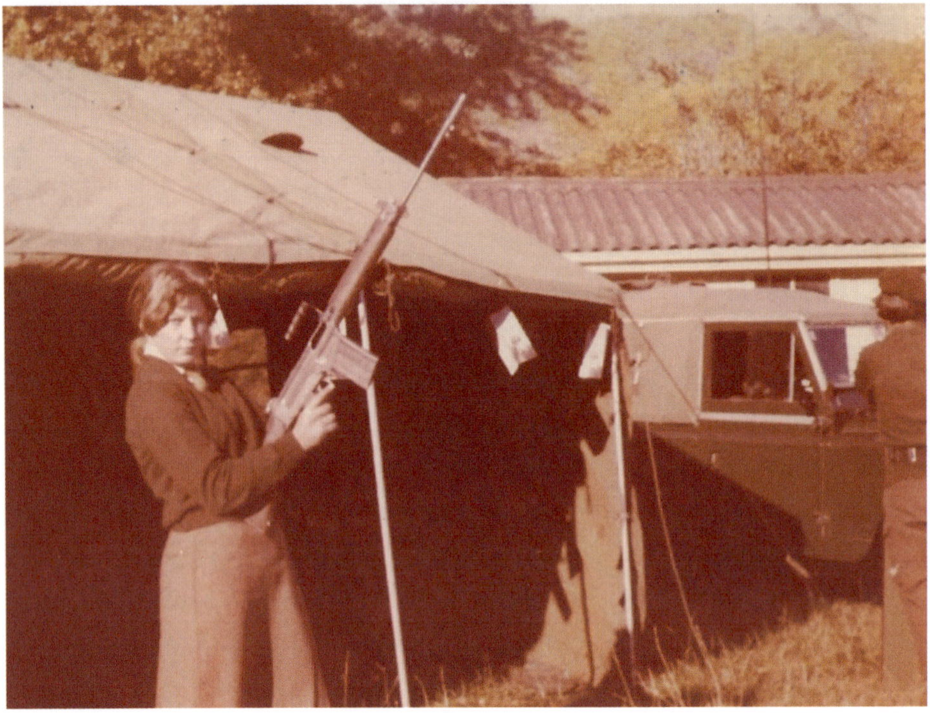

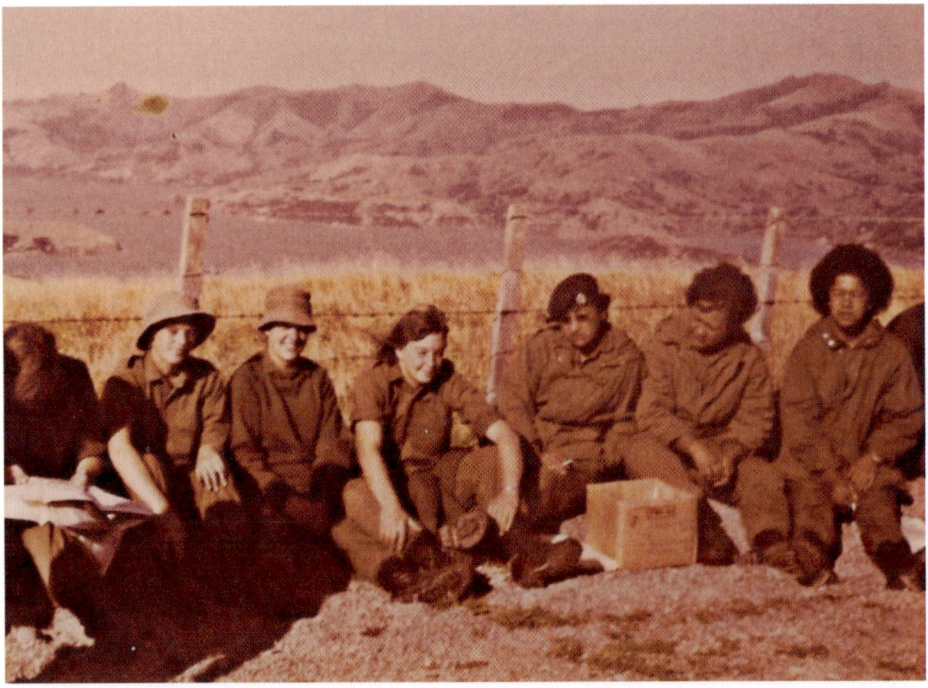

In some extraordinary way we felt love for our little unit — a sense of pride, you might say.

After seven weeks we graduated as efficient soldiers, and Jools and I remained Territorial soldiers for another four years, doing weekend manoeuvres with 2 Canterbury and 4 O South in Dunedin.

We felt really proud of what we had achieved, but we also discovered that not everyone was a fan of women being in the army.

At one annual camp everyone (men and women) had been camping out for five nights doing exercises and at the end of it we were ready for a decent meal and a shower. Straight after that, we were to be in a parade down the main street of town.

But when we got back to the main camp the women were suddenly ordered to clean the field toilets, which meant they had not enough time to get ready for the parade. There were clearly some big guns in the army (no pun intended) who felt women had no place there.

In a display of solidarity and human kindness we will never forget, all the young men in our signals unit stepped up and ironed our parade uniforms and polished our shoes ready for us when we leapt out of the showers. There was no way they wanted us to miss the parade.

Thankfully we were never called upon to take up arms for New Zealand, but it was an interesting adventure and gave us some street cred when we started fighting a different kind of war — in the political turmoil of the early 1980s.

Opposite from top: Lynda with her M16 rifle; The team taking a lunch break while on manoeuvres. TOPP COLLECTION

Private Julie Bethridge Topp (left) and Private Lynda Bethridge Topp.
TOPP COLLECTION

JOINING THE ARMY

Now what?

I vividly remember the phone call. We were 17 now, and Jools and I had talked a lot about it while we were doing our training at Burnham.

Dad answered, and the conversation went something like this.

'Hi Dad, we've finished our basic training and Jools and I would like to come home now to work on the farm and eventually take over.'

There was a short pause.

'Well, your mother and I have decided you should go and see the world. If you come home now, you'll be stuck here milking cows for the rest of your lives.'

It was not the answer we'd been expecting.

We found a little café in Colombo Street, Leo's Coffee Lounge, and ordered mince on toast and a cuppa. What were we going to do?

'The farm is a tie,' Dad went on. 'You've got your whole lives ahead of you — just get out there and live it.'

I hung up and told Jools the bad news. We had no home and no jobs.

We found a little café in Colombo Street, Leo's Coffee Lounge, and ordered mince on toast and a cuppa. What were we going to do?

The priority was to find somewhere to stay, and after an hour of traipsing around the streets of Christchurch we found a boarding house opposite Cranmer Square. We had enough money for one room for two weeks, so we dossed down and decided we would figure out the next step tomorrow.

We clearly needed to find work. My eye caught on a sign outside Cooper Henderson Motors, dealers in second-hand cars.

Hiring Now.

The job entailed washing cars on the lot every morning, cleaning and small repairs to trade-in vehicles, and driving vehicles to the WOF station. They seemed impressed by my ability to replace a tail-light bulb and change a tyre, skills acquired from Dad. They said I could start the following Monday.

The next few weeks were pretty rough. We lived on fried cauliflower and white bread with lashings of butter, and we walked around Christchurch a lot because we didn't have a car. On the first Sunday we ended up in Cathedral Square, listening to the Salvation Army Band. We were spellbound by a young woman playing tambourine and singing.

By the end of the second week we had found a house to rent in Ōpawa, and the following Sunday we headed back to the Square to watch the Salvation Army again. I'm not sure whether she ever knew that we were her devoted fans, but she had a profound impact upon us. That gal could sing.

The music scene in Christchurch was flourishing at this time, and soon enough we found our way upstairs at the Gresham Hotel, where we discovered Nancy Kiel and her band.

That gal could sing too. She was a gorgeous, tall American redhead and we fell madly in love with her stylish performances. We would sneak up the stairs on a Friday night and dance the night away to Nancy and the band. I say sneak because we were only 17 and the legal drinking age in 1976 was 21.

Nancy had a big lesbian following and Jools and I fitted right in. We seemed to be just like them. One night we invited Nancy and her friends back to our place in Ōpawa for a party. By the time we got home there were about 40 people milling about waiting — we still didn't have a car and had walked home! We made a note that it was time to purchase a vehicle.

> We'd never really thought much about how we sang but she said we were unique and had a sister harmony to die for.

We lit the big fire in the lounge and did what we knew from our old days back home on the farm — got out the guitar for a sing-along. It wasn't too long before Nancy turned up and listened to us sing for the first time. We'd never really thought much about how we sang but she said we were unique and had a sister harmony to die for.

I threw in a yodel or two and that seemed to impress our guests.

We spent the next two years living, working and playing in Christchurch. Jools got a job at the Aulsebrooks biscuit factory, I worked at the car yard, we got a puppy — a black foxy cross we called Wild Oats — and every Friday night we headed to the Gresham to watch Nancy.

One morning I arrived at work just as an old guy drove into the yard to trade in his old vehicle. The olive-green Standard Eight was the cutest car I'd ever seen, and by five o'clock that day it was ours. We called her Olive. We were moving up in the world.

When Nancy offered us the small flat at the back of her house we jumped at the chance and that was where the gang was born — Nancy Kiel, lead singer; Dianne Cadwallader, probably the finest woman guitarist in New Zealand and former manager of Mr Lee Grant; and the divine Miss Janice Gray, cabaret singer, who was going out with a sheep stealer at the time and had just got out of finishing school (code for women's prison). She'd been caught importing Buddha sticks from Australia.

Top: Lynda and Jools carving up the dance floor. NANCY KIEL

Bottom: Di Cadwallader, Lynda (centre) and Jools in full voice. MARK WILSON

A few other amazing women called in from time to time, such as Canadian Sandi Hall; writer and feminist Lee Hatherly, the sexiest voice in radio; and Annie Davies, folk singer extraordinaire. For the first time in our lives we were surrounded by women musicians — women who identified as feminists and political activists. Di was a lesbian, Nancy and Janice were not but it didn't matter. We all felt a connection that was fuelled by the joy of singing.

Lynda and I were the youngest in this group of weird and wonderful women and it just felt so natural. This was our tribe, and they felt like family.

Nancy encouraged us to get a job singing, and before long we had landed a gig singing at the Victorian Coffee Gallery on a Wednesday night. The pay was $5 each and as many toasted sandwiches as we wanted — what a deal.

We ordered extra sandwiches and brought them home to heat and eat over the next few days. The Victorian seemed to be frequented by university students, lesbians and chess players — there were a lot of duffel coats and roman sandals.

We were invited to sing at the International Women's Day rally in Cathedral Square and debuted our first protest song, 'Freedom'. It was a call to women to stand up and fight for what they believed in, and seemed to have the desired effect on women at the rally.

> We'll fight for our freedom,
> We'll never be wrong.
> We'll just keep on fighting,
> No matter how long
>
> Our sisterhood is strong again,
> Fighting one and all,
> Bringing together all the women
> Standing strong and tall.

Nancy and Di played at that rally too; it was the first of many. Di was hugely important in helping us forge our career in those early days. She knew the ropes and helped us become professional performers. She showed us how to use a mic, how to string a guitar properly and to always tune your guitar with a tuner, be on time for a gig — all the things that mattered in the entertainment game.

This was the 1970s. Feminism was taking New Zealand by storm and here we all were, strong women, making our way in the world and having fun doing it.

Jools and I were approached by Trevor Spitz, the big Christchurch agent/promoter at the time. He needed an act to play at some of the smaller pubs on the outskirts of Christchurch and hired Jools and me to do a gig at the Yaldhurst Hotel. This was a totally different vibe to the Victorian Coffee Gallery — mostly country people and horse trainers frequented the Yaldy and we had a pretty good first night. Nancy arrived as we were singing our last song and we all hugged and kissed and had a celebratory beer.

We were called into Trevor's office on Monday morning and promptly fired for being openly gay in a country pub. This was the first time we had personally encountered any sort of discrimination. It was also weird because Nancy was not gay. In fact for just about every young man in Christchurch she was the girl of their dreams.

The thought of someone being demonised for loving someone of the same gender was hard for us to accept — actually hurtful. But if anything, it made us stronger and probably more outspoken.

We made a few appearances at the Christchurch Folk Club and every now and then we joined Janice Gray at one of her many hotel gigs. Janice knew the special knock on the door of late-night

Jools (left) and Lynda return to the Victorian Coffee Gallery in 1983, six years after their first appearance there. STUFF LIMITED

bars where the party continued into the night. Sometimes there were more people in the bar after hours than there were during regular trading. We always felt special when Janice took us out on the town; she knew everyone and always looked after us, making sure we met all her friends and always had a drink in hand.

We really thought we'd made it when Red Mole asked us in 1977 to perform in their show at Carmen's Balcony, an infamous nightclub in Wellington. Red Mole was at the time New Zealand's most avant-garde theatre group. We loaded up Olive, drove to Picton, caught the ferry the next morning and arrived in Wellington excited for our first theatre show.

Red Mole had put together a cabaret and they needed someone to yodel — all those years of me howling like a cat in heat to perfect the Swiss sound was finally paying off.

Jools and I carried our guitars up the stairs to Carmen's Balcony, thinking we had made the big time. Caterina De Nave, the group's money taker and unofficial bouncer, was sitting in the ticket office. She had long dark hair and an air of confidence — I thought she was pretty good-looking. She told us to go through for a sound check, and there was Red Mole in rehearsal.

Deborah Hunt, Sally Rodwell and Alan Brunton were the original members of Red Mole, and they were joined by different musicians in their shows around New Zealand. Beaver and Jan Preston were the two main singers at the time, and now we were there too.

The show was loosely based on a New Zealand A&P show, and we were to come out and yodel in a talent quest sequence. I remember Deb did a fire-eating performance as part of the talent quest and we reckoned she should have won it hands down. Her stage presence was commanding and she held the audience in the palm of her hand.

Sally could turn her hand to anything, portraying sadness and then switching to happiness in the blink of an eye. The next minute she was a puppeteer, and between shows she made the masks and costumes. Her partner Alan Brunton was a poet and writer/performer who helped pave the way for local material to be seen as acceptable in New Zealand.

Our three nights with Red Mole were exhilarating. They created a space where performers could experiment and explore their own original ideas, and Jools and I realised at that point that there was more to the entertainment world than a few songs at the local coffee house.

It was also our first performance outside Christchurch, and Wellington audiences seemed to like the fresh-faced farm gals who could yodel.

We must have made an impression on the bouncer, too, as Caterina later invited us, Di and Nancy down to Dunedin for a weekend to record some songs. She had access to a studio as she was now working as a script editor for a new kids' television show called *Play School*. In the end it was only Jools and I who went, as Di and Nancy had a gig.

———

So we packed up the Standard Eight again and headed for an adventure down south. And what an adventure it was. The prospect of spending a weekend with Caterina was both exciting and a little frightening for me. I had thought she was amazing when we met her in Wellington with Red Mole, and when we pulled into the driveway of her terraced house in Great King Street my heart was going flat out like a lizard drinking.

Caterina answered the door and greeted us like old friends. She wined and dined us, gave us a guided tour of Dunedin — although we drove as she had never got her licence. She was funny, she was charming, and by Saturday night I was in her bed.

Next morning Jools was having a cuppa in the cobblestoned garden that opened off the kitchen. As I sat down, her first words were, 'Well, I guess we really must be lesbians now.'

On the Sunday we waved goodbye to Caterina as we drove away in Olive, and all the way home I had this weird knot in my stomach — you know, the one you get when you've just had your first lesbian encounter.

Funnily enough, we didn't record any songs while we were down there.

She was funny, she was charming, and by Saturday night I was in her bed.

Back in Christchurch, we were approached during a Victorian Coffee Gallery gig by two young guys who had watched us perform. They had started up a coffee lounge in Dunedin called Governor's Café, just around the corner from the famous Captain Cook Hotel near the campus of Otago University. Would we like to come and play there every Wednesday night?

Was it fate or was it just coincidence that three weeks after my weekend with Caterina we were offered a job in Dunedin?

We said yes, loaded up the car with everything we owned, including Wild Oats and her four puppies, hugged Nancy and Di goodbye and we were off.

We had nowhere to live, no full-time jobs, no money and five dogs.

7

Dunedin: The Topp Twins are Born

We slept in the car on our first night in Dunedin, then went to the Governor's for our first gig. Halfway through the evening the door opened and in the glow of the streetlight I saw the silhouette of a woman with long hair. In stepped Caterina.

It was good to see her. She sat and watched for a while, then walked over and said, 'There's room at my place if you'd like to stay.'

And we did. For a year and a half.

Dunedin was a blast.

You could stand in line at the supermarket checkout between a granny in a knitted cardigan and tartan scarf and a young punk rocker with a pink mohawk and a nose chain pinned to their jacket.

University students ruled the day. Everyone was drinking coffee, everyone bought their clothes at second-hand shops, and tea cosies

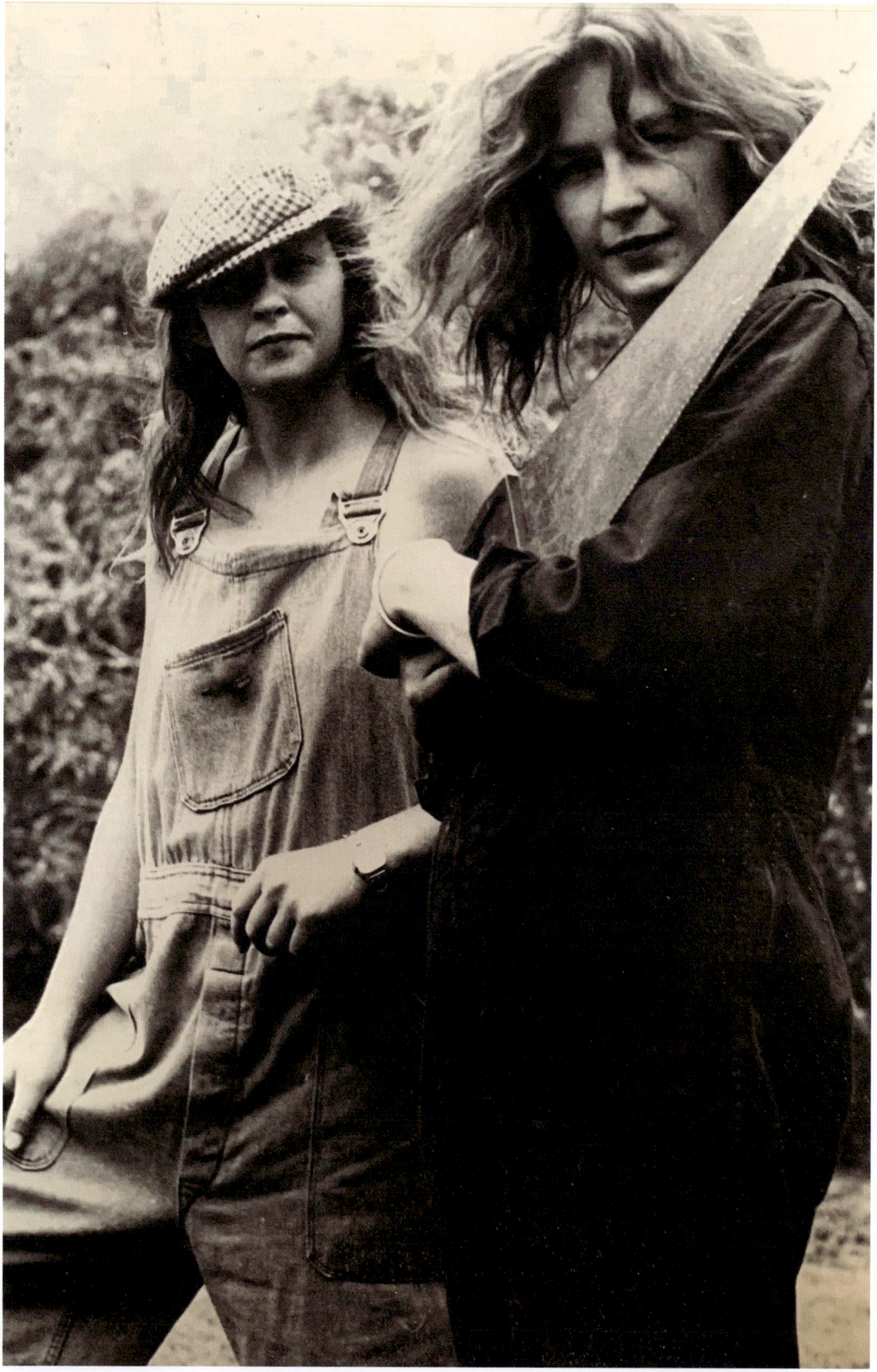

sold out fast as they made good hats. The local lesbians lived in a big old house that had once been an establishment of ill-repute.

Caterina organised a new house for all of us and we settled into a charming little bungalow called Rose Cottage in Macandrew Bay, overlooking the harbour and on the way to Larnach Castle. There was (of course) a rose garden right along the front — it looked like something out of Somerset Maugham.

The local lesbians lived in a big old house that had once been an establishment of ill-repute.

I got a job as a gardener in a local park, which I loved, mainly because I was outside, and Lynda became New Zealand's first woman tyre inspector. The ad in the local paper read:

Man Wanted
Training offered to become a Tyre Inspector
Firestone Tyre Shop

Lynda rocked up for the interview, saying she could work and learn just as well as any man. She got the job, started out unloading tyres off trucks and moved on to re-treading truck and car tyres. She patched holes in the sides of tractor tyres with a rubber bung that looked like an old-style iron. Eventually she worked her way up to becoming a tyre inspector.

We ended up buying a second car, as Olive had developed an annoying habit of sometimes deciding not to start. One day, parked outside the local dairy, was a truly remarkable find: a Standard Ten, the next model up from the Standard Eight. It was a little beauty.

Opposite: Young lesbians, 1979. ROMI CURL

Now we even had twin cars.

Problem was that neither of them was particularly reliable.

One day we managed to get one of the old girls going but she broke down on Portobello Road, the long and winding route around the coast into Dunedin. A young man in a purple Dodge Charger stopped to ask if we needed help, and after a look under the bonnet he said it might be a mechanic's job and offered to tow us into town.

We were grateful for his help but honestly, it turned into the hairiest ride of our lives. I think he forgot we were hooked to his tow rope as he flew along the road reaching speeds of 80–100 ks. Several times we were strewn across the white line in his wake — it's a total wonder we didn't collide with an oncoming car. We were both hysterical with nervous laughter for about 8 kilometres.

We made it, but we learnt a valuable lesson that day: *never* on *any* account accept the offer of a tow behind a young man in a purple Dodge Charger.

Dunedin was a great place to be for music at that time — many a good New Zealand band came out of the Dunedin music scene. We remember seeing Toy Love at the Captain Cook, and The Chills.

We began to find our own style, Lynda's yodelling got even better, we started writing more of our own songs and began to get noticed in the burgeoning café scene. We couldn't make a living from our music, but it was the thing that excited us the most. We decided we really needed a name if we were to get ahead in the music world.

After discussing numerous options we eventually came up with Homemade Jam.

The Homemade bit was about our country roots and a play on the meaning of made or assembled by oneself, and the Jam was about playing with other musicians. We thought it was great and used the name for a good six months, until someone rang to book us for a birthday party, asking for Homo Jam.

> Then Lynda said out of the blue, 'We're the Topp twins. How about we just stick to our real name?'

Now we were not afraid of being openly gay, but Homo Jam just felt weird, so it was back to the drawing board. After about another week of tossing around suggestions we finally asked ourselves: who are we and what do we want people to know us as? Then Lynda said out of the blue, 'We're the Topp twins. How about we just stick to our real name?'

And so from that day on we were simply known as the Topp Twins.

And it was the Topp Twins who were asked to perform at the United Women's Convention in Hamilton in 1979. Jools and I were excited because the whole gang from Christchurch were going to be part of the big concert on the Sunday night and there would be a big contingent of lesbians from all over New Zealand.

The agenda was packed full of speeches and workshops, involving women from all different walks of life, political agendas and ethnicities. A lot of Māori women attended, many of whom identified as lesbian. There was a sense of a new era dawning for women to control their own lives and destinies.

But even in this environment there was no time allocated for lesbians to speak or share their fears, concerns and ideas. We felt invisible, unheard, and even untrusted by the women in charge of the agenda. Why was there no place for us at a convention that was supposed to celebrate women?

We decided to stage a girlcott, and demanded a lesbian speaker among the final evening speeches. Our bargaining power included the refusal to stage the concert that closed out the convention.

Talk about radical: a bunch of us even staged a sit-in on the green outside the main building. Eventually the organisers agreed to have a lesbian representative speak. Rosemary Ronald was the chosen one: she was a mother and a schoolteacher, eloquent, proud, clear, and sexy to boot. Lesbian visibility had arrived, but we also thought: if it is this hard to get through to the conservative women among us, how hard is it going to be to change the establishment and the men in charge?

The concert went ahead, and we sang 'Paradise', which celebrates lesbian love. We wanted to show that being lesbian was something to be proud of. As we told the media at the time, many lesbian women felt trapped in heterosexual relationships. The 1970s was a time when lesbians started to express solidarity, but many still felt isolated and disempowered. We wanted to reach out to them.

> When will you come to me and touch me on the cheek?
> And when will you come to me and say let's sleep
> And when will you come to me and take me by the hand?
> And when will you come to me and take me to Dreamland?
>
> In Paradise
> In Paradise
>
> I saw you in the park today, too scared to cross that road
> Cos I was here in Paradise and you out in the cold
> So come on into Paradise where women feel all right
> So come on into Paradise, we'll do just what we like

DUNEDIN: THE TOPP TWINS ARE BORN

In Paradise
In Paradise

And then I saw her turn around and she slowly smiled at me
She walked across that road today, she walked defiantly
She said I've come to Paradise, I've come to be set free

In Paradise
In Paradise

She touched me on the cheek that day, she said I want to be
   with you
So women cross that road today — there's a Paradise for you

In Paradise
In Paradise
In Paradise

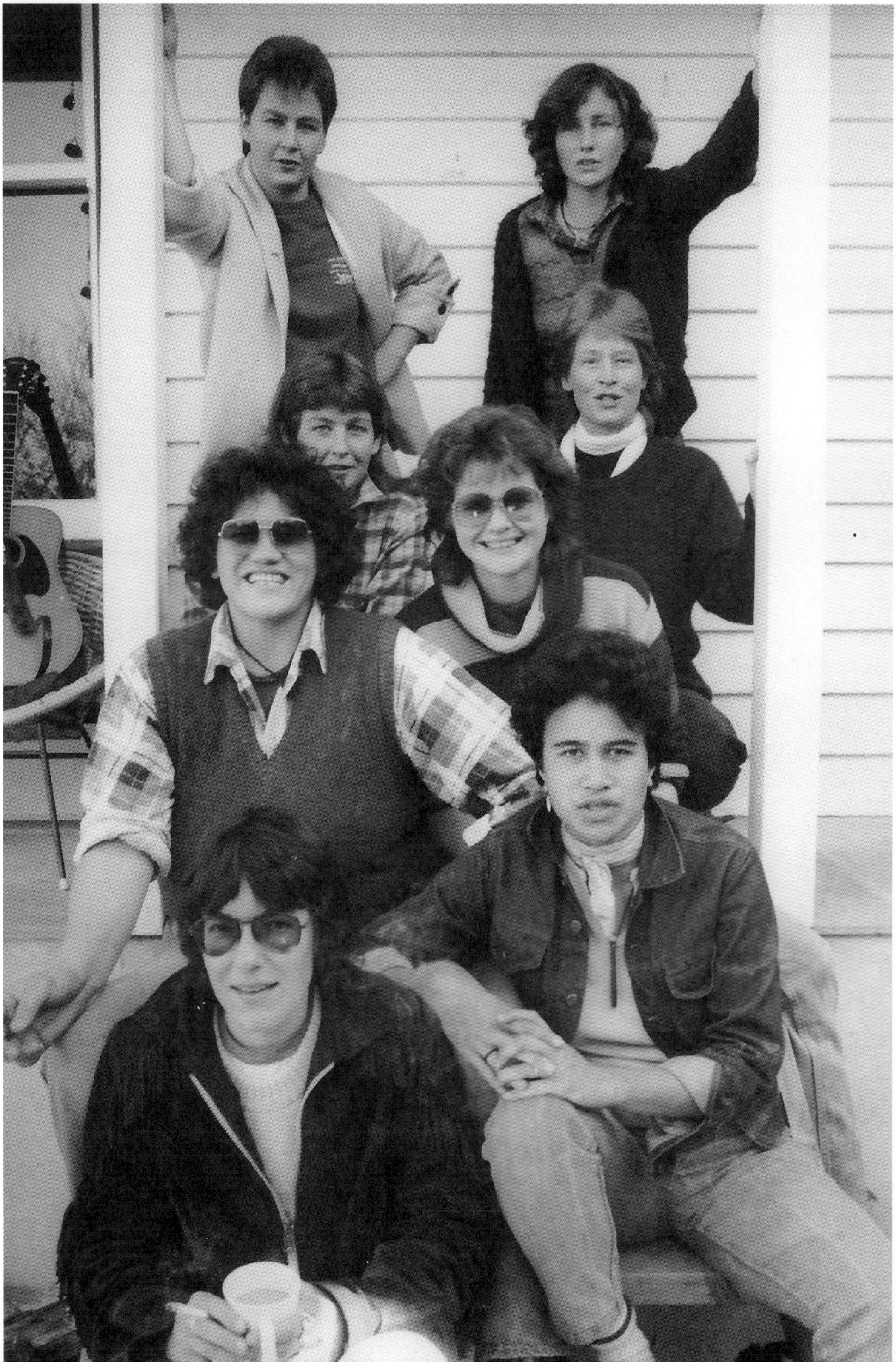

8

Auckland: The Place to Be

The 1979 Women's Convention changed our lives in many ways. It was our first real taste of being immersed in a large group of political women who identified as lesbians. There was a large contingent there from Auckland and these women were amazing — strong and articulate, out and proud.

So without too much discussion we decided Auckland was the place to be. Things were happening there and we wanted to be a part of that story. This meant Lynda and Caterina agreed to part ways, as Caterina was moving up in the world of television and wanted to stay in Dunedin.

I was happily in love with Nik Lancaster, who I'd met in Christchurch. She was a nurse at Christchurch Hospital and was learning to play the drums. We ended up living for a while in her

Opposite: The twins and some of their Auckland gang. (Clockwise from top left) Lynda, Margie Palmer, Di Cadwallader, Nancy Kiel, Tracy Huirama, Jess Hawk Oakenstar, Mereana Pitman and Jools. GIL HANLY

parents' studio — they were an amazing family who accepted me into their tight-knit unit. Nik was up for an Auckland adventure too.

We'd heard on the grapevine that Ponsonby was the lesbian capital of Auckland, so that's where we landed.

Life in Ponsonby was good. We had a house, dogs, a guitar, and a mob of young lesbians who became lifelong friends. What we didn't have was money. Even though we had made an impact at the evening concert at the convention, we knew we'd never make enough money singing — we both needed jobs. I found work packing men's shirts into boxes, and Jools landed a dream job as a gardener at Auckland Zoo.

Ponsonby was different back then, much less middle class, and very multicultural. It was not long after the terrible dawn raids, a dark chapter in New Zealand history, when cops stormed the homes of Pacific Island families to crack down on overstayers. Many of these raids happened in Ponsonby. Unlike some other Auckland suburbs, Ponsonby was home to many alternative types — and we were among them.

Ivan's restaurant was our local. It offered sausages, fried onions, steak, eggs and chips, white bread and butter, and all washed down with free cups of tea from a big urn. Ivan, the chef, was Yugoslavian and his sister Mary waited tables. She was always immaculately dressed, her hair swept up into a soft bun. She would take your order with a slight tilt of her head and never ever wrote anything down. Then she would shout out the order to Ivan as she walked into the kitchen and, in what seemed like only minutes, she would arrive with six plates up her arm and deal them out like a pack of cards.

Ivan's stayed open till the early hours of the morning and we ate there on many occasions after returning home from a late night out. It would be full of shift workers, cab drivers, musicians grabbing a feed after a gig, and assorted drunks. Mary didn't put up with any troublemakers. She never kicked anybody out; instead she would ring their family to come and get them. Jools and I thought she was amazing: she reminded us a little of our mum. And the food was glorious.

Just down the road from Ivan's was Bhana Bros, where we bought our groceries, and of course way down the other end of the street was The Gluepot Tavern.

We frequented the downstairs public bar. By late afternoon Friday it would be pumping; by 8 p.m. there would have been a fight of some sort, especially if someone knocked someone else's jug over. The lesbians had a bar leaner just to the right as you walked in, so we could get out quickly if the fight spilled over, but they never lasted too long — the management were pretty onto it. Everyone stayed in their groups. We were accepted there — no one gave us a hard time.

The lesbians had a bar leaner just to the right as you walked in, so we could get out quickly if the fight spilled over.

It took us three months to find our way upstairs to the music venue. The manager had recently introduced entertainment by way of up-and-coming acts on Monday to Wednesday nights, and we climbed the stairs one night to check out The Sam Ford Verandah Band. Trudi Green was belting out an original in her raspy Cockney accent. As we ordered our beers no one could keep their eyes off the blonde bombshell in her amazing outfit, a cross between a Playboy Bunny and a 1950s cowgirl.

Sam played guitar and keyboards. With his cowboy hat and embroidered jacket he was straight out of Sons of the Pioneers from the Grand Ole Opry. We loved them and became good friends. Many parties and jams went down at their big house down on the waterfront, and then we got the gig: a double act at The Gluepot featuring The Sam Ford Verandah Band and the Topp Twins. Those early-week performances at The Gluepot really kick-started our careers.

Nancy Kiel and Di Cadwallader eventually found their way to Auckland too. Nancy introduced us once again to her dear Canadian friend Sandi Hall and for a while we all lived in her house in Remuera, a beautiful big villa that had been restored, unlike most of the houses in Ponsonby at the time.

We got a gig on Thursday nights playing at La Cava, a small downtown restaurant, and life was sweet. The music scene was exciting and there was a series of women's concerts at the Island of Real café: so many amazing women performers belting out their own original songs, and a huge women's audience just waiting for those shows to happen.

Di and Nancy were our favourites of course, and Hilary King, a teacher with an incredible crop of red hair, was high on our list. Mereana Pitman had a beautiful strong voice matching her strong commitment to Māori struggles at that time. Her integrity was amazing, and she was inspiring to be around. Mahinārangi Tocker was truly one of New Zealand's best singer-songwriters, and Clare Bear was a great all-rounder who could sing, play guitar and bass, and was a brilliant sound technician. She did sound on many of our early tours.

Val Murphy was already a legend — she could belt out a blues number, then make you cry with a sweet original. Di McMillan on ukulele sang some mean tunes with Gloria Hildred, an amazing jazz/blues guitarist; Tracy Huirama had a sexy soulful sound, Hattie St John had been on the music scene in Auckland for some time, and Jess Hawk Oakenstar, originally from the US, was a folk/rock hero who wrote great originals and did a mean version of 'Sweet Transvestite' from *The Rocky Horror Picture Show*.

We were the matriarchs of music, the feminists of folk, the lesbians singing lesbian love songs and, as the late, great Aretha Franklin once sang, 'Sisters are doing it for themselves.' Our concerts at the Island of Real with all these women were always sold out, with feminists, artists and lesbians making up the bulk of our audience.

In 1982 the Web Women's Collective came into existence, and under the label Web Records put out the very first New Zealand album written, performed and produced by women. *Out of the Corners* was recorded at Harlequin Studios in Auckland, in the cut-price midnight-till-dawn shift, and we presold 500 copies to cover our costs. This had never been done before — it felt like we were part of a musical revolution.

But we're getting a bit ahead of ourselves. After a stay in Remuera we moved back to Ponsonby. The Karangahape Girls Club (KG Club), a lesbian nightclub, was in full swing at the top of K Road and it felt as if most of the lesbians in Auckland lived in or around that area. Lynda and I had started playing soccer for the lesbian soccer team Circe, and we were part of a thriving community. It was cool to be a dyke.

We were all intent on changing the way women were treated and we wanted to tell the world, but we had no media platform and cellphones hadn't been invented. Our only possible means of communication, it seemed to us, came in the form of a can of spray paint.

Tagging came later, as a way for young people to identify themselves and make their mark, but we were into painting political slogans that identified social problems.

Ponsonby and Grey Lynn had some perfect graffiti walls, which ended up with some of the most amazing slogans. The song 'Graffiti Raiders' was written around then.

The cover of darkness was our secret weapon when it came to ensuring we weren't arrested or challenged when we had something important to say. One night down by Three Lamps shopping mall at the corner of Pompallier Terrace we sprayed a pretty confronting slogan on a big white wall because we were sick of women being attacked and raped in our biggest city.

> The cover of darkness was our secret weapon when it came to ensuring we weren't arrested or challenged when we had something important to say.

DEAD MEN DON'T RAPE. It was like the Me Too movement before social media. As we were writing our latest message to the city, a middle-aged man came out onto the porch of an old wooden villa and yelled, 'Hey! What are you girls doing?' Lynda replied, 'We're writing "Dead Men Don't Rape".' Even in the dark we could see him look a bit taken aback. He shouted back to us, 'Right then. Well, I'll leave you to it.'

The door slammed as he made a hasty retreat.

We felt like we'd made our point and headed down College Hill.

At the bottom of the road was a huge billboard advertising a new TV murder mystery series called *Twin Peaks*, and right in the middle of it was a naked mannequin of a dead woman wrapped in plastic. Talk about a red rag to a bull.

Lynda slammed on the brakes and read out the catchline at the bottom of the billboard: 'Who killed Laura Palmer?' One of our gang in the back seat yelled out, 'Michael Hill, Murderer', a play on the successful ad campaign for 'Michael Hill, Jeweller'. It was agreed. We went to work, then all stood back to admire our handiwork.

It was 2.30 in the morning and all good dykes were snuggled up in bed.

Home time for bad girls.

Years later we met Michael Hill, who was guest speaker at an event we performed at. We rocked up and told him what we'd done in our early Ponsonby days. He took it rather well, stating that any publicity was good publicity.

We performed at the first Sweetwaters Festival in January 1980 near Ngāruawāhia. This festival had the banner of a Festival of Music, Culture and Technology. We played the smaller stage in the afternoon and had a great time with our audience, but we mostly remember checking out all the other acts.

This was much more of a rock show than the alternative-lifestyle vibe of Nambassa. We got to see The Swingers, Split Enz, Hello Sailor, Midge Marsden, The Crocodiles, Toy Love, The Dudes, Elvis Costello, Mi-Sex, Renée Geyer, The Wide Mouthed Frogs, and Red Mole's *Punk Evangelical Show*, and Billy TK and Powerhouse.

Those three days had a profound effect upon us — the sounds, the lights, the performances, the massive audience. We were beginning to realise that this might be something we could do for the rest of our lives. A career in music was actually a possibility.

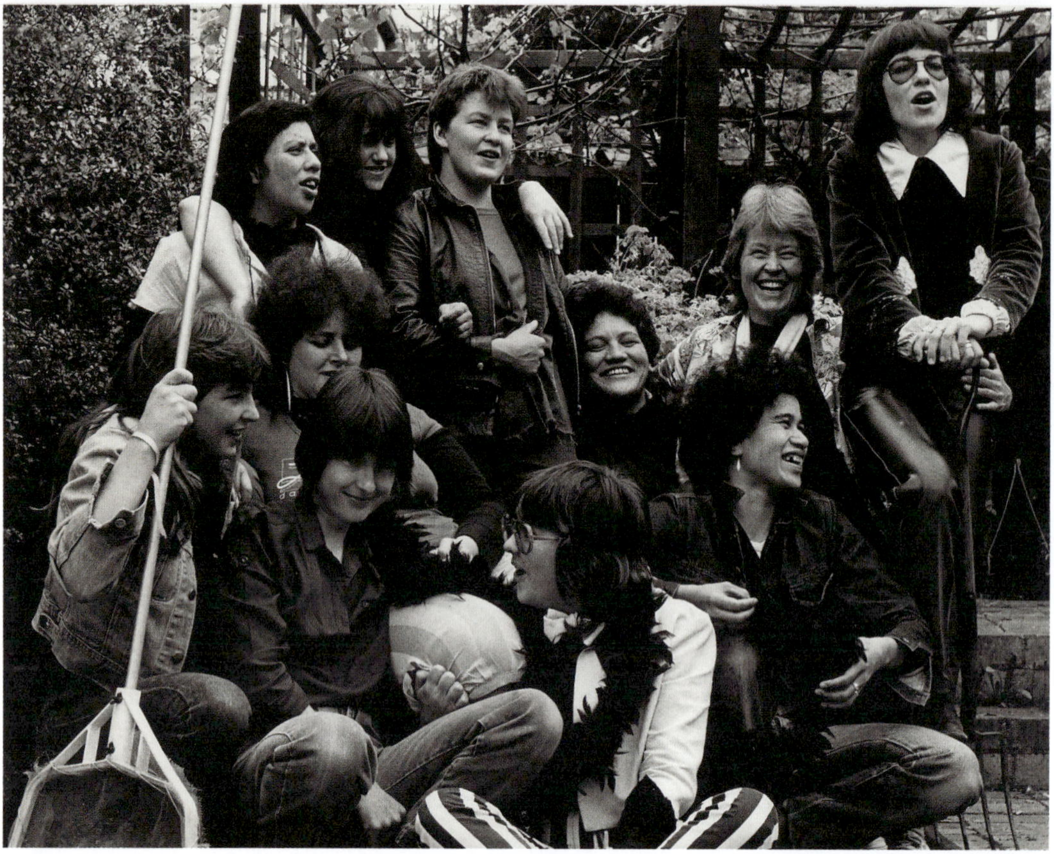

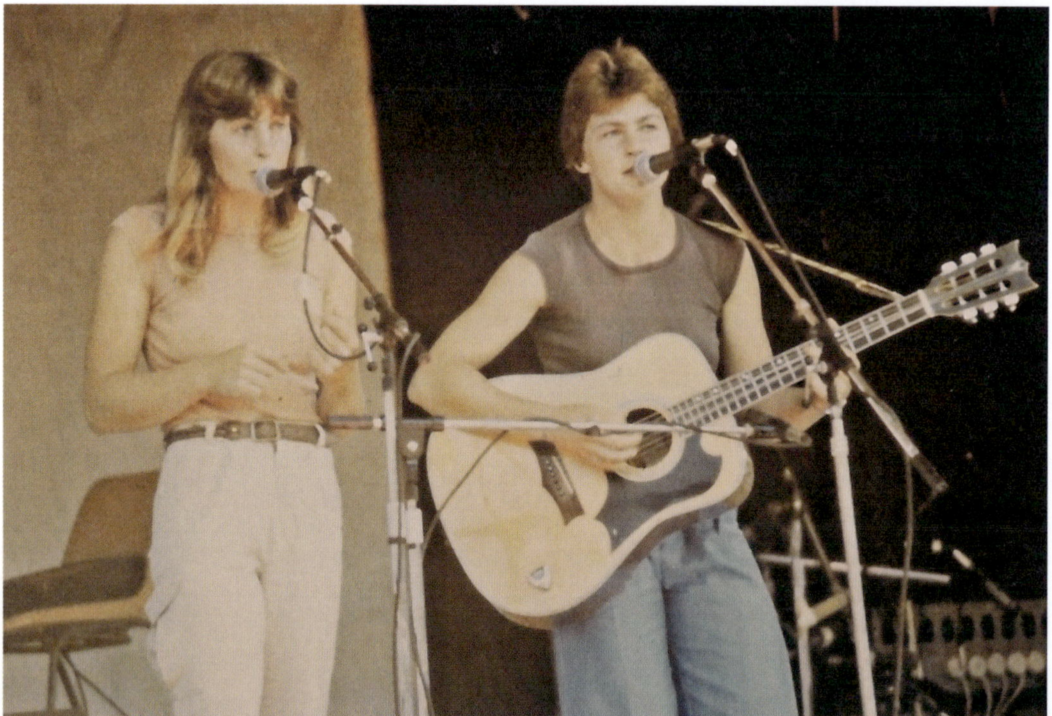

Later that year we performed at The Gluepot as the support act for The Swingers, who were big at the time. We arrived early on Saturday afternoon for our sound check. The guy behind the desk took one look at us and called out to his mate, 'It's just a couple of sheilas with a guitar — we don't need to do a sound check for them.' We begged to differ, arguing that the sound check was important for us to make sure we got a good sound on stage. He was unmoved. He wandered off to get a beer and left us standing there.

That night, just before we were to perform, we saw two mics on stage and told the sound guy we only wanted one. He seemed a bit confused — he had assumed we needed two for vocals and a direct input for our guitar.

Meanwhile, the lights dimmed and we heard 'Please welcome up-and-coming act the Topp Twins!'

We strode on stage, and I grabbed a mic and announced to the Gluepot crowd that the sound guy had been a dork and refused to give us a sound check, so we needed everyone to quieten down because we were going to play acoustically.

We then proceeded to jump up on tables and blast out a punky version of 'Graffiti Raiders', throwing in a yodel that brought the house down. We followed up with 'Freedom Song'. By the time we finished, the whole Gluepot was with us.

I have no idea how the career of the sound guy panned out, but we've never been refused a sound check since.

Opposite top: The amazing women's collective who created the album *Out of the Corners*. (Clockwise from top left) Mahinārangi Tocker, Val Murphy, Lynda, Mereana Pitman, Di Cadwallader, Jess Hawk Oakenstar, Tracy Huirama, Hilary King, Clare Bear, Jools and Hattie St John. GIL HANLY

Opposite bottom: Performing at Sweetwaters in the early 1980s.
GRAHAM HOOPER

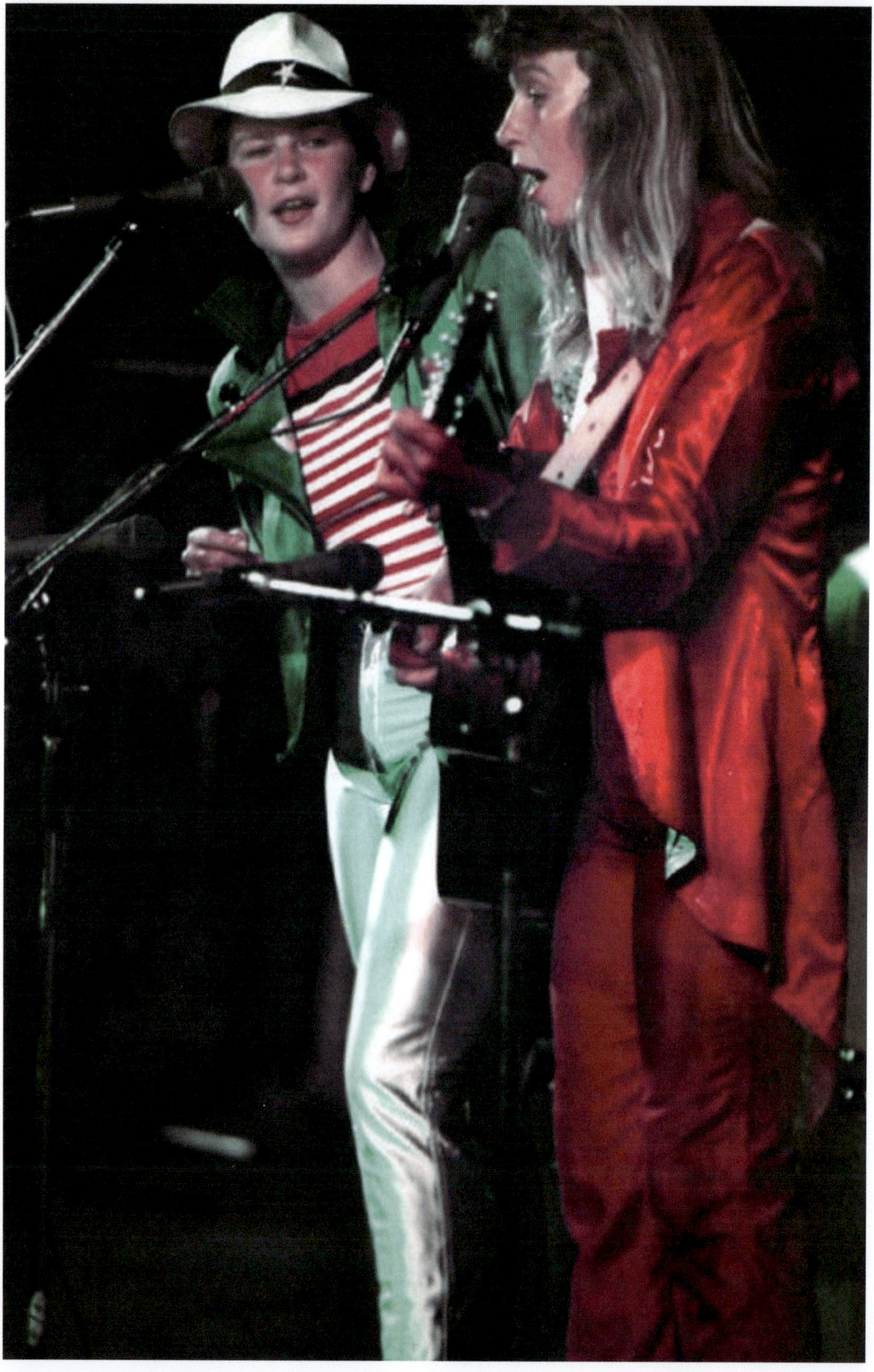

9

1981: Part of History

No doubt about it, 1981 was a big year.

We were at Nambassa in January for the third and last of the hippie-themed festivals celebrating music, arts, alternative lifestyles, peace, love, the environment, holistic health and natural foods. We arrived at Waitawheta Valley in our green van the night before the crowds arrived, and parked under a stand of trees about 300 metres from the main stage. We had a couple of mattresses in the back and had figured on eating at the festival's many food stalls. It was all vegetarian, as the Nambassa festivals banned sales of meat and alcohol, though you could bring your own. We had a box of beer under the front seat.

Soon after we arrived, a Hare Krishna van pulled in beside us. They set up a tent with a hand-painted sign above the front opening, from which they sold barfi, a fudge-like milk-based sweet from the Indian subcontinent. It was made from full-fat milk, sugar and ghee, which did not seem to us to square with the whole healthy

Opposite: The Topp Twins at Nambassa. HEATHER BYARS / COURTESY OF PETER TERRY / NAMBASSA FESTIVAL COLLECTION

vegetarian theme of the festival, but nevertheless it became our food of choice for the entire five days, mainly because they offered us an unlimited free supply since we were their neighbours.

After a couple of bars of barfi that first day, Jools and I headed out to get our bearings and suss out the site. The food stalls were putting finishing touches to their signage and clothing stalls were arranging their wares on hangers artfully created from tree branches or driftwood.

We drifted over to the house-truckers and admired the workmanship in their design and carvings. They were a friendly lot. Even though we didn't mix in their circle, we had a respect and sometime longing for their lifestyle, involving abandonment of the conventional life. Later, we did take to the road in a tractor-drawn Gypsy caravan, but that is another story.

Stage crew, sound and lighting techs were all busy in the main stage area and there was a feeling that something big was about to happen. And it was.

This year Jools and I were to perform on the main stage, which would showcase over 60 groups. The two big overseas acts for the Saturday night were Dizzy Gillespie and The Charlie Daniels Band, with the Topp Twins slotted between them. It was a great spot and an acknowledgement from the organisers that we had built a strong following among counterculture festival-goers.

Backstage were three dressing rooms side by side, separated by tarpaulins. Each act was allowed backstage two hours before their scheduled start time, and Jools and I had been allotted the middle dressing room. Dizzy Gillespie's band were already in one of the others. The tarps were not very high: if we stood on tiptoe we could see over.

We had hung up our costumes and Jools was tuning the guitar for a quick warmup. I nipped outside for a toilet stop and saw a stretch limo pull up into the backstage area. Charlie Daniels stepped out and surveyed the scene, and a minute or so later a bus arrived with the rest of the band. Weird that Charlie was the only one in the limo, I thought, and scooted off to find the toilets.

> Nambassa out the front was all peace and love and barfi, but backstage that night it was a whole different story.

By the time I got back, The Charlie Daniels Band was heading into dressing room No. 3, but meanwhile something was going down in No. 1. Festival organisers were in a heated discussion with Dizzy Gillespie, who said — loudly — that he wasn't going on till he got paid. Jools and I decided to practise the yodel we had on our set list, and as we launched into the chorus both Dizzy's band and Charlie's band peered over into No. 2 to see who was yodelling. It was a moment of weirdness: an African American New York jazz band, The Charlie Daniels Band from the American deep south, and the yodelling lesbian twins from New Zealand.

Both camps complimented us on our sound, and then suddenly a war of words broke out between Charlie and Dizzy over the top of us. Nambassa out the front was all peace and love and barfi, but backstage that night it was a whole different story. Dizzy was adamant he wouldn't perform without his money up front, Charlie said he was full of shit, and the shouting went on for a good 10 minutes, with us literally stuck in the middle.

Eventually, to break the impasse, the MC flipped back our 'door' and said, 'We're going to put you girls on first, so get ready.'

Wait, what?

'No, we don't want to go on first — they're expecting Dizzy Gillespie! It would be the worst gig we've ever done in our lives!'

By now the main stage had sat idle for about 20 minutes and organisers were desperate to fill it. So eventually we said, 'Okay, but give us five minutes.' We dashed off to find our friends Hilary, Di (McMillan) and Gloria, who we knew were in the audience. Remarkably, we found them almost straight away and told them we needed them to be our backing singers for the night. Troopers that they were, they leapt at the chance and we all hurried backstage.

By now crew members and the MC were yelling at us, 'You've *got* to go on. We need someone on that stage *now*.' Jools grabbed her guitar, and the gals, now wrapped in Hilary's feather boa, became the Boa Consisters. We walked out onto that stage and the crowd went absolutely nuts — it was our best gig ever. We had a wonderful time with that audience, who loved our political songs and our lesbian love songs. Jools and I and the Boa Consisters sang our hearts out to the massive Saturday-night crowd at the last-ever Nambassa.

The New Zealand Students Arts Council (NZSAC) was set up to tour bands and theatre shows around all New Zealand's universities, especially during orientation, and many famous performers got their big break with NZSAC.

In 1981 it was our turn. Brian Sweeney, the chair of NZSAC, saw us perform at a lunchtime student gig at Auckland Tech (ATI, as it was known then), and offered us an Orientation tour. He paired us up with a classy political comedy duo called Slick Stage. Actors

Opposite top: Slick Stage and the Topp Twins. PETER MOLLOY

Opposite bottom: The Topp Twins on tour. BRUCE CONNEW

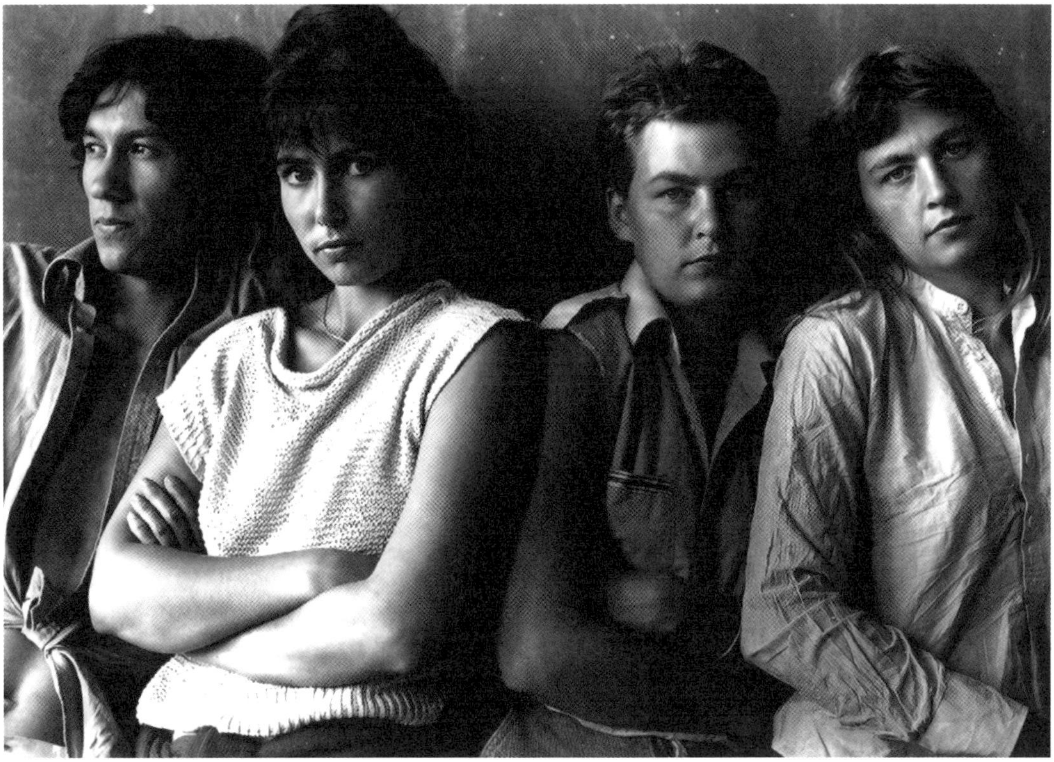

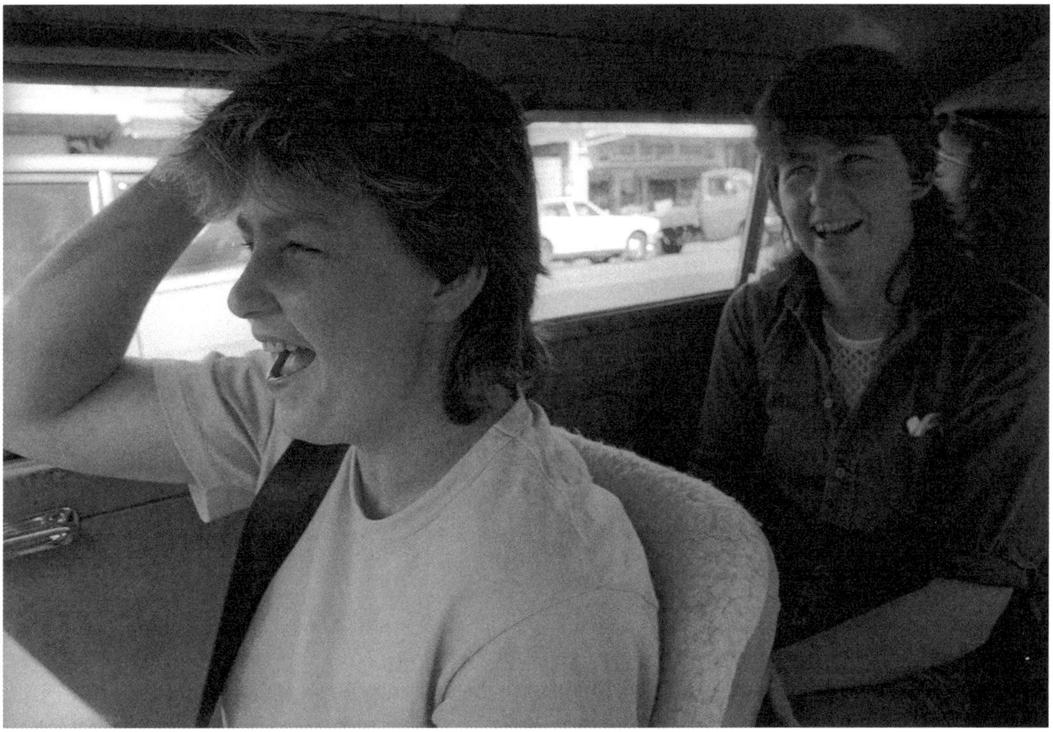

Peta Rutter and Peter Rowell (now known as Peter Turei) did political skits and we sang our original songs. We worked really well together.

We travelled from Auckland to Dunedin performing at every campus along the way. During the day we played the university café and at night we played a public show in the local theatre. We worked out that we got paid $30 each per performance, but we didn't care. We were out there doing it and we had a lot of fun on the road.

The students thought we were a bit crazy. I remember once we started taking pies out of the warmer in the cafeteria and giving them away to poor students . . . We ended up paying for a lot of pies at the end of the gig but the students thought it was brilliant.

Other acts toured early in their careers by the NZSAC were poets Sam Hunt and Gary McCormick, Blam Blam Blam, Limbs Dance Company, Split Enz and Red Mole. There were dozens more.

The tour helped set us up as Kiwi entertainers and Brian came on as our manager. We were very lucky to have him help launch our careers. He really believed in us, and we loved hearing him out in the audience laughing. Over the next five years, he organised tours around New Zealand, our first TV appearance on *That's Country* and a gig opening for a Split Enz tour. Finally, in 1985, Brian arranged our first appearance in Sydney at the Belvoir St Theatre.

He went on to found the global public relations company SweeneyVesty with his go-getter partner, Jane Vesty, and they now live in New York. Brian and Jane kindly helped fund our documentary *Topp Twins: Untouchable Girls* in 2009. We will always be grateful for Brian's generosity and support in our early years.

Greg Fahey, who managed the 1981 NZSAC tour, took on the role of tour manager for our successful Gypsy Caravan Tour in 1989 and was an absolute joy to work with.

Brian and Jane, along with Greg and his late wife, Anna Cahill, became our dear friends. These two men were there right at the

1981: PART OF HISTORY

beginning of our careers, and have continued to support us for more than 40 years now. Our love for them is immense.

———

There was no time for shows or touring in the winter of 1981. South Africa's racially selected national rugby team, the Springboks, were to tour New Zealand in July/August, and thousands of Kiwis were committed to stopping them.

The 1981 Springbok tour was one of the most momentous events in New Zealand history. The whole country was divided and they were a tumultuous few weeks.

Jools and I knew where we stood. We were living in Auckland by then and the protesters would meet every Wednesday and Saturday — match days. Every time there was a game there were protests up and down the country. Jools and I were part of Patu Squad, made up of dedicated anti-apartheid activists who were prepared to do anything to stop the game, including being arrested if it came to that. Patu Squad was mainly radical Māori, radical lesbians and other staunch individuals. We were hands-on — the planning group would come up with the action and we would implement it on the day.

Early in the tour the Springboks were scheduled to play Waikato at Rugby Park in Hamilton, on 25 July 1981. The planning group spent some time organising for this game, as it was the first one that South African audiences would get to see live on TV. The plan was simple: get on the field. Our mates Goss, Shar and Linden travelled from Auckland with us in our old green van.

Unbeknown to the rugby crowd, about 200 protesters were on the inside. They had paid for tickets and dressed as All Blacks supporters (with wire-cutters in their back pockets). The rest of us

Left: The Topp Twins, ready to take on the world in 1981. STUFF LIMITED

Below: The twins at a Springbok tour protest in Auckland, 1981. Jools and Lynda can be seen in the front row at far right, with their friends Shar, Nik, Shane and Linden. GIL HANLY

met at Garden Place in Hamilton. Our group of girls was directed to the fifth row from the front of the march, and had been given orders to push the people in front of us when the order was given.

The atmosphere at the beginning of the march was a mix of excitement and trepidation. As we neared the stadium entrance the lead group (including us) veered off towards the wire fence around the grass stand. We grabbed the wire and pulled it up to reveal a massive hole cut by the inside team. The word went out to push, so we leaned against the row in front of us to get them up the steep embankment. We in turn were pushed by the row behind us, and so on down the next 20 rows.

I remember seeing a nun and a priest running beside us carrying a big wooden cross, and rugby supporters trying to wrestle it off them.

The next minute we were all inside the field. It was pandemonium for the first few minutes as all the protesters started running towards the centre of the field. I remember seeing a nun and a priest running beside us carrying a big wooden cross, and rugby supporters trying to wrestle it off them, and thinking should we help. Players on the field for the curtain-raiser game were running in all directions to get out of there.

About 350 of us made it onto the field and formed a big circle right in the middle of the park. We linked arms and looked out to the stands to see 30,000 rugby supporters staring angrily back at us.

As I looked down the line of linked arms I saw all of our team of girls had made it onto the field. Linden's face said it all. This was her first-ever march and she smiled as beads of sweat dripped into her eyes. I remember it being hot. Most of us were wearing heavy clothing and motorbike helmets as protection. I had a thick coat on top of my overalls and as we stood there all packed together I remember getting hotter and hotter.

At this point a line of police entered the field. A small contingent of high-ranking police approached us, and their boss spoke to the two big Māori boys who were walking around the circle encouraging us to stay together and stand fast. After a few minutes of intense discussion the police headed back to the stands, and then out they came, for the first time ever in New Zealand: the Riot Squad. Helmets, full shields and long batons at the ready.

I was thinking oh shit, we're going to get the crap beaten out of us, but in reality it wasn't the cops we needed to fear — it was the rugby supporters, who were becoming more and more frustrated at the lack of rugby.

We didn't know it at the time but apparently a small plane had been stolen from Taupō and was heading towards Hamilton. Police had no idea what the pilot's plan was, but with that unknown risk and the protesters on the field who were going nowhere, they made the call to cancel the game. This was announced over the loudspeaker and the frustrated rugby supporters quickly became a very angry mob. Chants of 'We want rugby!' rang out around the grounds, and some started throwing cans and bottles onto the field.

We replied by chanting 'The whole world's watching!' 'The whole world's watching!' The amazing thing is that the whole world *was* watching. TV footage of the drama unfolding in Hamilton was beamed live around the world, and right into the living rooms of South Africa. Springbok supporters who had got up early in the morning to watch their team trounce Waikato were shocked to learn that anti-apartheid protesters had stopped the game, and South Africans who had spent their lives trying to end the apartheid regime knew they were not alone.

Back on the field we had been surrounded by the Riot Squad, who formed an outer circle about two metres from us. When I look back now, I'm not sure if it was to stop us getting away or to protect us from rugby supporters.

They started arresting us one by one, and most of us were resigned to this. A police truck drove in and protesters were escorted to the back of it.

As we ran the gauntlet, pepper bombs, cans of beer and fists were raining down on us. It seemed like everything went into slow motion.

A few minutes later the rugby supporters breached the field. I remember the Riot Squad telling us to run, and directing us to the far corner of the field, away from the stands. Then the police were gone.

The protesters started running for the open gate but by the time we were about 200 metres away from it, a massive crowd of rugby supporters was waiting there for us. Jools and Linden were in front of me and as they ran the gauntlet, pepper bombs, cans of beer and fists were raining down on us.

It seemed like everything went into slow motion. Jools and Linden seemed to be dodging all the artillery and I remember thinking, it's okay — we're all going to be okay. Then I came to an abrupt halt. Someone had grabbed the back of my overalls and punched me in the side of my head. I remember seeing another woman being punched in the face, and suddenly all around me protesters were falling and being punched and kicked, while others trampled over them trying to escape.

Then I saw Shar and Gossy — they had come back to look for me. They grabbed the front of my overalls and a tug of war proceeded.

Something had to give, and thankfully it was my overalls, which split right down both sides. The rugby supporters were left holding the entire back of my overalls and in that moment we were free and bolted to the gate.

Ironically, I had pulled on a pair of rugby shorts that morning in case it got hot, and now they were the only thing covering my butt. We made it onto the road and straight into another war zone. Residents across from the stadium had allowed injured protesters onto their front lawns to wait for ambulances, but rugby supporters started ripping out gardens and smashing fences. An ambulance that had pulled into a driveway was now being rocked by them.

> **Ironically, I had pulled on a pair of rugby shorts that morning in case it got hot, and now they were the only thing covering my butt.**

Meanwhile, full cans and bottles of beer were being directed at us from the tiered seating in the stadium above us as we took off down the road. One of those cans hit a woman in front of us and caused a terrible L-shaped gash in the middle of her forehead as she turned. I could see a big flap of skin hanging down. There was no blood but her face had gone completely white. We all just kept running; it now felt like a life-threatening situation.

I'm not sure how far we ran or how fast, but eventually we had to stop to catch our breath. At last there was calm. We were far enough away from the stadium and as I looked around I saw that Jools, Linden, Goss and Shar had all made it out alive.

There was a big mob of protesters now all regrouping and trying to figure out what to do next when the word went out to get out of

Hamilton. We headed back to the van and drove out in silence, all in a state of shock. Eventually we decided we needed a drink and pulled off the main highway into Huntly, stopping in the carpark of the pub known locally as The Trough.

We pushed through the swing door of the public bar and stood in a line. The TV above the bar was showing footage from the stadium, and the locals who were watching all turned to look at us. It was like that scene from *Gunfight at the O.K. Corral*. The barman broke the silence. 'Best you girls get outta town,' he said.

We didn't need to be told twice. We started backing out the door as the verbal abuse began, and suddenly we were on the run again. We hurtled into the van and I remember Shar trying to shut the sliding door as I took off around the back of the pub, down the lane where they delivered the kegs. I drove like the wind and didn't slow down until we got to Rangiriri, about 20 ks away. We all burst into hysterical laughter — not because anything was the least bit funny but because we felt like we'd cheated death.

Later that night we sat on the old couch we'd found in the inorganic rubbish collection, propped up with beer crates, and watched the day's events unfold on the nine o'clock news. We all realised we had just become part of New Zealand history.

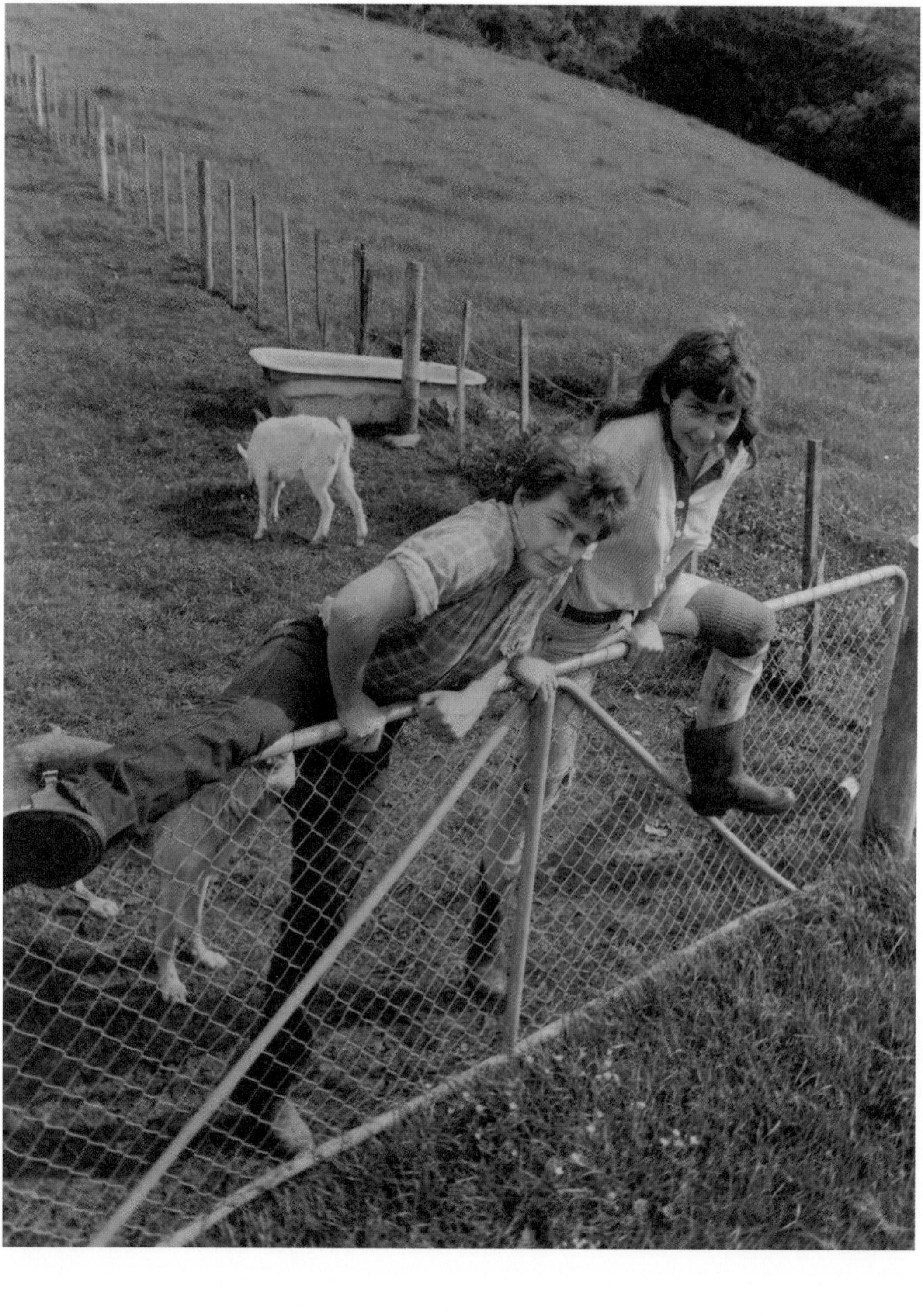

10

Outlaws in the Bush

We were living in Brown Street in Ponsonby, trying to make enough money to pay the rent, feed the dogs and ourselves. Even though we were busy in the music scene now it was a struggle to make ends meet. The repo man was after our green van and we had to park it in a different street every night so he couldn't find it.

We'd been in Auckland for about three years now and we missed living in the country, so we started looking for somewhere out of town to live, thinking we might be able to save some money as well. Someone told us about a piece of land out at Huia, West Auckland, that had been a commune in the early 1970s. Tim Shadbolt and his wife at the time, Miriam Cameron, had helped establish the commune but it had been abandoned for a few years now.

We got hold of Tim, who we'd seen a few times speaking at protests and lunchtime rallies at Auckland University, and asked if Jools and I could live out on the land for a while. 'Go for it,' said Tim.

Opposite: Rural radicals at Te Henga (Bethells Beach), early 1980s.
ANNE CROZIER

We drove out towards Huia and managed to identify the block of land by some concrete steps in the middle of nowhere. This had to be the place. Tim had been a concrete contractor and Huia was a 'concrete collective'. Tim later famously towed his beloved concrete mixer (named Karl Marx) behind the mayoral Daimler when he was mayor of Waitemata City.

We climbed up through the bush and down into a small valley, where we found the remains of the Huia commune: an old two-storey hall in desperate need of repair, with a rusted and collapsing outside kitchen and a rotting door hanging off the long-drop.

We set about tidying up the site and made a start on a new outdoor kitchen. I'm not sure where we had acquired our building skills, but it just seemed to come naturally. We heard about someone chucking out an old coal range and managed to get a few friends to help us get it out to the site and in place under the corrugated-iron roof of our new kitchen.

The next step was to dig a new long-drop and fix a few leaks in the roof of the old building.

We'd started living there the day we arrived, sleeping on the floor of the old hall. We decided to build a loft at either end of the building to be our sleeping quarters, and set about making stairs up to them out of mānuka we cut from the surrounding bush. If we had ever fallen out of bed we would probably have crashed to a horrible death as our loft beds were about 7 metres up.

We loved living at Huia. We would head down to the beach to collect shellfish, and seaweed for the vegetable garden we planted. Every month we headed into town for basic supplies, to meet up with friends at The Gluepot for a drink, and to do a bit of busking. Back at Huia we sat around in the outdoor kitchen singing and writing songs. 'Outlaws in the Bush' was one of them, and the first verse summed up our anti-establishment views and how we felt about city life.

We're outlaws in the bush
We're outlaws in the bush
We ain't gonna pay no taxes
We ain't gonna pay no rent
Cause living in the city
You're gonna end up bent
We're outlaws in the bush

It was great to be living off the grid and bucking the system, but we still needed money to feed ourselves and our dogs. We've always had dogs in our life and we had two out at Huia — Wild Oats, the black fox terrier cross we'd brought up from Christchurch, and Kelly, a German shepherd.

There was a Kiwanis Camp down near the beach at Huia and we came up with this hare-brained scheme of taking 15 kids on overnight adventures in the bush. We convinced the Kiwanis boss, emphasising our army training, and he thought it was a great idea. We agreed on a fee that would nicely solve our cashflow problem.

We came up with this hare-brained scheme of taking 15 kids on overnight adventures in the bush.

The plan was that the kids would walk up to the commune and we would spend the morning giving them some basic training on how to make a bivouac and what to eat in the bush. Then we would walk them about 20 minutes into the bush and they would have to make a camp for the night's sleepover, heading back home the following morning.

The first lot of kids probably thought they had arrived at some crazy boot camp. Jools and I greeted them as they came over

Top: Jools (left) and Lynda with Gladys the pig and loyal dogs Bear and Kelly. ANNE CROZIER

Bottom: Kids are always a great audience. STUFF LIMITED

the hill and down into our outdoor kitchen. We were dressed in T-shirts, football shorts and gumboots, and each had a knife and steel hanging off our hips. We were flanked by our two dogs.

Suddenly an altercation broke out between the dogs, and a dog fight rolled through the kids like a storm. It was mostly a lot of noise, but Oats, the little foxy, took off into the bush and disappeared. After checking that the kids were all okay, Jools went off to look for her. She returned after 10 minutes having seen no sign of Oats. We reassured the worried kids she would be fine, but we were both concerned about her, and now we had 15 kids to look after as well.

This was not the start we had planned. We set off for our overnight experience in the bush and the kids spent the whole time walking along the track calling for Wild Oats (who did not show).

The first job was to gather material to make the bivouacs, so we set about teaching them how to use low branches and weave fern fronds to make a shelter. The kids were amazing — they loved being out in the bush, and the prospect of sleeping overnight in their clothes intrigued them. The fact that they didn't have to put on pyjamas or brush their teeth appealed to their inner rebels, and building their own shelter gave them a sense of confidence.

With the shelters finished, we gathered old leaves to lay on the floor and then set about making a fire for billy tea. We told them stories of how early settlers had lived in the bush and used bullocks to haul timber for building houses, and how important it was that we looked after the bush and protected it.

Jools and I had invested in 15 enamel mugs so we poured all the kids a billy tea, got out the guitar and sang a couple of songs for them, and then at about 8 p.m. we told them it was time for bed. They were incredulous that there was no dinner but we told them that was part of the experience — to survive in the bush you had to find edible plants or go hunting. Within half an hour every one of them was fast asleep; it had been a big day.

At first light we woke the kids and said we were all going on a search and rescue mission to find Wild Oats. We split into two groups: Jools headed back up towards our outdoor kitchen, and I headed further into the bush, teaching the kids to keep to the ridges and stay in sight of one another so we didn't lose anybody.

Wild Oats was nowhere to be found.

When the bus arrived to pick up the kids they piled on and we said our goodbyes. Then just as the bus pulled away, Wild Oats came trotting out of the bush. The kids saw her and the bus came to a grinding halt. Every one of those kids got off the bus and ran to hug our little dog.

It was a good outcome, and one that Jools and I have never forgotten. Every now and then I wonder if any of those kids from that first trip remember their time with the two outlaws in the bush.

The Students Arts Council offered us another tour in early 1982 and this time it was just the Topp Twins. We loved touring New Zealand — it seemed more like a lifestyle than a job. Students back in those days were very political and we got amazing support at the lunchtime concerts.

We had also realised we loved living in the country. At the end of the NZSAC tour we were offered an old farmhouse to rent on a five-acre block near Bethells Beach, so we headed out to the west coast, and busked every Friday night in Queen Street to fill the coffers.

11

Busking and Busted

One of the most adventurous and rewarding times in our singing career was busking downtown in Auckland's Queen Street.

It was a busy and vibrant place in the early 1980s and we never failed to get a big crowd gathered around on Friday night. Back then, shops closed at 5.30 p.m. most nights but on Friday nights you could shop until 9 p.m.

It all began with one of our Friday trips into town from Huia for supplies and a catchup with our mates. We did our grocery shopping and then realised we didn't have enough petrol for the ride home later in the evening — or enough money to buy any.

With some quick thinking, we got the guitar out of the car and set up outside the National Bank. We put our empty guitar case on the ground in front of us and started singing.

Well, we created quite a stir in that old town. Busking wasn't really a thing back then and people were crossing the street to see what all the commotion was about. Suddenly we were a big hit, leaping about in our gumboots and bush clothes. There were mums out shopping with the kids, workers finishing their day, young people looking for some action and suddenly there we were.

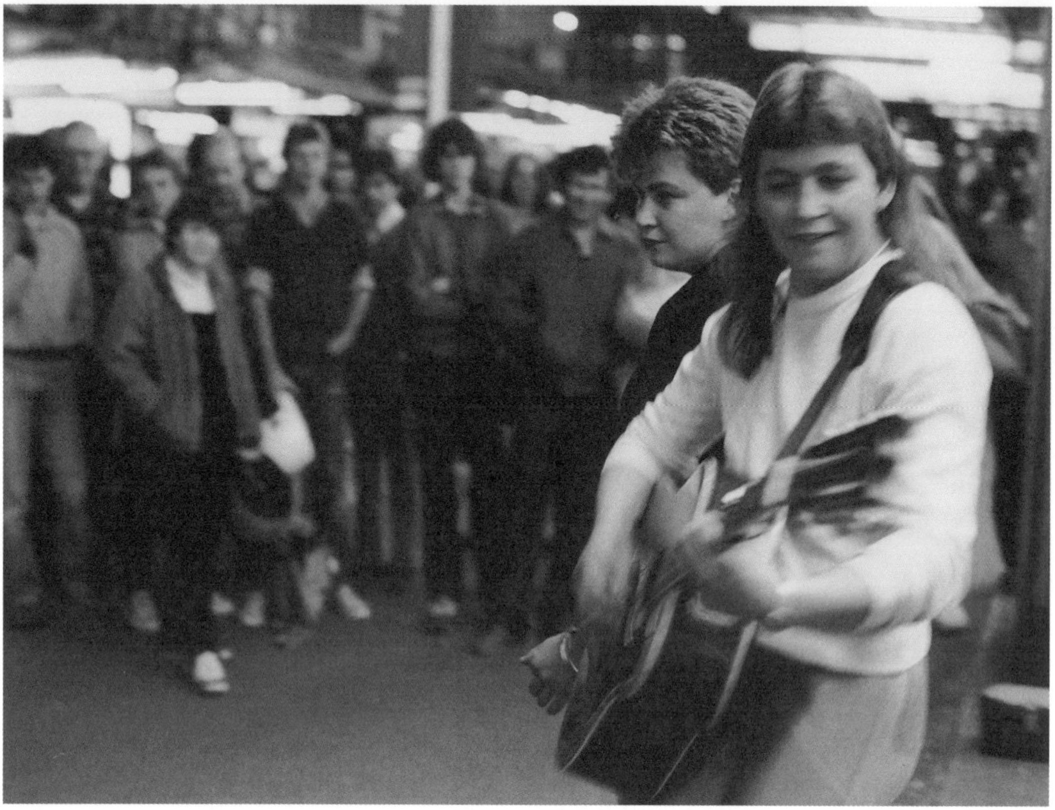

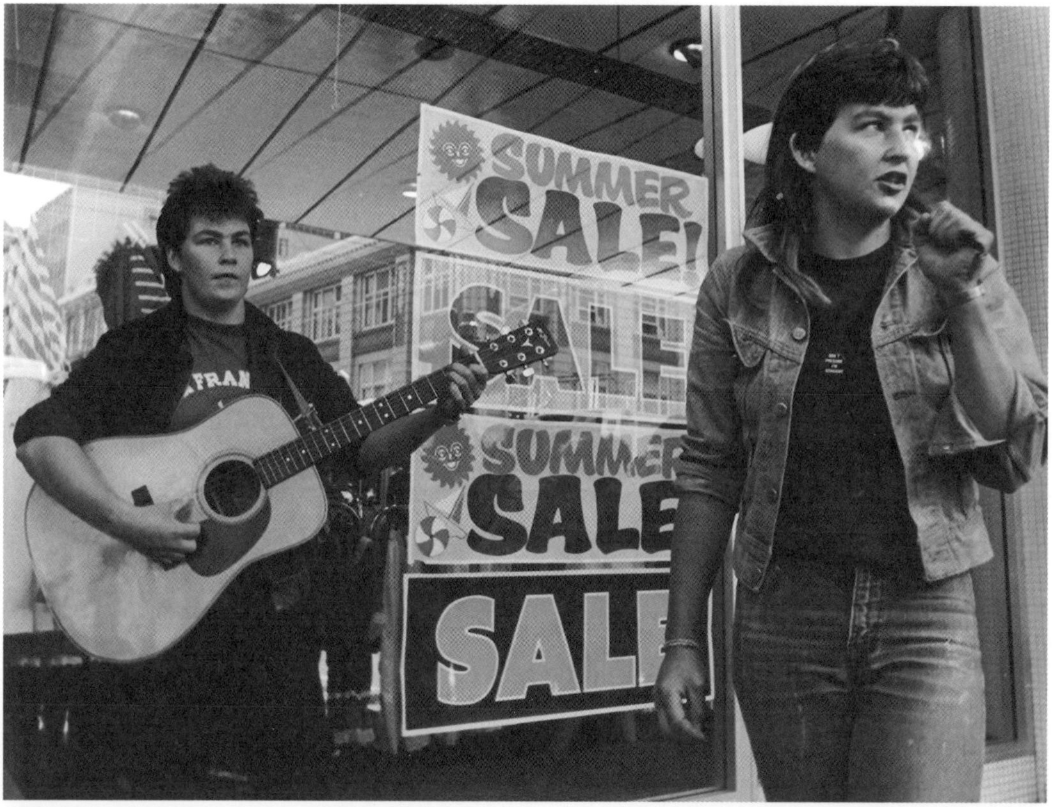
SUMMER
SALE!

At that time a lot of hotted-up Cortinas, Escorts and Holdens cruised Queen Street and it all felt rather exciting and pretty risqué. When we stopped singing, people gathered around to put money in our guitar case and when we counted it all up, we had made $105, which was a lot of money in 1983. We thought we were millionaires. The Bernina sewing shop nearby loved us — they took all our coins for Saturday shopping and gave us back notes.

From that day on we came into town pretty much every Friday for our stint on the street. Sometimes people would be waiting for us to arrive. We did this for about six years, and it really was our apprenticeship — learning how to work a crowd, how to persuade people to throw money at us, and how to reach all the different sorts of people who happened to stop and watch us for a moment.

There was one group who could drown us out, and every so often we had to stop singing to let the Hare Krishnas go by. It all added to the general street craziness; sometimes we'd jump in behind them and dance and sing their song as well. It was all good fun.

There are two occasions that we remember quite well. One night we already had a pretty big crowd on the edge of the street and things were going well when we heard a ruckus up the road. Cops were chasing a young man down the footpath towards us. He charged right through our audience and as he did, he chucked a brown paper bag in the guitar case. The cops, none the wiser, continued after him in hot pursuit.

We stared in silence at the paper bag for a good minute or so, the crowd waiting in suspense to see what would happen next.

Well, of course Lynda couldn't resist. She went over and very

Opposite from top: The twins busking on the city streets in Auckland (BRUCE CONNEW), and in front of a store in Wellington (MARK WILSON).

cautiously opened the bag — it was like street theatre of the very best kind — and she pulled out a brightly coloured waterproof motorbike outfit.

It looked about the right size so Lynda pulled it on. The leggings and the jacket fitted perfectly and the crowd were in hysterics. We went back to singing, and just as we started, the police came back through, minus the sprinting thief. We nodded to them and they nodded back. No one in the crowd said a thing, and to this day Lynda still has the motorbike outfit.

The second occasion also involved the police but this time they were after us — not for the bike suit but for busking on the street.

No one — including us — could believe we'd been arrested. We made the ten o'clock TV news that night.

We had a large crowd around us and the cops came along to tell us we were obstructing the footpath and had to pack up and leave.

The crowd got angry, yelling at the cops to leave us alone. We stood our ground. When people started throwing coins at them, the police arrested us both and led us towards their car. I had my dog with me, and our guitar was on the footpath along with the case with money in it, but the cops wouldn't let us take any of it. I yelled to a friend to please take my dog and our gear home.

It was very stressful and quite a palaver. No one — including us — could believe we'd been arrested.

Opposite: Lynda (left) and Jools honing their busking routine at a lunchtime concert for students. JOCELYN CARLIN

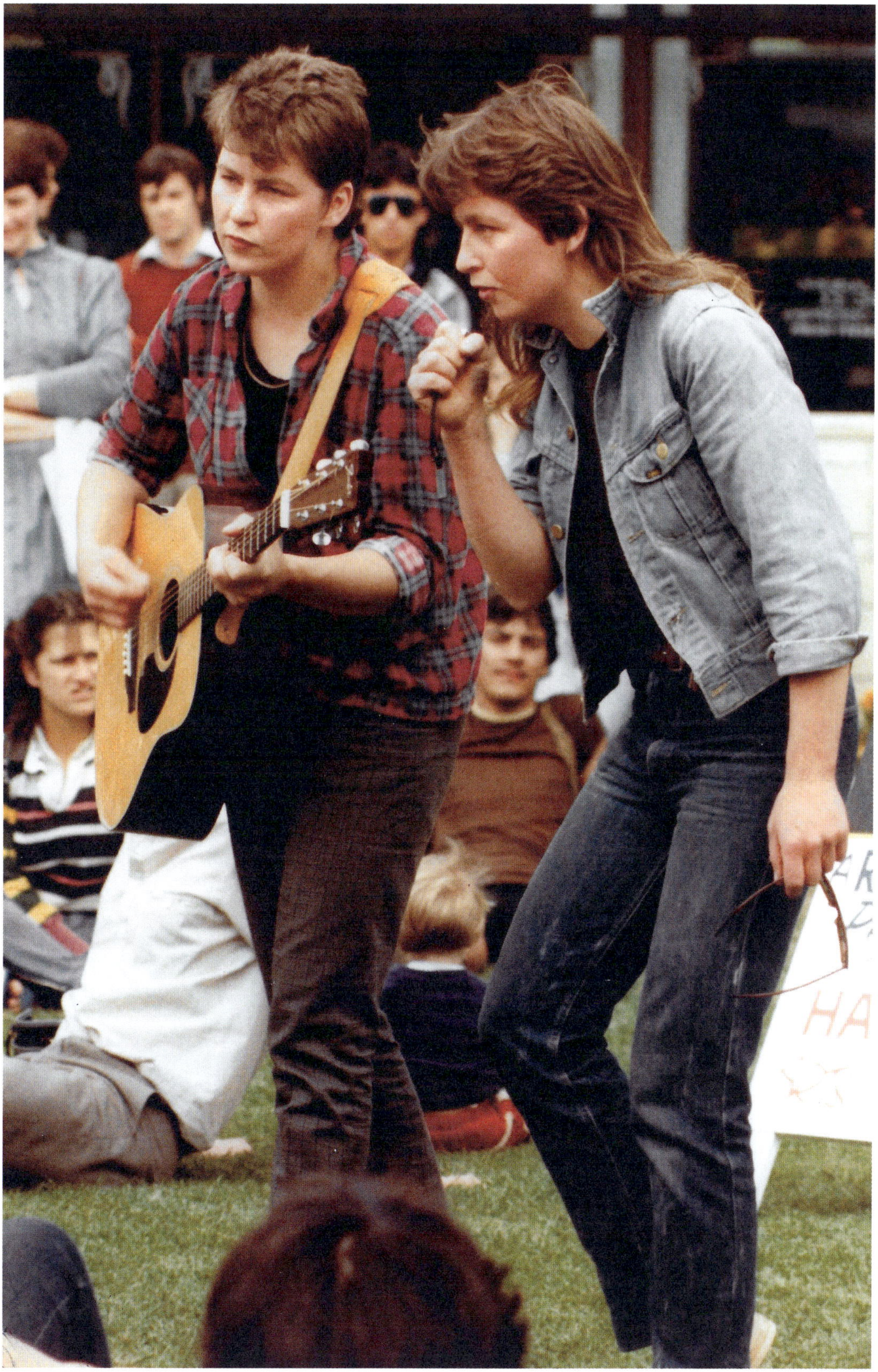

We made the ten o'clock TV news that night when a note was handed to news anchor Angela D'Audney at the end of her broadcast. She read: 'In news just to hand, the Topp Twins have been arrested on Queen Street.' No other details were given. Mum and Dad were sitting at home watching the late news and were quite upset that their girls were on the wrong side of the law. Overnight we became household names.

When we arrived at the police station we thought they might just chuck us out of the car and tell us to go home, but no, we were charged with obstructing the footpath and sat in a cell until we were released at 4 a.m. During that time one cop asked if we might like to perform at the police Christmas party. We politely declined.

The cop who processed us was a surly sort of bloke. We told him we would give our names but no other information. He got mad with us and at one point a matronly-looking policewoman nearby called out to him to go easy on us. 'They're in for busking, not murder,' she said. We had a good old cackle, pleased to have an ally in the cop shop.

One cop asked if we might like to perform at the police Christmas party. We politely declined.

The next day, 7 October 1989, we appeared in court.

When you've been watching the courtroom TV drama *Perry Mason* for the past 10 years you've got a pretty good idea about how things go down in a court of law. Short of sleep though we were, we decided to defend ourselves.

We put on suits, slicked our hair back and carried leather briefcases into the Auckland District Court. The *New Zealand Herald* later reported Lynda telling them the briefcases contained our lunch, and the suits were our own. 'All good young butch lesbians of that time had suits in their wardrobes,' she said.

Our court case drew a lot of attention and I remember a bunch of law students turned up to view the proceedings.

Our spin on the case was that the first officer who arrived hadn't handled the situation well. As things escalated he called for backup, which immediately upset the crowd, and things grew from there. Also, we were charged with obstructing the pavement but in reality it was the crowd that impeded movement on the footpath, not us. It was a minor technical point but we thought it was worth arguing that we'd been charged with the wrong offence.

The police had someone from the city council as an expert witness on city bylaws, but we argued that since we had been charged with a criminal offence, not a civil offence, council bylaws were not relevant. The judge agreed with us and disallowed the council's evidence.

One–nil to us.

The prosecution called the constable who had been the first officer at the scene. In cross-examination Lynda was brilliant. She asked him if he had the power to arrest, to which he replied yes. 'Well, why didn't you arrest us?' Lynda went on. 'Instead you called for backup, which meant there were three cop cars double-parked on Queen Street. If anyone was obstructing the flow of traffic and pedestrians it was the police.'

In classic Perry Mason style she ended her questioning with a statement: 'I put it to you . . . that you were incompetent and it was your inability to act that escalated a minor situation into a full-scale police call-out.'

This sent the university law students into an uproar and the judge warned them that if there were any more outbursts they would be asked to leave.

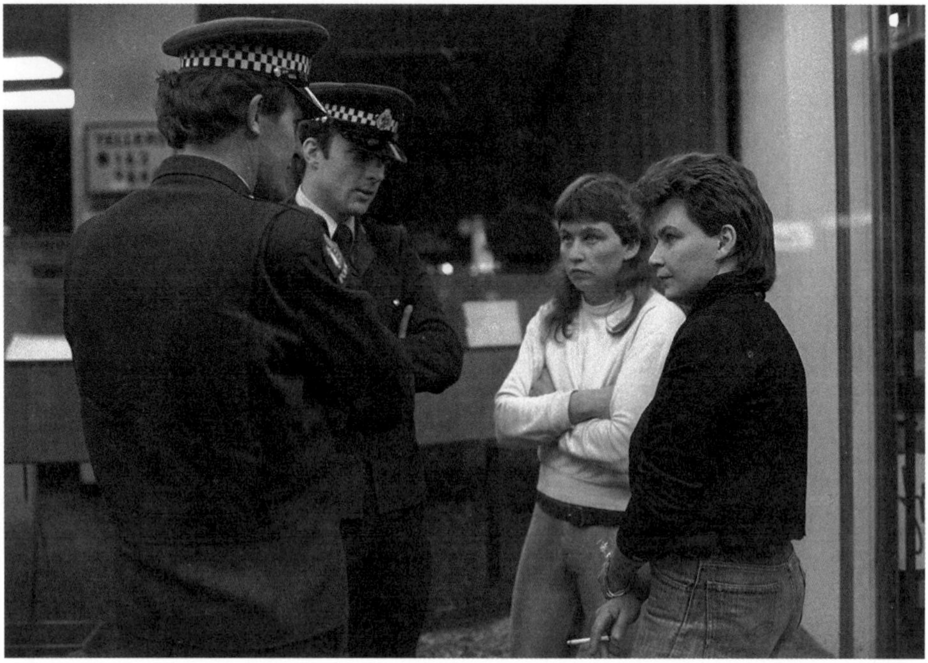

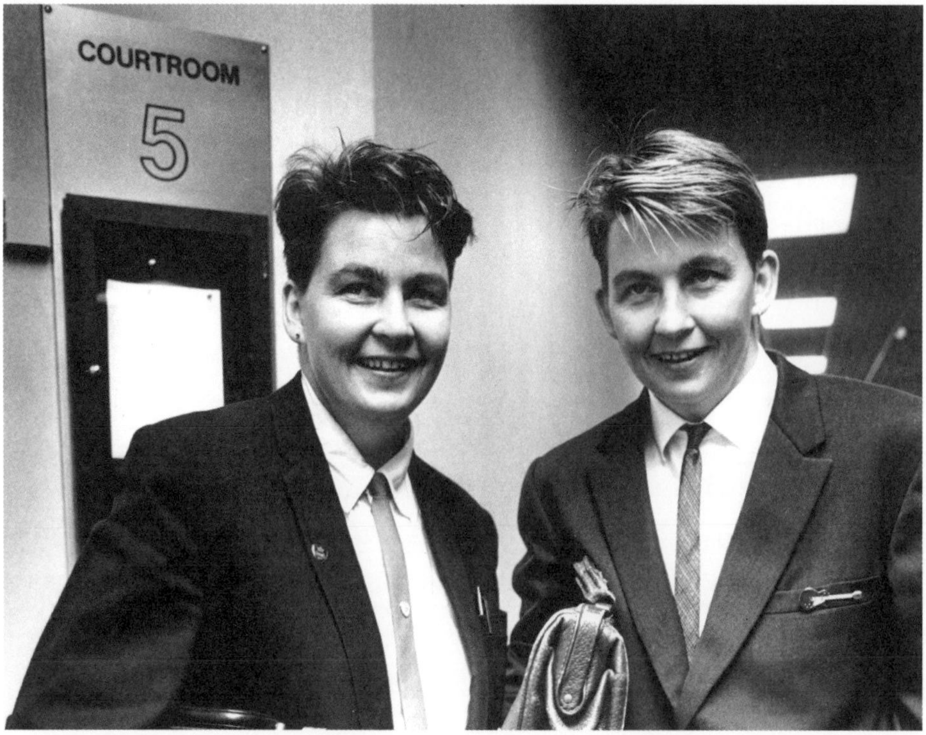
COURTROOM
5

Two–nil to us. Perry Mason would have been impressed.

We told the court we had been entertaining on the streets for a number of years and hoped that our music and entertainment brought some joy to the folks in Queen Street and made it a livelier place. Auckland's mayor at the time was Dame Cath Tizard, and she had hastily written a letter stating that Queen Street was a lot brighter when we arrived on Friday nights to entertain, and she hoped to see us back there soon.

The court adjourned for lunch and the judge would sum up afterwards.

More law students poured in after lunch.

As the judge began speaking it sounded like he was going to throw the book at us. He said it had been an interesting event for the police to handle, and they had a job to keep the streets safe and clear. But he also said that many people obviously enjoyed our busking performances, and went on to hand down a ruling that still stands to this day.

If we or anyone else want to busk in Queen Street we have to contact the police and tell them when and where. They will then send two officers down for crowd control.

It was a victory in that we were not convicted, but in some weird way the ruling took the spontaneity out of busking, and our busking days on Queen Street came to an abrupt halt.

All in all, we reckon our arrest on Queen Street gave us about 10 grand's worth of publicity on TV, radio and in the *New Zealand Herald*. Not a bad day's work.

Opposite top: The police shutting down the Topp Twins on another occasion in Auckland. BRUCE CONNEW

Opposite bottom: The twins' big day in court for busking.
NEW ZEALAND HERALD

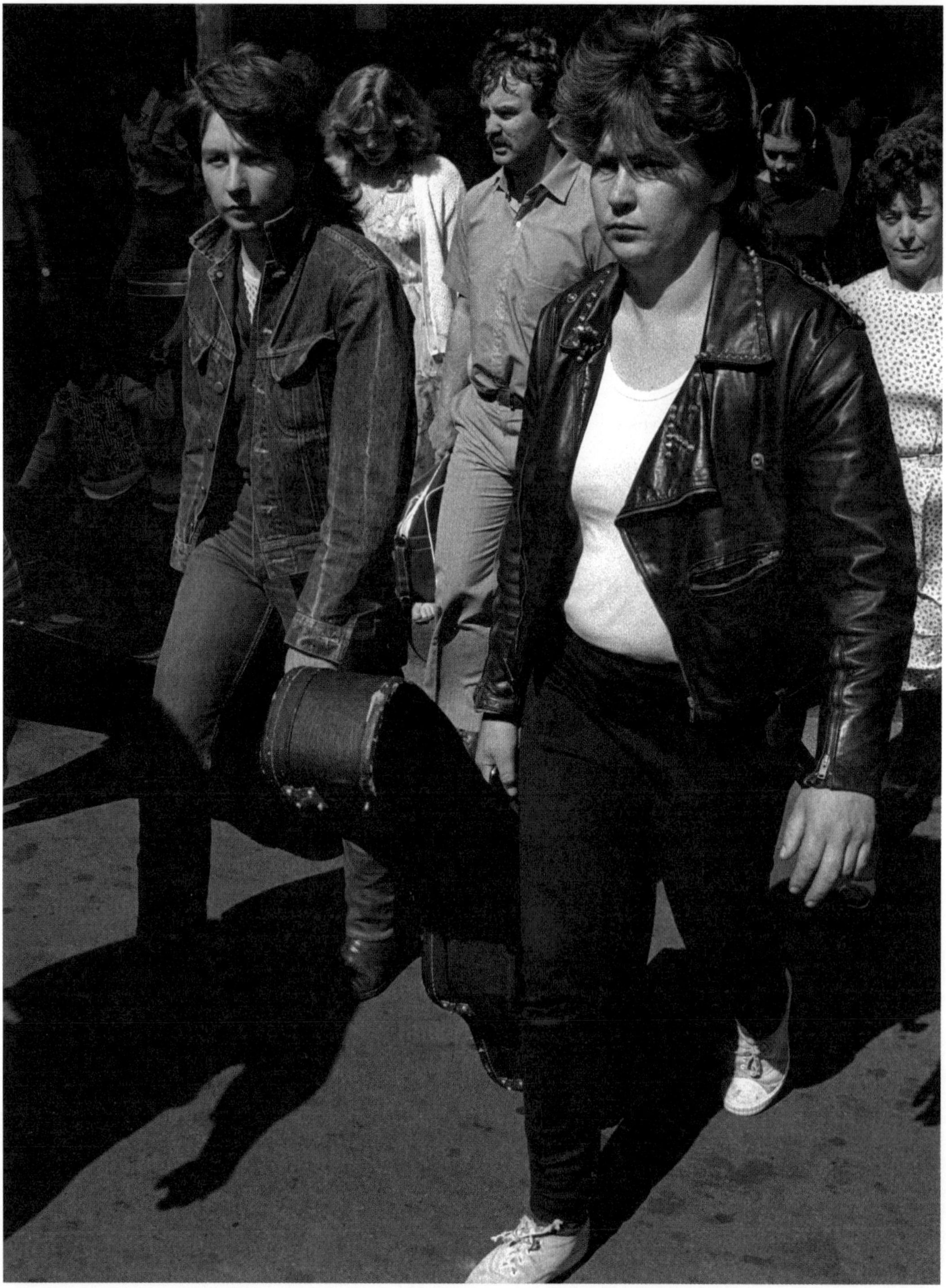

12

The Art of Political Protest

By 1982 we'd been performing for over four years and had made quite an impact in that short space of time, not only for our music but also for our politics. Jools and I decided it was time to record some of our songs. We asked Di Cadwallader to co-produce our first album — she knew about recording and ended up playing guitar on some of the tracks.

The album was an EP titled *Topp Twins Go Vinyl*. It was such a blast walking into Harlequin Studios to lay down our first song. It was also a tricky recording for our sound engineer, Paul Streekstra, who had to figure out how to get separation between the guitar and two vocal tracks. Jools laid the guitar track down first and we tried to lay the vocals down separately while listening to the guitar track, but maybe because we had only ever sung live, or maybe because it was a twin thing, we just couldn't sing without each other. In the end Paul used polystyrene sheets as a buffer between the mics and we recorded all the songs live.

Opposite: Young radicals in the 1980s. BRUCE CONNEW

We couldn't afford to print colour album covers so we printed the design in black and white on paper, and glued them onto 250 blank album covers. We had a glue party (not that sort) and friends came around to help. It was all part of trying to make it as entertainers back in the day. *Topp Twins Go Vinyl* went to No. 34 in the charts.

The late 1970s / early 1980s was a time of heated political protest on several fronts, among them race relations. A lot of lesbians felt a strong affinity with Māori, mainly because we, like them, felt unheard and discriminated against. We were also friends with some Māori lesbian women and we felt it was right to support their demand for the Treaty of Waitangi to finally be honoured. Many lesbians, Māori and other activists always travelled to Waitangi in the Bay of Islands to protest against Treaty breaches at the Waitangi Day commemorations on 6 February.

At that time protester numbers were well into the hundreds and there was a lot of conflict with police. On one such occasion we had arrived for a protest at the old Te Tii Marae, just down the road from the main Treaty Grounds. Police had surrounded the meeting house and a number of Māori women were protesting out the front, performing a pretty intense haka.

A single lightbulb on the roof of the old meeting house cast a dramatic light on the scene that was unfolding. More protesters arrived and the police stopped them from going onto the grounds.

One by one the women were arrested and carried off by the police. Those remaining continued their haka until there was only one woman left. It was an eerie sight and sound in that dark night.

It was also the most surreal and inspiring protest we had ever witnessed.

There was no resistance, no violence from the protesters, just a dignified resolve to be heard — to stand up and be brave and believe in their culture.

After the women had been taken away, we got word to go to another marae that was quite a drive out into the countryside. We arrived about midnight to find a big feed waiting for us, and a place to rest our heads for the night.

> There was no resistance, no violence from the protesters, just a dignified resolve to be heard — to stand up and be brave and believe in their culture.

New Zealand has come a long way in 40 years. I remember one politician speaking at Waitangi, saying: 'We are one nation with one people.' He really didn't get it: only when we honour our differences can we work and live together.

So much has changed since those days. Finally the New Zealand government said sorry and began a Treaty claims process. It would be long and protracted, but slowly the wrongs and injustices were publicly acknowledged and began to be put right.

A new generation of Māori are now reclaiming their culture, the moko has made a comeback, and te reo is part of our daily lives.

In saying that, there is always more work to be done.

I remember watching the six o'clock TV news. It was 25 May 1978, and on the orders of Prime Minister Rob Muldoon around 800 police

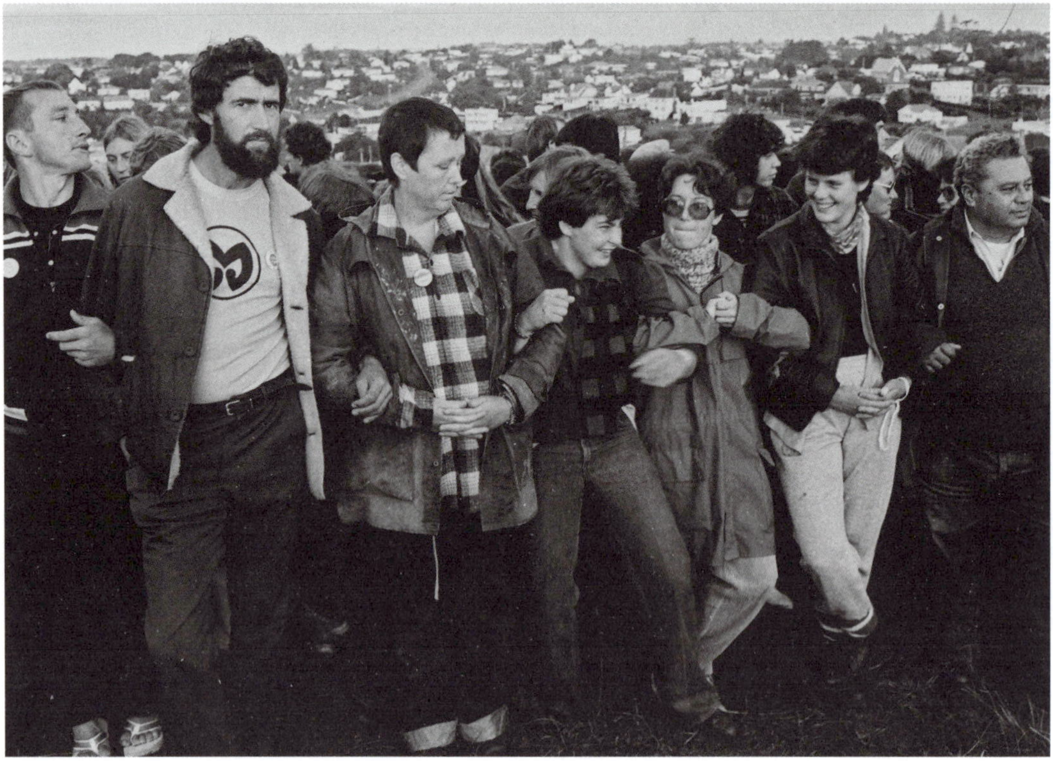

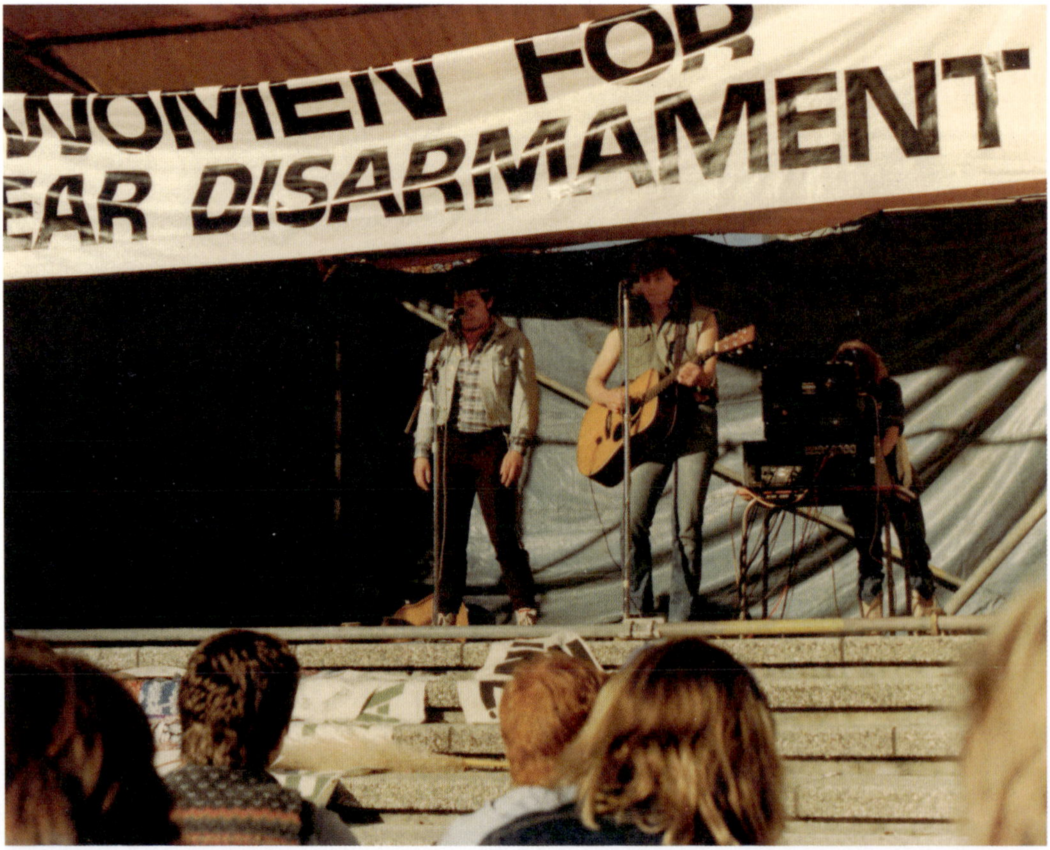
WOMEN FOR
EAR DISARMAMENT

and army personnel had forcibly removed over 200 people from Bastion Point, ending an occupation that had lasted for 506 days. Those arrested were protesting against the Crown sale of land alienated from Ngāti Whātua Ōrākei.

Jools and I had spent some time up at Bastion Point. We supported the protest and helped out with a few jobs that needed doing, like sabotaging some of the sewerage pipes that had been laid by the government for the housing development it planned for the site.

We had pre-measured packets of quick-set cement and hot-water bottles filled with water tied to us, and we crawled along on our bellies, army style.

We had arrived very quietly late at night, as there were police and security on site. We had pre-measured packets of quick-set cement and hot-water bottles filled with water tied to us, and we crawled along on our bellies, army style. We dragged ourselves and our tools of destruction to these square grates above the pipes, dropped a packet of quick-set and a bottle of water down each grate, and moved on to the next one.

We were out there for about an hour, and by the following morning every pipe at Bastion Point was buggered. Job done. We were pretty buggered too — it was exhausting work.

Opposite top: Lynda (centre) links arms with other protestors on Bastion Point. GIL HANLY

Opposite bottom: The twins perform a concert supporting nuclear disarmament at Aotea Square, Auckland, in the early 1980s. ARANI CUTHBERT

I remember one day we were up there with the protesters and the police moved in to try to stop protesters from occupying a particular area. Jools and I had decided we were prepared to get arrested that day, so we joined the lineup against the cops.

Suddenly a booming voice could be heard above the crowd: 'You twins get out of there! We're going to need you to sing at the concert to raise money for the people who are going to get arrested!'

And that became our role in relation to Bastion Point. A week later we were playing at The Gluepot to raise funds to pay fines and legal costs. Our song 'Bastion Point is Māori Land' got pretty well thrashed. We knew this was not our fight, that our role in relation to the Bastion Point protest was to be there when we were needed, to offer the support we could. We'll never forget what Mereana Pitman said about us when she was interviewed for *Untouchable Girls* (the movie):

> *They are true friends and companions and true allies and there was never a time that we didn't trust them. That was an unusual relationship at that time for Māori activists. Pākehā people were the butt of our activism. But they [the Topp Twins] were not included in that. They knew where the boundaries were.*

The nuclear-free movement had been active in New Zealand since the 1960s, but we weren't involved until around 1982/83. There were some amazing, dedicated people who did most of the hard work — Maire Leadbeater from the Campaign for Nuclear Disarmament (CND) was one, along with Jacqui Barrington at Greenpeace. There were many unsung heroes in the peace movement too.

Top: Jools (left) and Lynda busk outside the Beehive (parliament buildings), circa 1982. MARK WILSON

Bottom: The twins at Whenuapai Peace Camp in 1984. Anne Crozier's daughter Emma is in the centre. GIL HANLY

Once again, our contribution was mostly through performing at rallies. One of the first was in September 1982 in Auckland's Aotea Square, with Herbs and other bands, organised by supporters of a campaign to make Auckland City nuclear-free. The concert was held a week ahead of an Auckland City Council vote on the issue. The council voted down the proposal 13 to 7.

We performed at several more rallies that year, with a strong nuclear-free message in several of our songs. It was that message that prompted our invitation to join the speaking tour of Australian activist Dr Helen Caldicott. She was a twinset and pearls kind of woman, with a wealth of knowledge on nuclear arms, and we were radical lesbians with a simple message. It looked like an unlikely combination but we were all pursuing the same goal: a nuclear-free New Zealand.

I still remember the emotional reactions of all the women watching — there was anger and there were tears as the credits rolled, and I was inspired to write a song.

Helen was a celebrated nuclear critic and former president of Physicians for Social Responsibility. She was articulate, intelligent and able to fire up an audience with her talks. As MP Marilyn Waring once said, 'She helped guide us to become a nuclear-free country.' It was a real privilege to be touring with Helen Caldicott.

A nationwide Women's Day for Nuclear Disarmament was called for 24 May 1983. The week before, I attended a women's peace camp held over four days in Devonport. Maire Leadbeater was on hand to lead workshops, and on the last day we watched a film about the bombing of Hiroshima and Nagasaki. I still remember the emotional reactions of all the women watching — there was anger and there were tears as the credits rolled, and I was inspired to write a song I called 'Radiation Burns'.

The following week over 20,000 women marched up Queen Street, most carrying white flowers, some with banners and many with faces adorned with peace signs. The march was silent, and the power it created was deafening. The largest women's demonstration in New Zealand history ended in Aotea Square where Jools and I debuted 'Radiation Burns', which went on to become something of a peace anthem.

It took another three years but on 8 June 1987 the New Zealand Nuclear Free Zone, Disarmament, and Arms Control Act was finally passed into law.

We like to think our small contribution helped inch New Zealand towards adopting that courageous position, which still stands today.

The Peter Garrett and Topp Twins tour was organised by Peace Movement Aotearoa (PMA) in 1985.

Our big lanky mate of Midnight Oil fame was full of energy and raring to go.

It was a whirlwind seven-day tour of sometimes two shows a day — lunchtime at a university campus and a public show at night. Endless radio interviews and publicity calls kept us busy when we weren't performing.

Margi Mellsop, our tour manager, organised the finer details while PMA set up venues and arranged transport. From Auckland to Hamilton was a tight time-frame so they hired a small fixed-wing plane. During the flight Peter Garrett took over the controls for a while as he had his pilot's licence.

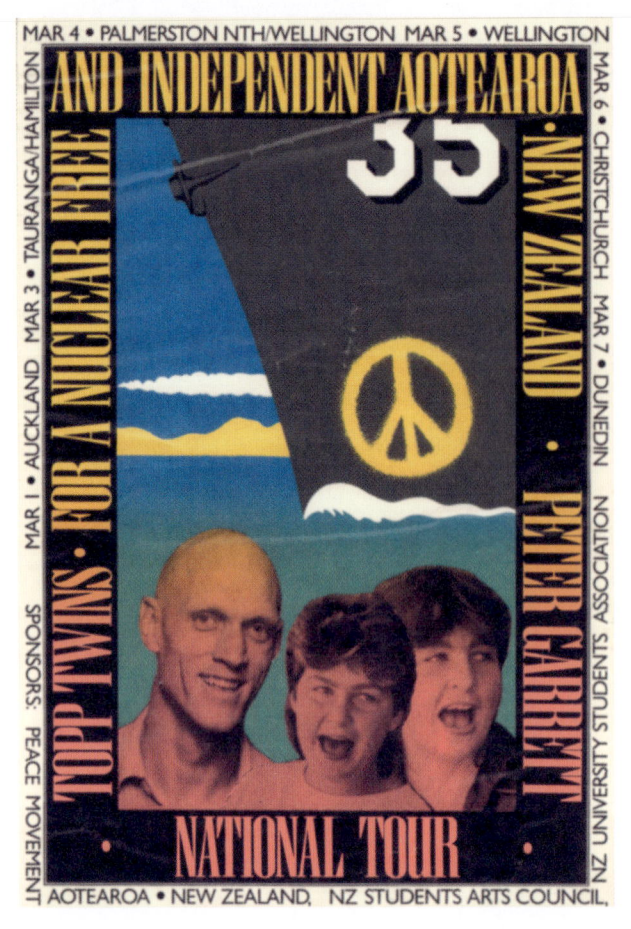

Left: A poster for the Peter Garrett / Topp Twins tour in 1985, 'for a nuclear free and independent Aotearoa'.
COURTESY OF TAPUAKA HERITAGE & ARCHIVE COLLECTIONS, TE HERENGA WAKA — VICTORIA UNIVERSITY OF WELLINGTON

Below: Lynda (left) and Jools on the road during the Peter Garrett tour.
LARRY ROSS

He spoke like he sang, all arms and legs and really intense; he was amazing to watch as well as listen to. He threw away the speech he'd written in Australia and basically just congratulated New Zealand for being world leaders in the fight against nuclear war and nuclear power.

In Wellington, Peter was to give a talk at the Wellington City Art Gallery about politics and art. We were told we weren't needed for that show — it was to be only Peter or no show at all. That came as a surprise to us. There was talk that the Wellington City Council did not want the council-run art gallery to host a show for nuclear disarmament, but gallery managers denied that.

We decided the most important thing was to get the message across, so we didn't make a fuss. Jools and I watched on as Peter told his audience that art is the one thing we have that can bring us together and change the world. He also made a point in his talk of saying he couldn't understand why it was okay for him to *talk* about politics in the gallery, but not for the Topp Twins to *perform* about politics.

We are proud to have been able to use our art to fight for a nuclear-free Aotearoa. New Zealand has been a world leader in seeking peaceful outcomes in a world full of conflict. We applaud all our fellow citizens who stood up to be counted.

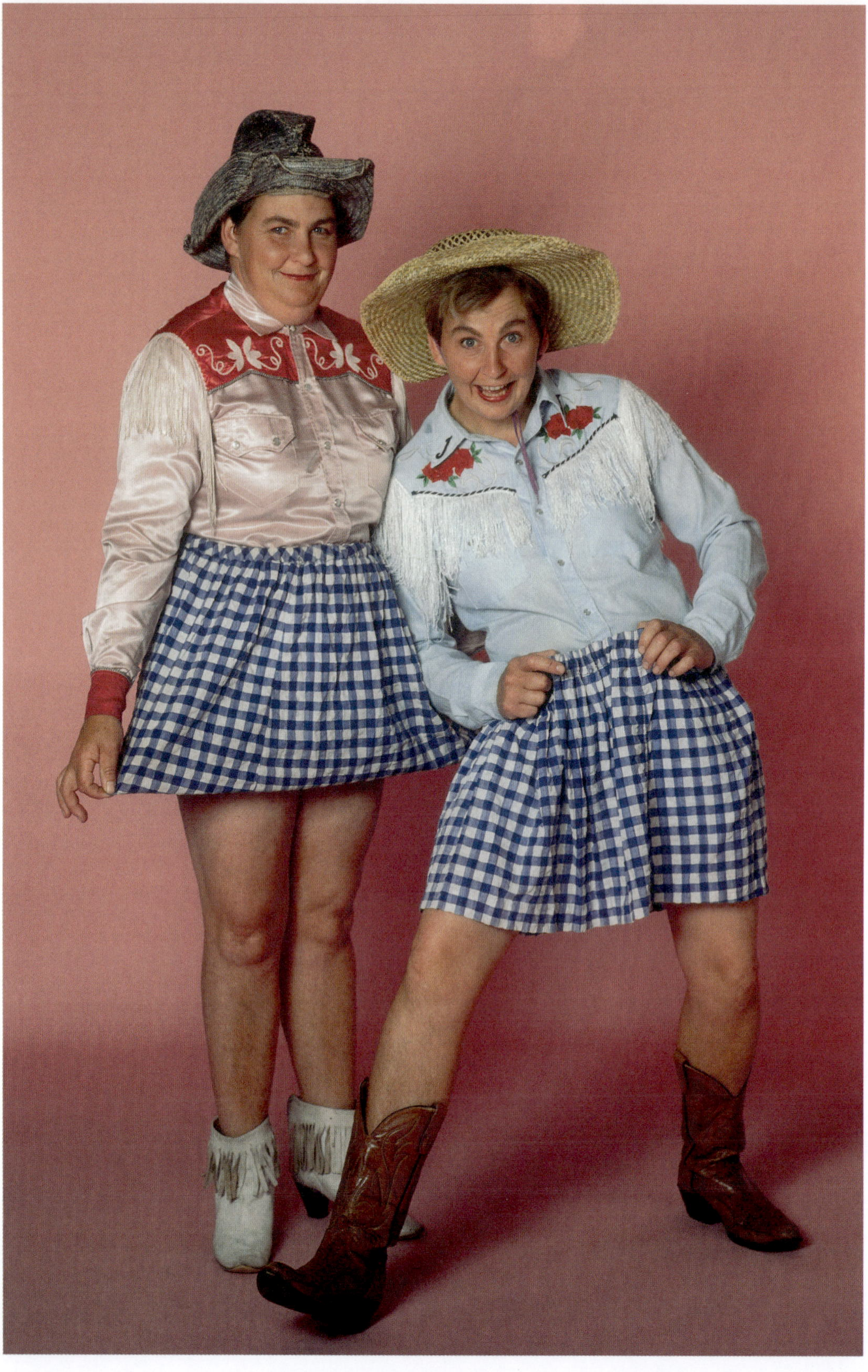

13

The Gingham Sisters

Jools and I were pretty exhausted by the end of 1983. There had been so much going on, and so many issues that we'd jumped into because we wanted to be a part of them. When we were asked to MC and perform at the New Zealand Music Awards in Wellington in November, at the Michael Fowler Centre, it felt like it came out of left field. Here was the mainstream entertainment industry inviting a couple of radical political lesbians into their midst. This felt like a major kind of acceptance: how could we refuse?

Live on stage at the televised show would be Body Electric, Coconut Rough, DD Smash, Brendan Dugan, Allison Durbin, Tim Finn, Herbs, Hogsnort Rupert, Shona Laing, Monte Video, Pink Flamingos, Patsy Riggir, Craig Scott, Shane, Jodi Vaughan . . . and the Topp Twins!

We drove to Wellington in our new wheels — a blue Holden stationwagon. The repo man had finally found the old green van in a shed out at Bethells — God knows how. We had an amicable

Opposite: The Gingham Sisters. SALLY TAGG

discussion in which he told us it was one of the longest repo jobs he had ever done — it had taken him four years.

After driving all night we pulled into Wellington in the early morning, nipped to the railway station for breakfast, then headed to the Michael Fowler Centre to find out our schedule for the day.

Patsy was country music royalty, and Brendan had won just about every award you could win in country music, and here we were right in the middle of them.

We were assigned a dressing room in between Brendan Dugan and Patsy Riggir. It was surreal: we were the new kids on the block in country music but we were also radical political lesbians; two things that don't really go together. Patsy was country music royalty, and Brendan had won just about every award you could win in country music, and here we were right in the middle of them — and we were the ones that would be performing and handing out the award.

What do you wear to your first New Zealand Music Awards . . . well, how about top hat and tails with glitter? Our sound check was scheduled for around 2 p.m. and we sang a song called 'We've Got Country Music Coming Out Our Ears'. All went according to plan, and we had enough time to head back to our hotel, have a quick feed and be back at the theatre by 6 p.m.

As we headed out to the carpark our friends from Herbs were in the foyer, so we offered them a ride back to the hotel. We managed to squeeze eight of us into the old stationwagon. Then, as we pulled out onto the road, there was Patsy Riggir waiting for the artists' bus. We knew that the last bus back to the hotel was at 2 p.m. and by now it was closer to 3 p.m., so we pulled in beside her.

'There are no more buses, you'll have to jump in!' I yelled out. Two Herbs got out of the back seat and ushered Patsy into the middle, then the first Herb sat on the second Herb's knee. Meanwhile the other Herbs had lit up a big joint and were passing it around.

I looked in the rear-vision mirror, and what a sight it was: Patsy surrounded by four big boys in a cloud of illegal smoke. I thought it was one of the funniest things I'd ever seen. The radical political lesbians, New Zealand's finest reggae group and the queen of country music, all in our old stationwagon. Oh, for a camera.

We all made it safely to the hotel. Patsy did not partake in the handing round of joints, but I believe that on that night she was the happiest we ever saw her.

The awards were great and we had a blast. We also held a party in our room that night and of course Herbs were there, and for the first time in our careers we rang room service for beer and toasted sandwiches for everyone. The next morning at checkout it cost us $650, but it was worth every penny.

About five doors down from our house in Brown Street, Ponsonby, Limbs Dance Company had just moved into a new rehearsal studio. We'd met some of the dancers at festivals and Limbs was making big waves in the arts scene. Jools and I would sometimes head up the three flights of stairs and watch the choreography being thrashed out for their next show.

Mary Jane O'Reilly, Douglas Wright, Shona McCullagh, Leonie Kaywood, Kilda Northcott, Bruce Hopkins, Leanne Plunkett, Felicity Molloy, Sue Trainor, Brian Carbee, Glenn Mayo, Taiaroa Royal and Mark White were just some of the dancers who performed with Limbs over those years. Sue Paterson was their manager, and the talented and funny Phee Phanshell was the production manager.

It was Phee who asked if I'd like to go on tour with Limbs as their stage manager/technician and I jumped at the chance. I didn't really have much relevant experience but I learnt pretty quickly once we were on the road — rigging lights, setting up sound systems, laying the dance floor, calling the show, cueing the music and packing out . . . The first tour was a steep learning curve.

I also fell head over heels for the gorgeous Shona McCullagh. I found out the feeling was mutual and we danced through a beautiful love affair, until she met her future husband John Gibson. I sang at their wedding, and I'm godmother to their beautiful children, Arlo and Vida. We are all family now and the best of friends.

I wondered about creating a character who was a bit shy but also funny — I thought this might be a character the audience could relate to.

Jools and I had been asked to perform at one of Limbs' fundraising concerts held in their rehearsal space, and we decided we needed something new in our act. We'd mainly been singing country music, and original protest songs.

I thought a bit of comedy might go down well. I'd recently done a couple of clown workshops with the very talented Maggie Eyre. My clown's name was Nobody, and halfway through we had to change our clown's name. I decided my new name would be Nobody's Friend. As soon as I said that name out loud all the other clowns wanted to be my friend.

Anyway I wondered about creating a character who was a bit shy but also funny — I thought this might be a character the audience could relate to. And so the very first characters Jools and I created were the country and western comedy duo the Gingham Sisters. My character, Belle Gingham, was a direct product of my first clown workshop.

We discovered early on that to put something down you don't have to know much, but to send something up you have to know your target very well, and we'd spent our childhood learning all those old country tunes and perfecting many difficult yodels.

The key to all our characters was to be not only funny but also bang-on accurate with the classic character type we were playing.

As Belle Gingham, Lynda could bring a whole audience to their knees with laughter with the ridiculous antics she perfected with her elastic-waisted blue gingham skirt. She'd pull out the elastic band and look down through the gap to the floor, and for some reason that just made people lose the plot.

My line in response was: 'She lost her marbles when she was young, and she's been looking for them ever since.'

Another thing we learnt was not to analyse things too much. If something works, don't fiddle with it, just keep it simple and keep it going.

The fact that Lynda's gingham skirt was a different shape to mine was definitely one source of the humour. We found a full-length gingham skirt in an op shop. My girlfriend at the time, Anne Crozier, was a dab hand on the sewing machine so she cut the long skirt in two and sewed an elastic waistband on each half. I got the top half and Lynda got the bottom half. Because the original skirt flared out at the bottom, Lynda's skirt looked hilarious.

These were matched with embroidered satin western shirts, hillbilly hats and white fringed cowgirl boots, and the Gingham Sisters were ready to yodel. It was the simplest outfit we ever came up with, but it really worked. Anne's beautiful daughter Emma, who was about three at the time, saw us and said 'Toppie is funny!'

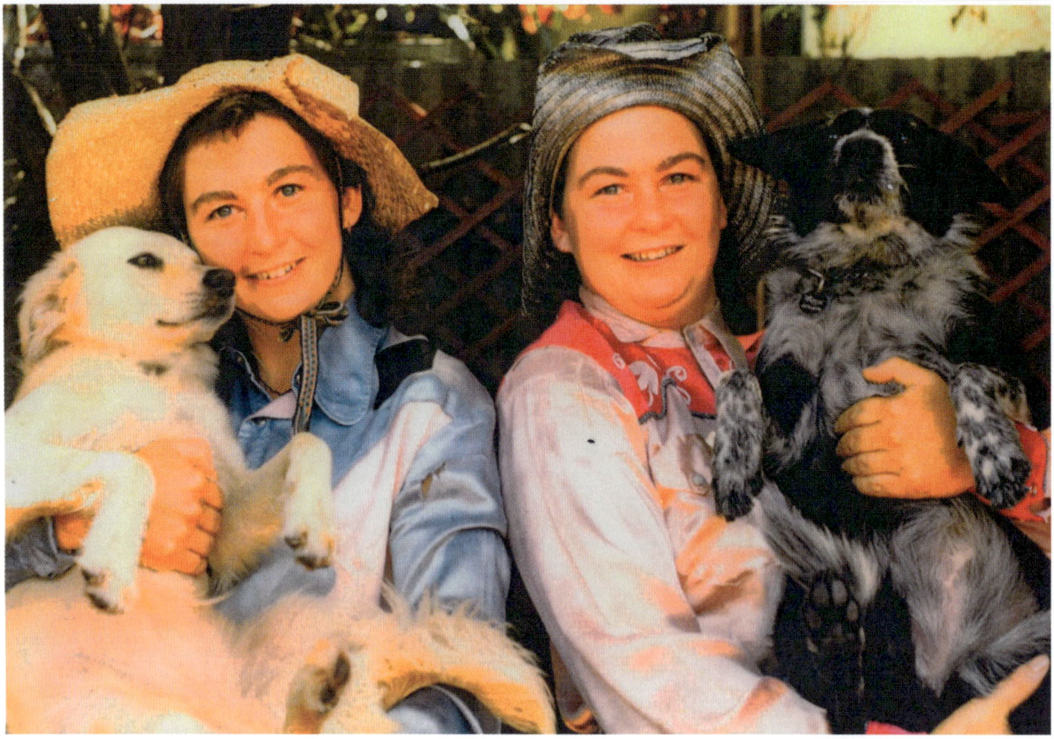

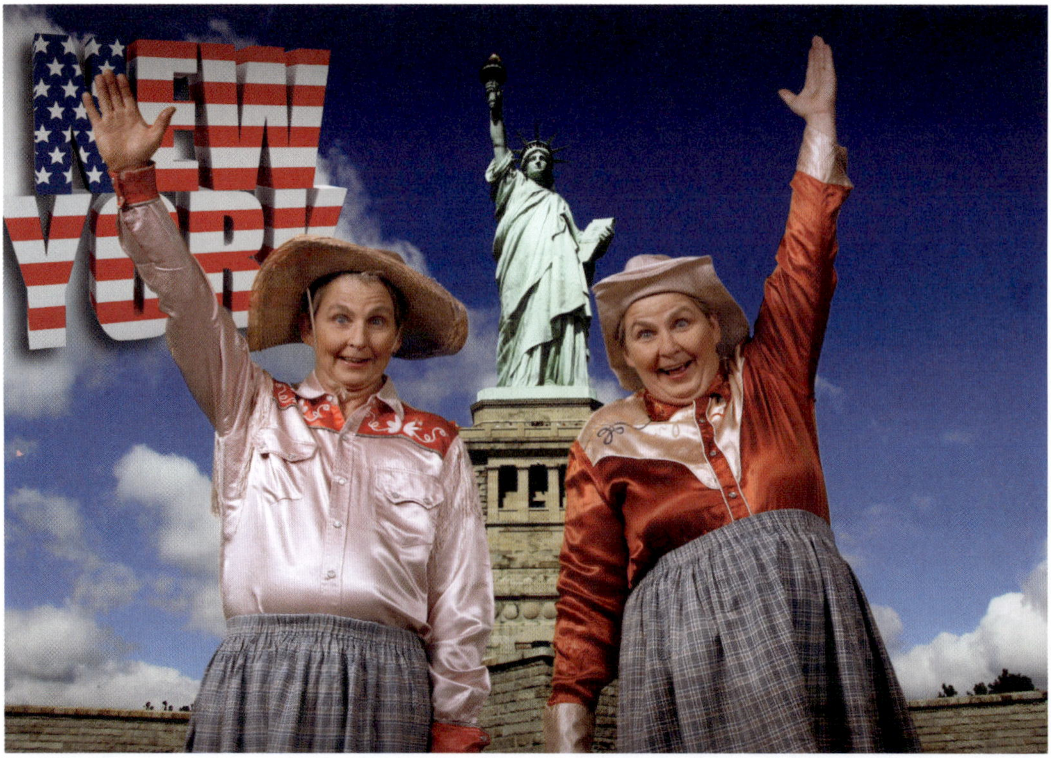
NEW
YORK

THE GINGHAM SISTERS

We reckoned if the Ginghams made her laugh, we might be onto something.

Once while we were performing on Australia's Gold Coast we left one of our show bags in a car parked in a hotel carpark overnight, thinking it would be safe. But the car was broken into and we ended up losing my gingham outfit and Camp Mother's pink outfit as well.

You can't buy those outfits off the rack, but luckily we had a few days to find replacements. Lynda sent an urgent call back to Arani, our manager, in New Zealand to get a spare Camp Mother outfit from our house, and an Air New Zealand flight attendant carried it all the way to Brisbane and delivered it to us the next day.

Meanwhile, we spent all day trying to locate something that resembled a gingham skirt. The best we could find was a blue gingham shirt and a weird pair of short overalls with a bib and cross-over shoulder straps. During that night's show Lynda kept cracking up every time she looked over at me.

Sometimes when we were on stage I'd end up laughing with the audience when Lynda did something off-script. There was just no knowing when it might happen, but it was often when she was playing the spoons. If one of us cracked up, the audience always lost it. Laughter is infectious, and if it really is the best medicine we certainly dished out some good healing with those two characters.

We often wondered how the thieves reacted when they saw what was in the bag they took, and whether they were ever brave enough to put those outfits on. They probably wouldn't have looked out of place in Australia anyway.

―――

Opposite top: The Gingham Sisters in Australia with dogs River (left) and Bosie. DEB COLLINS

Opposite bottom: Many years later, the Ginghams travel the world (postcard from the *Untouchable Girls* documentary). SALLY TAGG / DIVA PRODUCTIONS

We had introduced characters, comedy and new songs into our act, but politics was never far away. In 1984 Lynda and I were invited to be part of the contemporary music contingent in the Aotearoa delegation to the Festival of Pacific Arts to be held in New Caledonia. The organisers in Nouméa had asked that all delegations write a verse for a waiata that would be sung by all attendees at the opening ceremony. They had provided the tune.

We had introduced characters, comedy and new songs into our act, but politics was never far away.

The song that our group came up with was written in a classroom at Rotorua Boys' High School on 29 September 1984. We called it 'Ngā Iwi E', and a star was born.

When we talk about a star we're usually referring to a person who has the qualities of those bright lights in the sky. They shine, they sparkle, and they remain constant. In this case the star is not a person but a song. 'Ngā Iwi E' became such a star, and now has a life of its own.

With us in that classroom (among others) were Hirini Melbourne, Taura Eruera, Robin Mohi, Kui Wano and Mereana Pitman. After about two hours of talking and writing we came up with not one but three verses of a song written in te reo that was intended to unite the Pacific festival.

We rehearsed as a group till we knew it off by heart, and later that day we helped teach that song to the 100-plus people in the

Opposite: Working on lyrics for 'Ngā Iwi E'. Hirini Melbourne is at the blackboard and (from left) Taura Eruera, Lynda, Jools and Mereana Pitman sit at the desks. JOHN MILLER

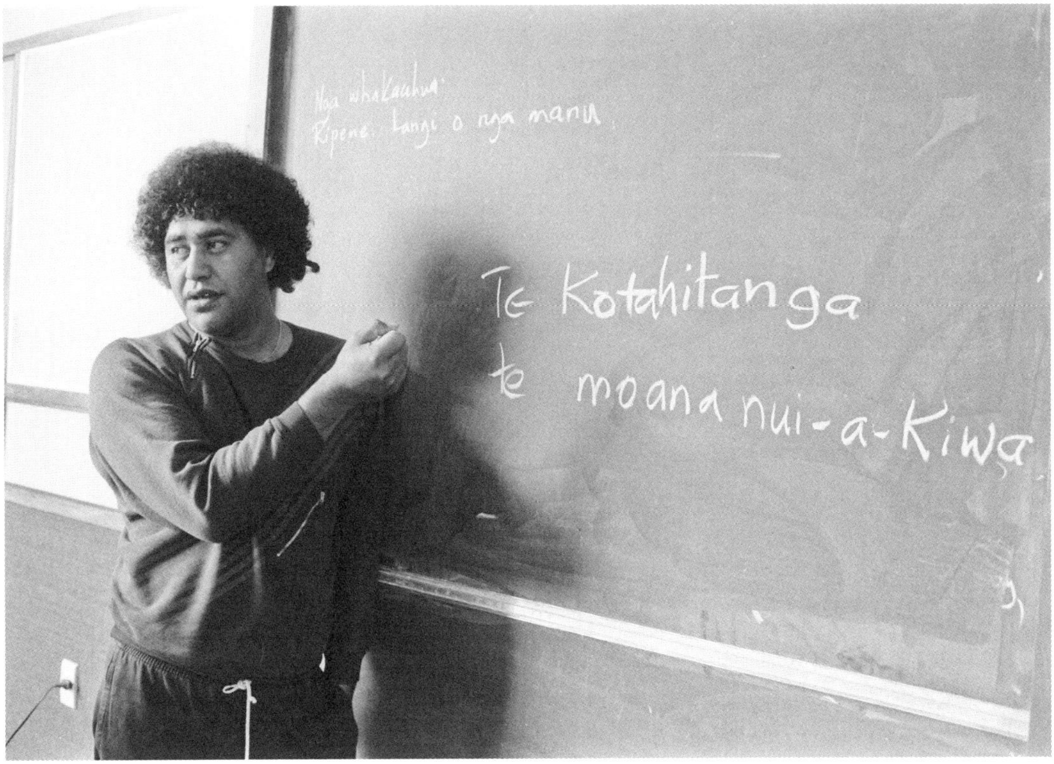
Te Kotahitanga
te moana nui-a-Kiwa

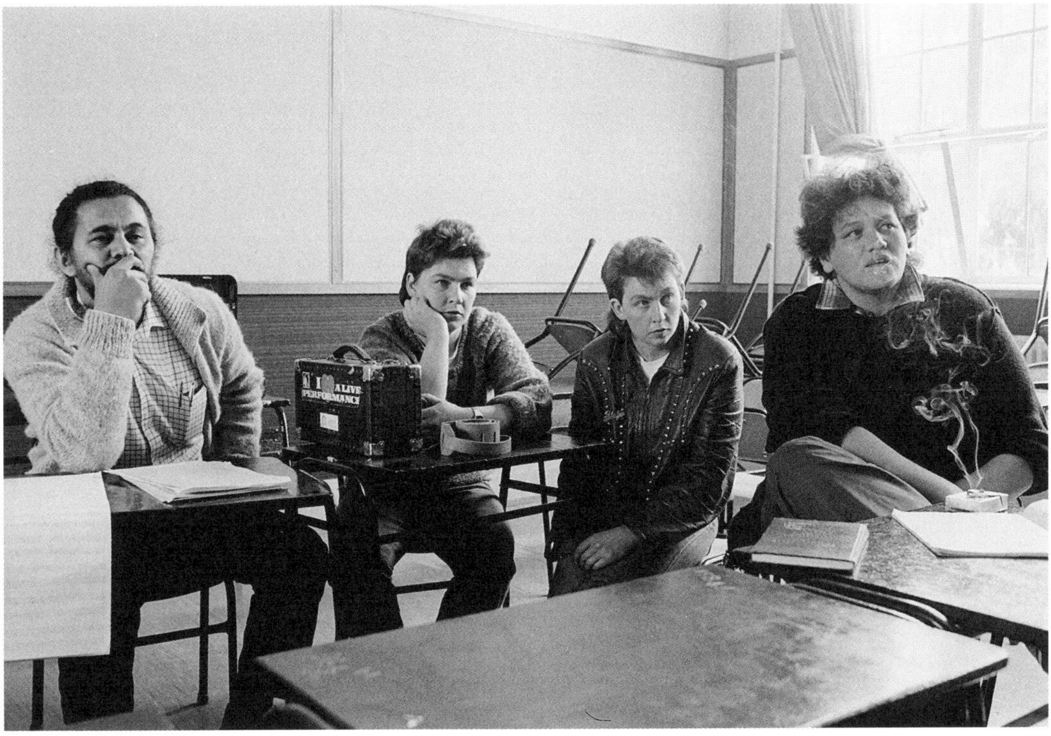

delegation at a local marae. We loved singing it, and the big group learnt it really quickly. Everyone who had worked on it felt proud.

Unfortunately that song was never sung at that festival by us. The French High Commissioner to New Caledonia cancelled the whole event, fearing political strife between the indigenous Kanak independence fighters and the country's pro-French leadership.

But the Tahitian government raised their hand and invited the festival to be staged there the following year, in June 1985.

In the meantime, Tahitian independence activist Oscar Temaru visited New Zealand and requested that we boycott the event to show our support for the Kanaks of New Caledonia — and indeed the indigenous inhabitants of all islands under French rule. A small number of us agreed to the boycott but the majority of the New Zealand delegation went.

> A song that would have been sung only once, at a Pacific festival, became a catchcry for a movement of change and struggle for all the people of the Pacific.

In honour of the indigenous people of New Caledonia who struggled to be heard under French rule, we agreed to sing that song everywhere we went. So a song that would have been sung only once, at a Pacific festival, became a catchcry for a movement of change and struggle for all the people of the Pacific.

The star was not only born, but had packed its suitcase and was on tour.

I don't know how many times we've sung that song, but it would be in the thousands. We performed it with the Auckland Philharmonia Orchestra and recorded it on *Honky Tonk Angel*. We know it will go on forever in Aotearoa and around the world.

Ngā iwi e, ngā iwi e	People, people
Kia kotahi rā	Unite as one
Te Moana-nui-a-Kiwa	Like the Pacific Ocean
E-i-a-i-e!	E-i-a-i-e!
(Whakarongo, tautoko)	(Listen, support)
E-i-a-i-e!	E-i-a-i-e!
Kia mau rā, kia mau rā	Hold fast, hold fast
Ki te mana motuhake	To your sovereignty
Me te aroha	And to love and compassion
Wāhine mā, wāhine mā	Women everywhere, women everywhere
Maranga mai, maranga mai	Rise up, rise up
Kia kaha	Be strong

Lynda (left) and Jools on Auckland Harbour in the 1980s. BRUCE CONNEW

14

The End of the Rainbow

We'd had a full-on time of activism and singing at protest rallies, so it was a joyous moment when we got the call to tour with Split Enz in 1984 as their support act. Moments like these were so helpful in forging our career — and were proof that people in the industry believed we had the talent.

It was the first time we'd ever had a backstage rider, guaranteeing us the likes of clean towels and our own security team. Scruff and Foot they were known as. It felt like we were living the rock-star lifestyle.

Nelson was a sold-out concert but unfortunately it was an outdoor venue and it pissed down with rain. But that audience was so loyal — they weren't going anywhere, even though they were soaked to the skin.

As we came on stage a gush of rain came pouring through a gap in the stage roofing and a wall of water hit the drum kit behind us. I was playing guitar and hoping I wasn't about to be electrocuted. Meanwhile Lynda told the audience they were amazing, then walked over and stood under the waterfall — the crowd went crazy. Lynda has always had an ability to connect with an audience, to sense what they want and to engage with them, almost on a personal level.

The Finn brothers had quite a similar background to us: they were country kids, and they're just great down-to-earth guys. There have been a few times over the years when we've all sat around with guitars and a few beers and sung party songs. It was a great privilege to be asked to their *Enz With A Bang* final party in Auckland on 7 December 1984.

It was an early-evening start, on the same day as the *Thank God It's Over* concert (students celebrating the end of exams) in Aotea Square featuring Herbs, DD Smash and The Mockers.

It didn't feel like New Zealand — this kind of stuff happened on television.

Jools and I were keen to catch the Herbs set, which was awesome. We listened to a couple of DD Smash songs, then left Aotea Square to head to the Enz party. It was while we were driving over the Harbour Bridge listening to the radio that we heard a news report about a 'riot' in Queen Street. Apparently, soon after we left the police had pulled the power to the stage and called the concert off. The 10,000-strong crowd were not happy, and by the time the police got things under control there was over $1 million worth of damage.

It just seemed so weird because it had been such a peaceful, chilled-out concert when we were there.

We had a great time at the Split Enz party and headed back over the Harbour Bridge around midnight. We decided to check out Queen Street on the way, driving from the bottom all the way up to Aotea Square. Everywhere shop windows were smashed, rubbish and broken bottles littered the street, cars had been upturned . . .

It didn't feel like New Zealand — this kind of stuff happened on television, not in our back yard.

Dave Dobbyn was subsequently charged with inciting the riot but eventually was cleared of all charges. We had been at a lot of protests that had made history in New Zealand, but this was one historical night that we were glad we missed.

―

Another event we were very relieved to miss was on the night of 10 July 1985, when French secret service agents bombed the Greenpeace ship *Rainbow Warrior* in Auckland Harbour. New Zealanders were all in a state of shock and disbelief at what looked to have been an act of terrorism in the harbour. It was headline news worldwide.

Greenpeace photographer Fernando Pereira was killed in the murderous blast, and there could easily have been more fatalities.

We had performed at many Greenpeace rallies and supported a number of their campaigns, and in return they had invited us to come on board the ship for a celebratory party that very night. We had declined as we had a gig booked elsewhere.

When we heard the news the following morning we all raced down to Auckland's waterfront. I remember seeing the bow raised out of the water and the rainbow and peace dove painted on the side visible above the waterline, as if to say: I may be down but you cannot kill my spirit. It was hard to believe something like this could happen in New Zealand.

The *Rainbow Warrior* had been about to lead a flotilla of protest vessels to Moruroa Atoll to protest against French government nuclear testing in the Pacific. The attack was clear evidence that the French saw what Greenpeace was doing as a real threat.

Top: The Topp Twins perform at a concert for the *Rainbow Warrior* at Mt Smart Stadium in Auckland. GIL HANLY / AUCKLAND WAR MEMORIAL MUSEUM TĀMAKI PAENGA HIRA

Bottom: The twins take to the stage in support of the Homosexual Law Reform Bill. DAVID HINDLEY

We were distressed to learn that another French agent, Christine Cabon (who went by the name Frederique Bonlieu), had infiltrated not only Greenpeace but also Auckland's lesbian community. She fled New Zealand six weeks before the bombing and never faced prosecution in France. Nor has she ever apologised.

But if the French plan was to shut down the Greenpeace movement, it backfired badly. The campaign to halt nuclear testing in the Pacific gained enormous public support after the bombing, and Greenpeace today is still championing the fragility of Mother Earth and the need to protect our oceans. Even back then they were talking about global warming and climate change. After all the extreme weather events on our planet lately — including in New Zealand — maybe more of us should be listening to what Greenpeace and other climate activists are calling for: an end to fossil fuels.

One contribution we were able to make was to sing at the *Rainbow Warrior* concert held a year after the awful event. Some big names flew in to raise money for a new boat to carry the Greenpeace flag into the high seas. We were honoured to perform alongside Neil Young, Jackson Browne, Graham Nash, Bonnie Raitt, Split Enz, Herbs, Dave Dobbyn, John Hore Grenell and Hello Sailor.

There was one bright political note in 1985–86.

Queen Victoria famously declined to outlaw lesbianism along with male homosexuality because, she said, 'Women do not do such things.'

But gay men have long been targeted by governments and moralists all over the world. Sexual activity between males was criminalised in the UK in 1885, and in 1893 New Zealand followed suit. Countless thousands of men were persecuted, prosecuted and punished over the years.

Almost a century later, the courageous Fran Wilde, a single mother and Labour MP for Wellington Central, introduced the Homosexual Law Reform Bill to the House of Representatives on 8 March 1985.

The backlash was predictably vile and offensive, but it did not stop the uprising of brave gay men who stood up to be counted and to confront the haters. Many lesbian and straight supporters stood with them.

Jools and I were asked to perform at several Homosexual Law Reform rallies and were in the Wellington Town Hall the night National MP Norman Jones spouted these infamous words:

Turn around and look at them . . . gaze upon them . . . you're looking into Hades . . . you're looking at the homosexuals . . . don't look too hard — you might catch Aids . . . Go back into the sewers where you come from. Let all the normal people stand up. We do not want homosexuality legalised. We don't want our children contaminated by those people.

What was said on that night was, in our view, the downfall of the opponents of this bill: the hatred expressed not only shocked the gays and lesbians protesting at this rally, but also allowed the general public to see the extreme lengths of discrimination these people would go to.

In contrast, the rainbow communities stood for love, and were seen to be celebrating their peaceful lifestyle.

The law passed on 9 July 1986 because gay men in this country stood up, risking jail and worse, and the right to love and to choose your sexual identity triumphed over hatred and abuse.

Our first television show, *Topp Twins Special*, was a live performance filmed in the Pumphouse Theatre in Takapuna in 1986. We played a variety of characters, including babies who emerged from a large white egg in the middle of the stage, wearing baby bonnets, long pink gowns and standing on our knees with slippers tied to them for our little dance routine.

The Gingham Sisters were well established by then so they were already a crowd favourite. We created several other new characters for the show. I played a ventriloquist and Lynda was my puppet — she stood behind a screen with a set of legs tied to it and I had my hand up her jacket. Lynda made a brilliant puppet; her makeup even had little lines below her mouth to make her face look wooden.

Most of those characters we never played again, including Topp Heavy, a couple of heavy-metal guitarists. My guitar was real but Lynda's was sponge rubber so she could smash it on the floor amidst smoke and flashing lights. We finished the show as ourselves in pastel-coloured suits and high hair in mullet style singing 'Untouchable Girls', which pretty much became our theme song.

Our old friend Di Cadwallader produced the TV special with Eloise McAllister, but it nearly didn't get made at all. We later found out that the first response from the top guns at TVNZ to Di and Eloise's pitch was that they thought the Topp Twins didn't have enough talent to do this kind of show. Enter Ruth Harley, who was the commissioner of entertainment at TVNZ, and a real mover and shaker. She had seen us perform live and believed we could pull this off. She convinced the powers that be to take a gamble on us, and it paid off. *Topp Twins Special* went on to win Best Entertainment Programme, Best Original Music and Best Entertainer in the 1987 *Listener* Film and Television Awards.

It was to be another 10 years before we were back on the small screen. And once again Ruth Harley, in her role as Head of Funding at NZ On Air, would be pivotal in getting us back on TV.

The twins at a peace rally in Melbourne.
PHOTOGRAPHER UNKNOWN

15

Australia and the World

Most Kiwi performers who do well at home eventually head to Australia to have a crack at the entertainment scene there, and we did that in 1986, staging shows in Melbourne, Sydney, Adelaide and Perth.

We had by now performed live heaps of times, recorded albums, helped change laws and filmed our first TV show, but would the Topp Twins cut the mustard overseas? There was only one way to find out, so it was onto a plane to Melbourne for Women 150, part of that city's 150 years celebration.

Holy moly — we really took off there. Reviews of our shows talked about people 'breaking down doors' to see us. We were a bit blown away. We also got a chance to see some great shows, and meet other women comedians — Liz Sadler, a lesbian comic, stood out — and see Aboriginal women from the Stolen Generation perform. We watched a heartbreaking one-woman show about an Aboriginal woman trying to find her birth mother, and it made us realise how powerful theatre could be. It also made us feel very lucky to have had such a wonderful childhood, with two parents to care for us and keep us safe.

Our next big show was at the Belvoir St Theatre in Sydney, and that did a lot to put us on the map in Australia. We were young and fresh-faced, with a new sort of theatre show that was both political and funny. We were in the right place at the right time. Our friend Deb Collins was our tech for the show, and that friendship has lasted a good 40 years.

Later on, we picked up many Australian Arts Council regional tours that took us to small towns and some of the outback areas. The big Aussie music festivals were great fun to perform at.

> We were young and fresh-faced, with a new sort of theatre show that was both political and funny. We were in the right place at the right time.

The Gympie Music Muster is held at the Amamoor State Forest in Queensland, and around 20,000 people turn up every year to camp and listen to all the big names in country music perform. It runs for four glorious days. People set up the most amazing campsites, with full-blown bush kitchens. There are a million utes covered in red dust, and festival-goers drink the local Bundaberg Distilling Company dry.

Port Fairy is a coastal town in south-western Victoria and their annual folk festival is another beauty. The smaller Blue Mountains Music Festival is attended by heaps of locals, along with plenty who drive or catch the train from Sydney. One of the best things about these festivals for us was the chance to see artists from around the world, many of whom have been touring for years, just like us.

The Tamworth Country Music Festival in north-east New South Wales is legendary. We performed there many times, which certainly boosted our other Australian shows — many people first saw us in Tamworth, then came to see us again when we hit their local town.

Unlike other festivals, Tamworth has no main stage, but venues all over the town stage performances — pubs, RSL rooms, bowling clubs, you name it — if they can fit in some chairs and a small stage, someone will be performing.

One year we played at the local RSL club, which held about 600 people and was packed out for every show. Mind you, this may not have had much to do with us: it was sweltering hot outside, and the venue had air conditioning and cold beer . . .

Another time at Tamworth we played the Gingham Sisters for the first half, and for the rest of the show performed as ourselves. We went downtown after the gig in our Topp Twins outfits (jeans, checked shirt and cowboy hat — standard attire for Tamworth). Some people who'd seen our show wandered up to say they loved our songs, and then one said, 'You should have seen the old scrubbers that were on before you!' We told them that was us too and they couldn't believe it.

We had a good old belly laugh about that one.

The super-duper Australian music festival, though, would have to be the Woodford Folk Festival in Queensland. It's the biggest folk festival in the world, with around 430 acts over six days and nights, and 120,000-plus people in attendance. The festival venue becomes like a small town, with thousands of tents among the trees, and restaurants, bars, marketplaces, workshops, street theatre and great music.

It's held at the end of the year and on New Year's Day there's a great fire event. Throughout the festival people make beautiful paper structures at the Fire Workshop; the year we attended, the theme was Noah's Ark. A huge boat and thousands of life-size animals, with candles inside to illuminate them, were carried on poles in a giant procession. From a hill above the stages they wound their way in the half-dark towards the mesmerised crowd. There were even a couple of misbehaving unicorns who refused to join the queue.

All the animals were then loaded onto the ark (a logistical challenge in itself) and the whole thing was set on fire. The unicorns could be seen cantering around on the hill as the fire slowly died out.

It was an amazing spectacle.

Much later we performed as part of the entertainment programme for the Sydney Olympic Games in 2000, and at the Rugby World Cup final when it was held in Sydney in 2003.

It was a privilege to sample a bit of the Australian music scene over the years.

On our second venture out of New Zealand we travelled to Canada for the Vancouver Folk Music Festival in 1987.

Several New Zealanders had featured over the years, and in 1987 we received an invitation to perform. One of the festival volunteers, our good friend Jo Morrison, had been pushing for us to be included. I'm pretty sure it helped our case that New Zealand had just passed legislation declaring the country a nuclear-free zone. This got a lot of publicity around the world and appealed to many folk-music types.

New Zealanders have a lot in common with Canadians. We're both Commonwealth countries, of course, with many 'alternative' folks, a large geographical neighbour that we often get confused with . . . and a passionate love affair with corduroy.

Lynda and I and our girlfriends, Shona McCullagh and Lidija Cukor, decided to grab the opportunity to visit Canada and see how our show would go down such a long way from home. We were just two gals and a guitar and we had no idea what to expect. The festival programme said this:

> *The Topp Twins are something brand new for us. All we know about New Zealand is that it is far away, has banned nuclear weapons, and considers Australia to be the world's most dangerous super-power. We think the Topp Twins are going to fill in the rest.*

We talked to the audience about being proud to be nuclear-free, sang original songs like 'Radiation Burns' and 'No War in my Heart', and played the blues. Lynda wowed them with her harmonica skills, we chucked in a few old-time country tunes and finished off with 'Untouchable Girls'.

We had them hook, line and sinker.

Also featured on the programme was Patsy Montana, the first female country singer to sell a million singles in the US with her song 'I Want to be a Cowboy's Sweetheart'. We were scheduled to play with Patsy and four other performers at one of the workshop concerts, aptly titled The Yodeladies.

That was a blast — we'd never had a yodel jam with so many performers before. Patsy and Lynda even had a go at duelling yodels, and we finished the set with Patsy announcing that she could retire happily, knowing that yodelling was in good hands with my talented, octave-swerving sister. And of course she gave us a signed postcard of her on her trusty pinto pony, which now hangs proudly in Lynda's Lady Cave.

Laurie Lewis, Michelle Shocked and Alison Krauss were also launching their careers at this festival, and it was so good to meet these artists and see them perform live.

From top: Lynda, Patsy Montana and Jools at the Vancouver Folk Music Festival; Billy Bragg gives Lynda a massage at the same event. PHOTOGRAPHERS UNKNOWN

One performer who caught our ear particularly, and with whom we became great friends, was Billy Bragg. We subsequently toured with the ever so sweet and talented Billy in New Zealand and in England and Scotland. I remember our first show with him in London in the late '80s. It was full of punk rockers, political activists and militant unionists, and we had decided to perform as the Gingham Sisters. What could possibly go wrong?

They didn't quite get us, thinking we were for real, and someone yelled from the back of the club, 'Sing something decent!'

Jools replied, 'If you don't like it, you can f--- off!', which was the first time I had ever heard her be rude to an audience member. I thought it all might turn to custard, but amazingly Jools' intervention seemed to do the trick. People down the front started repeating her line to the heckler down the back: 'Yeah, if you don't like it, you can f--- off!'

I looked down at our set list. The yodel was two songs away so I said to Jools, 'Let's do the yodel now.' Well, they must have thought it was some new kind of punk anthem because the whole crowd was soon pogoing to our yodel. We followed up with a couple of political songs, which we didn't normally do as the Ginghams, but it worked — we now had them eating out of our hands.

'Untouchable Girls' was our last song and, halfway through, out comes Billy Bragg dressed exactly like us in a gingham skirt, cowgirl shirt and hat, fringed boots and plaited wig. We were laughing so hard we could hardly sing and the crowd, who were really there for Billy, went nuts.

We wondered if he had done it to show the crowd that we were okay, but his crew told us later he'd got them to arrange the outfit for him a week earlier, so he had it planned all along. That's the kind of guy Billy is — down to earth and funny to boot.

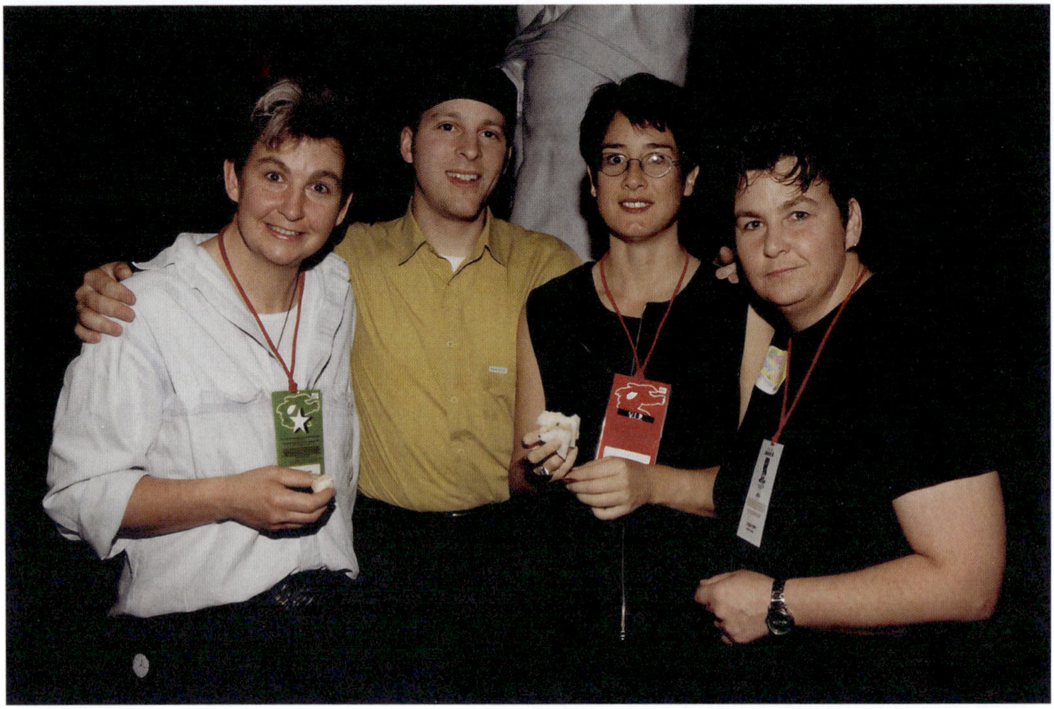

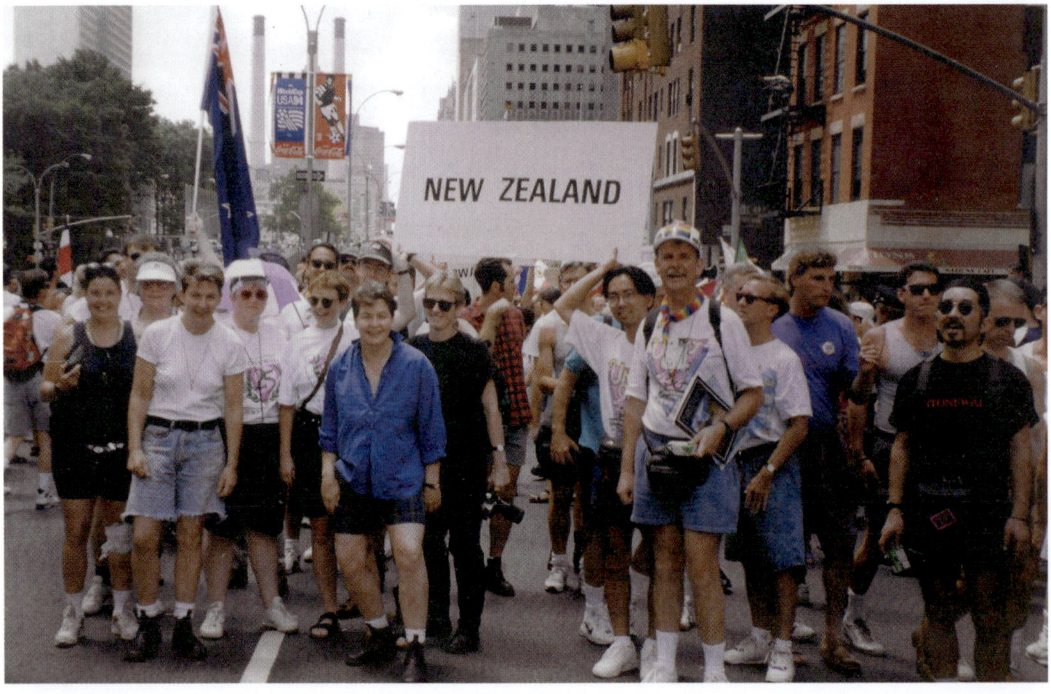
NEW ZEALAND

After the Vancouver Folk Music Festival in 1987 we were offered other shows at the Vancouver Cultural Centre in downtown Vancouver, and Patsy Montana also asked us to perform with her. Realising we had no merchandise to sell, festival co-founder Gary Cristall organised three days for us in a recording studio. He liked our sound and predicted that we were going to go places. The sound engineer, Simon Garber, was brilliant and certainly knew how we wanted to sound.

Day two we edited the whole lot, and day three we finished the artwork and had a cassette in our hot little hands titled *No War in my Heart* for the gigs that weekend. That's how ya did it way back in the '80s!

The event with Patsy was a sold-out show to a mixed audience of yodelling lovers, lesbians and folkies, and secured us a very loyal Vancouver audience.

We loved our time in Vancouver and stayed on a while at the home of our New Zealand friend Jo Morrison and her darling Canadian partner, Shelagh, over on beautiful Vancouver Island. We will always be grateful for their hospitality. In the years to come we enjoyed many fun times with them, and later their children, Jaime and Sasha.

Canada was good to us. We returned several times over the years, performing at various folk festivals in Edmonton, Calgary and Winnipeg, and twice at the prestigious Just for Laughs comedy festival in Montréal in the mid-1990s. Then, in 2009, we had the ultimate Canadian experience when our film *Topp Twins: Untouchable Girls* won the Cadillac People's Choice Award at the Toronto International Film Festival.

Opposite from top: The twins and Arani with Brent Schiess from Just for Laughs Montréal — the biggest international comedy festival in the world; Taking part in the 1994 Gay Games in New York. TOPP COLLECTION

Jools (left) and Lynda, spirits undampened by the rain, at the launch of their Gypsy Caravan Tour. STUFF LIMITED

16

The Gypsy Caravan Tour

We reckon we have circumnavigated the whole of New Zealand at least 20 times. Everybody loves a road trip, and we've had so many great experiences and met so many amazing Kiwis on our travels.

It's a glorious country to drive in, with the landscape changing all the time — and the magic hour of driving around dusk is often breathtaking. The sky fills with a light that shines at no other time; it's when day turns into night and the sunset reminds us how incredibly beautiful this Earth really is.

It's not often we ever see the sunrise, though — any self-respecting musician is sound asleep at that hour after a long night of performing and a bit of partying.

The Gypsy Caravan Tour in 1989 was a most memorable adventure, towing Lynda's beautiful Romany-carved Gypsy Caravan behind a big green tractor, top speed 20 kilometres an hour. (The caravan was originally owned by Gypsy Mike at Grey Lynn's Kelmarna Gardens, and was lovingly restored by Gregg Fletcher.) We called this our first lifestyle tour and only performed every third day, mainly because it took that long to get there.

I also had a cute wee caravan called a Starlett. We painted her up in the same colours as the Gypsy Caravan and, hey presto, we had ourselves a convoy. Greg Fahey was our tour manager, Clare Bear was our brilliant sound operator, Robyn Tearle the lighting guru and Martin McCullagh the tractor driver maintenance man. Clare, Robyn and I were also in a band at the time with our friend Gloria Hildred. We called ourselves Horsin' Around, and we were the opening act for the Topp Twins.

The crew and I travelled in the car towing my little Starlett, while Lynda rode on the veranda of the Gypsy Caravan in her rocking chair, being towed by Martin driving the Fordson Super Major tractor.

Lynda was in charge of the indicators on the Gypsy Caravan — two long pieces of wood with a carved hand and pointing finger operated by a long piece of string. We even put red reflector tape on the hands for night turning. I'm pretty sure we wouldn't get away with that these days.

Our first gig was at the Pūhoi hall. The only way out of Auckland was over the Harbour Bridge and Lynda decided the best time to go would be four o'clock in the morning because there'd be less traffic. She entered the Herne Bay on-ramp and puttered over the bridge. In no time, cop cars with flashing lights swooped into place behind her and beside her. Lynda just kept on chugging in the tractor as they escorted her over the bridge and directed her to the Takapuna off-ramp on the other side.

Lynda feared the worst: a ticket, or even being told the tractor and caravan were unroadworthy. But the cops were quite intrigued about our rig and the idea of the tour. They sent Lynda on her way with a wave and some sound official advice: 'Drive all the back roads and keep off the main drag.'

That had been our plan anyway — there's nothing nicer than travelling a country road in a Gypsy Caravan.

Pūhoi was sold out. The show was humming along until, right in the middle of a song, we lost power. Everything suddenly went deathly quiet and we were all plunged into darkness. Apparently a possum had climbed up the power pole next to the hall and damaged the lines.

Martin, an expert in number-eight-wire solutions, went into emergency mode. He unhooked the tractor from the caravan and drove her up the first few steps of the hall, opened the big double doors and put the lights on high beam. We finished the show unplugged but very well lit.

Wherever we parked, we would come back to find homegrown veges and home-baked goodies on the veranda.

What a start to our most interesting and fun-filled tour ever. Wherever we parked, we would come back to find homegrown veges and home-baked goodies on the caravan's veranda. The tour seemed to bring joy to every town we played at.

At Opononi, once home of Opo the friendly dolphin, we played at the local pub. In the last set we did a blues song and a young Māori guy jumped on stage and played duelling harmonicas with Lynda. It was spontaneous and amazing, which is always the best kind of show.

Disaster struck in Kerikeri, however, when our trusty old tractor broke down. Locals directed us to an old guy just out of town, a tractor whizz who could fix anything.

We dropped off the old Fordson to him and headed back to Kerikeri for the night.

When we drove out to see him the following day the entire tractor engine was in pieces on his workbench. He said he needed another day to put her all back together, but we had a gig further north the next day so Greg was wondering how we were all going to

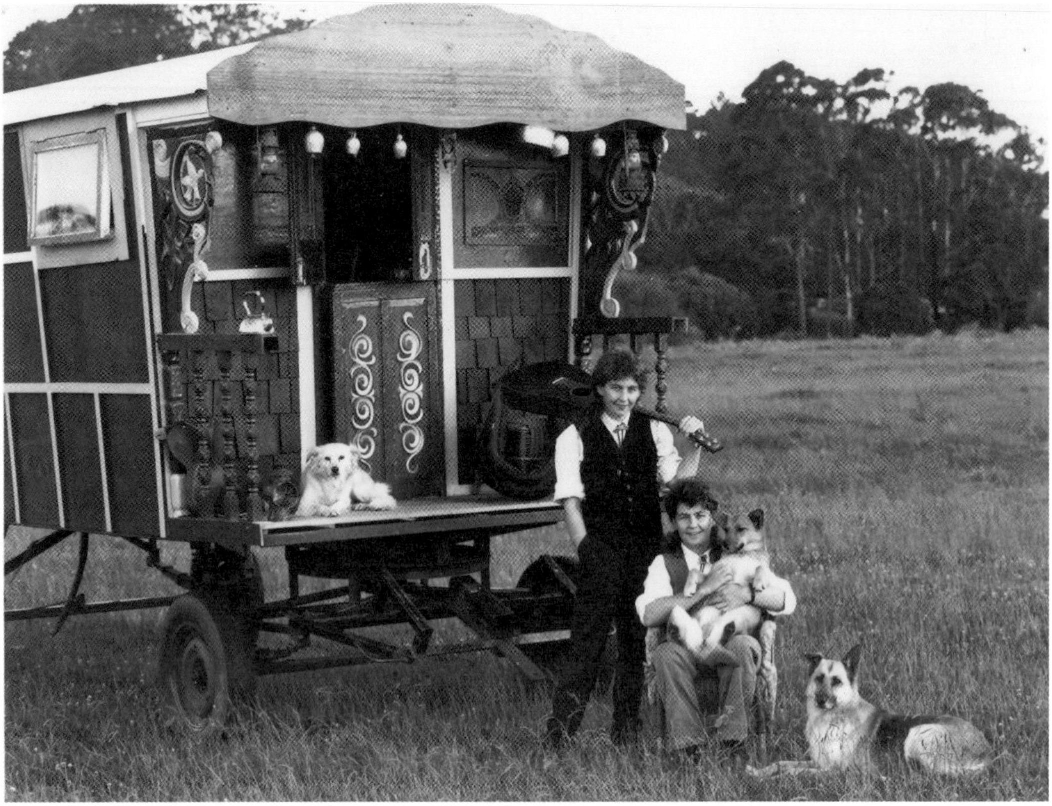

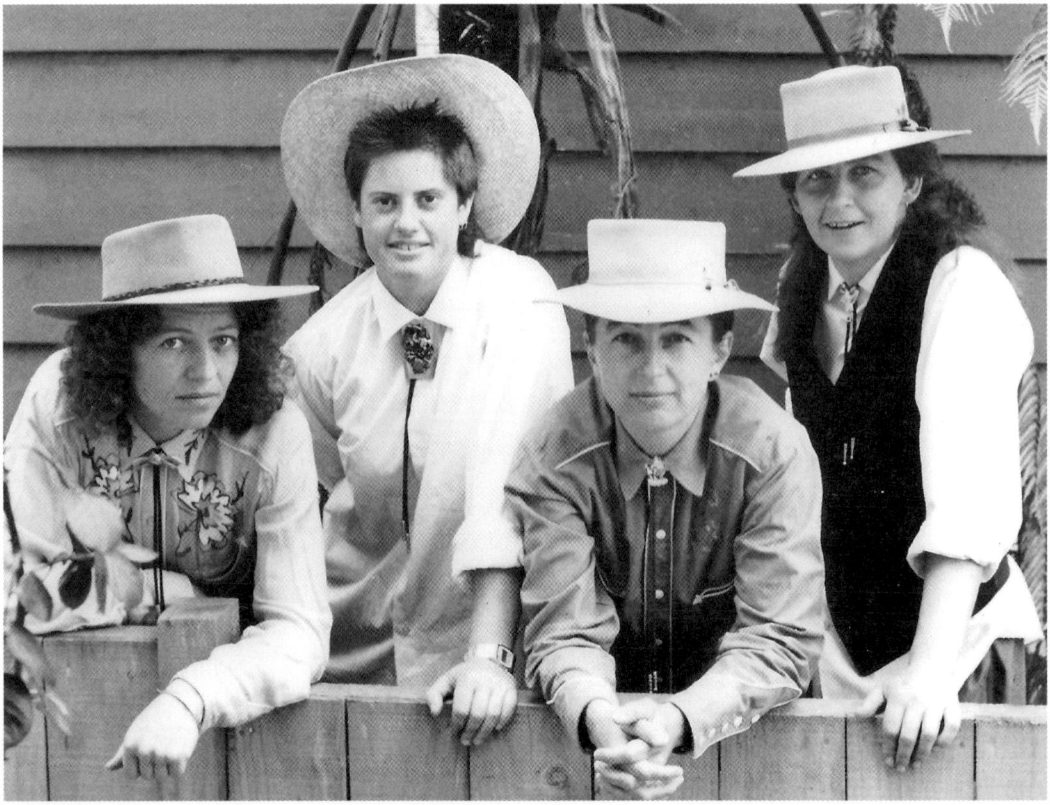

get up to Kaikohe. He needn't have worried. The old boy had already organised a mate's four-wheel drive for us to borrow. He was a true Northland legend.

My little Starlett was the star of the show in Kaikohe, standing in for the Gypsy as the ticket office.

We returned to Kerikeri desperately hoping our tractor would be back in one piece. To our delight she'd never looked better. In fact she was so clean she looked like she was for sale!

The old guy refused any payment but indicated that he wouldn't say no to having a beer with us. Greg raced into town to buy the old fella a slab of beer and we all sat around listening to a few yarns from one of Northland's old-timers. His skin was like leather from years of wandering around the farm shirtless, and he looked really fit and healthy for an older guy. He had never been to Auckland in his life and only went in to Kerikeri for groceries once a month.

Sometimes I'd ride with Lynda on the Gypsy's veranda and Greg would drive the convoy car. It felt magical to be on the road and we couldn't help thinking of all the real Gypsies and Travellers in the world who have been treated badly for their nomadic lifestyle. We certainly knew how lucky we were to have the freedom to travel and perform.

Opposite top: Jools and Lynda in front of the Gypsy Caravan. Lynda is holding Monday, Kelly is at their feet and River has the prime spot on the veranda. PETER MOLLOY

Opposite bottom: The members of Horsin' Around, the support band on the Gypsy Caravan Tour. From left: Gloria Hildred, Robyn Tearle, Clare Bear and Jools. PHOTOGRAPHER UNKNOWN

Then one morning in the suburbs of Whangārei that freedom was briefly taken away. Traffic officers in the old black and white patrol cars of that time pulled us over and asked for the Gypsy's warrant and registration.

They weren't impressed when we said we were just going from farm paddock to farm paddock so we didn't require any documentation. They replied that they wouldn't be letting us leave town until the Gypsy Caravan had rear lights.

We were very relieved when a local garage hooked up a big red light that ran off the tractor battery. Off we went again without a care in the world.

> All the lovely hippies came out of the bush to party in the local halls with us. We felt a sense of closeness to the people in those areas, both emotionally and politically.

There were three separate legs to the Gypsy Caravan Tour, with little breaks in between. After the Northland leg we had just enough time at home to do our washing, then we set off to the Coromandel.

All the lovely hippies came out of the bush to party in the local halls with us. We felt a sense of closeness to the people in those areas, both emotionally and politically. Colville was always a favourite: we'd protested against gold mining in that town in the past, and had also played gigs in support of protesters trying to stop the felling of native forests.

We hit Whangamatā on our birthday and played at the workingmen's club that night. It was another great night and after the show the staff produced a beautiful big chocolate birthday cake while our crew were having a well-deserved cold beer after packing up.

The tractor had been hard to start that morning, so Lynda started her up and left her running while we blew out the candles on the cake and got stuck in. We were having a great time until one of the bar staff came in and said it was nice that one of our crew was taking the tractor down to the camping grounds, where we were staying for the night.

We all looked at one another, noting that the whole crew was with us at the table. Then we all tore outside to see a young guy driving off in the tractor with the Gypsy Caravan in tow.

The good thing about that rig was that he couldn't exactly make a speedy getaway. We all took off running after him as fast as we could. He came to a roundabout and drove straight through the middle of it, which slowed him down a bit. Even though I always beat Lynda in the sprint races at school, she was the first one to catch up to the guy, running beside the tractor and yelling at him.

I was close enough to hear Lynda shouting: 'Get the f--- out of my tractor!' When he leaned down to hear what she was saying she grabbed him by the collar and hauled him out of the seat, climbed up and brought the whole rig to an abrupt halt.

He was trying to explain that he just needed to get home because he was drunk, and the tractor was already running . . . and it was just too big a temptation.

We let the young man walk home but the workingmen's club banned him from membership for two years for 'stealing the Topp Twins' touring vehicle'.

Justice had been done, and we had our cake and ate it too.

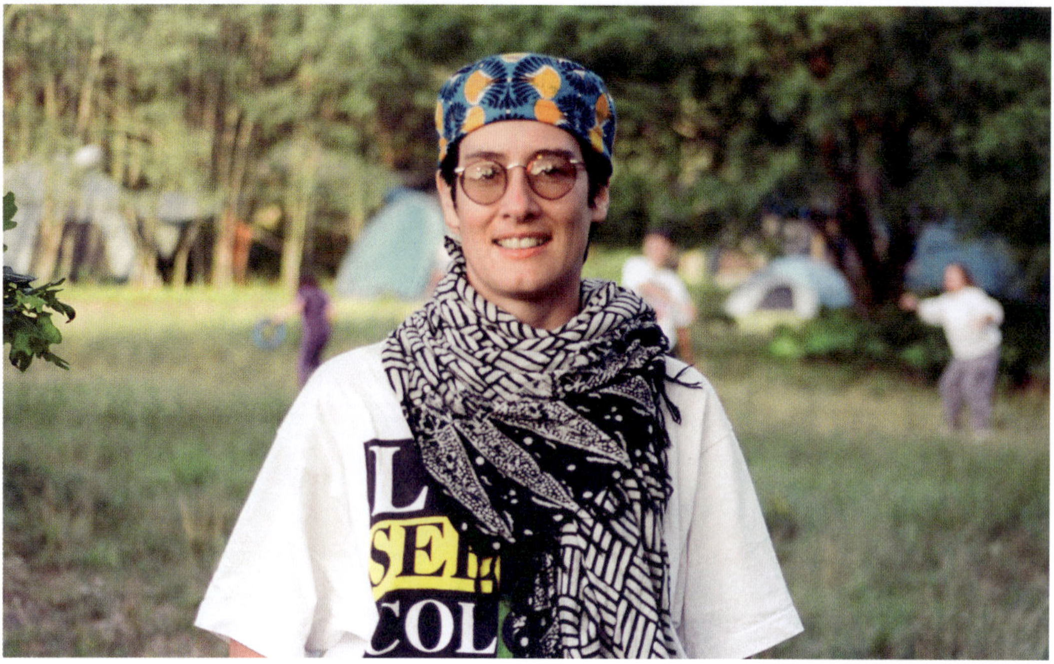

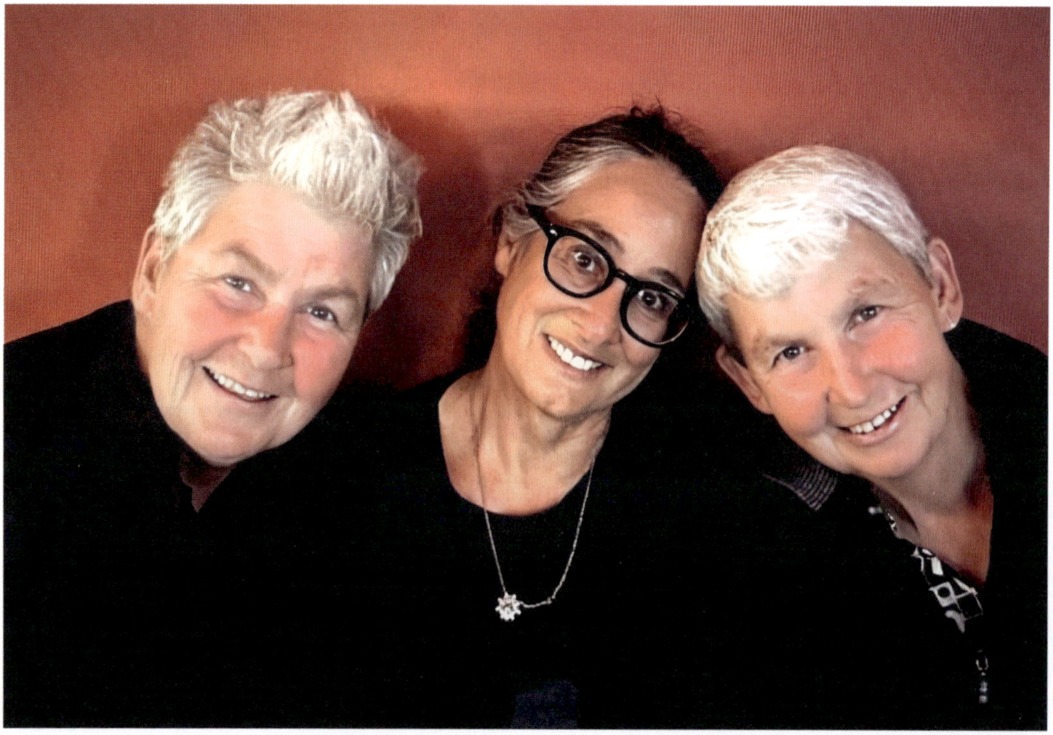

17

Arani Enters Our Lives

By 1990 we had been performing as the Topp Twins for 10 years, and with our involvement in the political events of the '80s and in the women's musical scene, along with our highly publicised arrest for busking, the phone was running hot with offers of work. We desperately needed a manager to book the gigs and handle publicity.

It needed to be someone who shared our ideals. We had met Arani Cuthbert a few times during our involvement with Greenpeace. She worked full-time for Greenpeace and was part of the team campaigning for World Park Antarctica. We got to know her a bit better when she asked me to help with the nuclear-free New Zealand campaign.

The idea was that the Greenpeace ship *Gondwana* would arrive in Wellington Harbour and we would simulate a nuclear explosion

Opposite top: Arani at the Michigan Womyn's Music Festival in 1992. TOPP COLLECTION

Opposite bottom: Lynda, Arani and Jools catch up in 2021, in between Covid lockdowns. FELICITY MORGAN-RHIND

on board. Protesters dressed in white hazmat suits would act as people affected by the disaster. My time as stage manager with Limbs Dance Company would come in handy for this protest, to create the effect of a nuclear explosion on board a ship.

I had made long metal boxes filled with wicks and diesel, to create black smoke, and these were placed on deck the entire length of the ship. Four gas cylinders with copper piping would create flames, and four smoke machines would pump out white smoke. As we came into the harbour my team and I lit the diesel wicks, ignited the copper piping and set our smoke machines in motion.

Arani was meanwhile coordinating the crew, who were strewn on the deck in various positions looking dead. As the ship docked, hundreds more protesters in hazmat suits lay in a sea of death on the wharf. It looked pretty impressive: the whole side of the ship was on fire and TV crews in helicopters and newspaper photographers captured the whole thing.

I was seriously impressed by Arani's ability to organise and publicise such a big, complex event. She was clearly a mover and shaker (with the added bonus of identifying as lesbian). We asked her if she would be interested in managing the Topp Twins. She said she was pretty exhausted after trying to save the planet, and ready for a change, but she'd never worked in the entertainment business. 'What would you want me to do?' she asked.

'Book us a gig,' we said. 'Make sure the venue suits our needs, do the publicity, and make a profit.' Arani was at a loss to start with, so I said, 'Find a country pub in the Yellow Pages and start there.' She opened the Yellow Pages randomly and pointed — at an ad for the Tūākau pub, just south of the Bombay Hills.

Here is Arani's account of this first foray into the entertainment business:

God knows why Tūākau caught my eye . . . perhaps because it is out of Auckland and would attract a different audience to the Twins' usual inner-city crowd. Also, it was only an hour away from the Twins' parents' house in Morrinsville.

The publican said yes but no fee, just cash takings on the door. I sent them posters but when we arrived, the day of the gig, we saw only one poster up: in the pub itself. It became a ritual to drive through small towns ahead of a show and spot posters. Not seeing any made me feel rather despondent.

The Tūākau pub is not a pretty place. Like many of New Zealand's rural drinking establishments, it's seen better days — and that was the day it opened. We walked in through the door and across a brown carpet sticky with beer, past the large pool table that dominated the room in which the Twins were to sing. On a large TV screen the Saturday-afternoon horse races ran with their monotonous commentary.

The bar was empty — apart from Nana Tui, a beautiful Māori kuia sitting in the corner with a couple of friends. 'Kia ora, Twinnies!' she called, and came over to greet them with a hongi.

We carried in the PA system and some lights from the back of the truck and did a sound check — Lynda and Jools operated their own sound. I rearranged the bar leaners and stools.

At 7 p.m. I positioned myself on the door. Cover charge was the huge sum of $10. The locals soon began arriving, Pākehā and Māori. I got the feeling this was uncommon; that the community did not usually mix. Most people paid obediently, but some just walked in, ignoring me.

The pub was packed when the show started. To my relief, the Twins seemed to be going down well. At half-time I did the rounds with a hat, hitting up some people I knew hadn't paid for a koha. Little did we know at that point that the Tūākau pub on a Saturday night was the drinking hole of the local chapter of the Mongrel Mob, which explained the rather anxious looks on some folks' faces as they came in.

Not only that, but apparently the head honcho was there that night. He was the scary-looking dude with a large tattoo up his neck, sitting on his own at a bar table. I brazenly (and unknowingly) went up to him asking for $5. He looked me in the eye and growled, 'F--- off, stinky c---.' I couldn't believe what I'd heard, but I did f--- off.

Then a beautiful moment happened when the Twins were singing 'Ngā Iwi E'. Nana Tui got up and started dancing, both arms stretched out, hands moving in slow circles, fingers articulating more than could ever be described in words.

The twins gave 200 per cent on stage, as they always did, and finished to rapturous applause. After the show they signed CDs and talked with people. As I finished packing up the merchandise, after most people had left, I looked over to see Nana Tui, the gang guy, Lynda and Jools all having a drink together.

I wandered over apprehensively and was amazed to see the man crying. This big patched black-leather tough guy had tears rolling down his face as he told the Twins about his life and how he'd just got out of prison.

That was the moment I realised the Topp Twins' music really did connect with people from all walks of life. I knew I'd found a new calling and wanted to be their manager.

That night in Tūākau will never be forgotten.

That was more than 30 years ago, and Arani is still with us today. For six years Arani and I were an item and I wondered if that would interfere with her manager's role, but she was always professional, diplomatic and dedicated.

18

Feathers, Leathers, Boas and G-strings

If you're gay, there's one event you should definitely try to attend, and that is the annual Sydney Gay and Lesbian Mardi Gras. Arani thought it would be a great gig for us, so she booked us to play at the 1991 Mardi Gras party.

I don't think we were really quite prepared for the spectacle that is Mardi Gras — we were absolutely blown away by the street parade. The costumes and floats were outrageous — we'd never seen so many feathers, leathers, boas and g-strings in our lives. The atmosphere was electric.

Dykes on bikes led the parade, with girls in black leathers riding about a hundred bikes, mostly Harleys, with their girlfriends and friends as passengers all in white dresses. They revved their bikes every time before they roared off and the deafening sound created great excitement among the thousands who lined the footpaths to watch.

Behind them was a smaller group of drag queens on scooters with a placard that read 'Queens on Machines', and behind them came a massive Kenworth truck with what seemed like a hundred

The twins showing a bit of leg at the Michigan Womyn's Music Festival.
TONI ARMSTRONG JR.

cowgirls taking turns to ride a mechanical bull in the middle of the flatdeck. The Marching Boyz were incredible, their tanned and oiled bodies crammed into gold budgie-smugglers, twirling rainbow flags.

Every gay and lesbian community group and club was there in an exuberant and wild celebration of the gay community.

We were convinced nobody would turn up but it was packed to the gunnels with people taking a break from the massive dance party.

The party afterwards was full of famous DJs, the drag shows were world-class, and up high on the main stage was the legendary gay Aussie icon Kylie Minogue.

Our show was scheduled for 1 a.m. (1 a.m.!) in the chill-out tent. We were convinced nobody would turn up but it was packed to the gunnels with people taking a break from the massive dance party.

In Sydney when they say 'all-night party' they mean it, and at our first Mardi Gras we partied all night long. Heading home around 7 a.m. we spotted a group of drag queens wandering down Oxford Street, high heels in hand, wigs a bit skew-whiff, the smudges of eyeshadow and lipstick confirming that a brilliant night out had been had. We'll never forget it.

New Zealand's own annual rainbow event, the Hero Parade, began in 1992 on Auckland's Queen Street and then moved to Ponsonby Road. Those early years were such joyous celebrations, with incredible floats and outrageous outfits.

The first year I rode my motorbike in the parade and Lynda watched with our friends from a big trailer we parked in Queen Street. A few parades later we hooked up the caravan to my Bedford

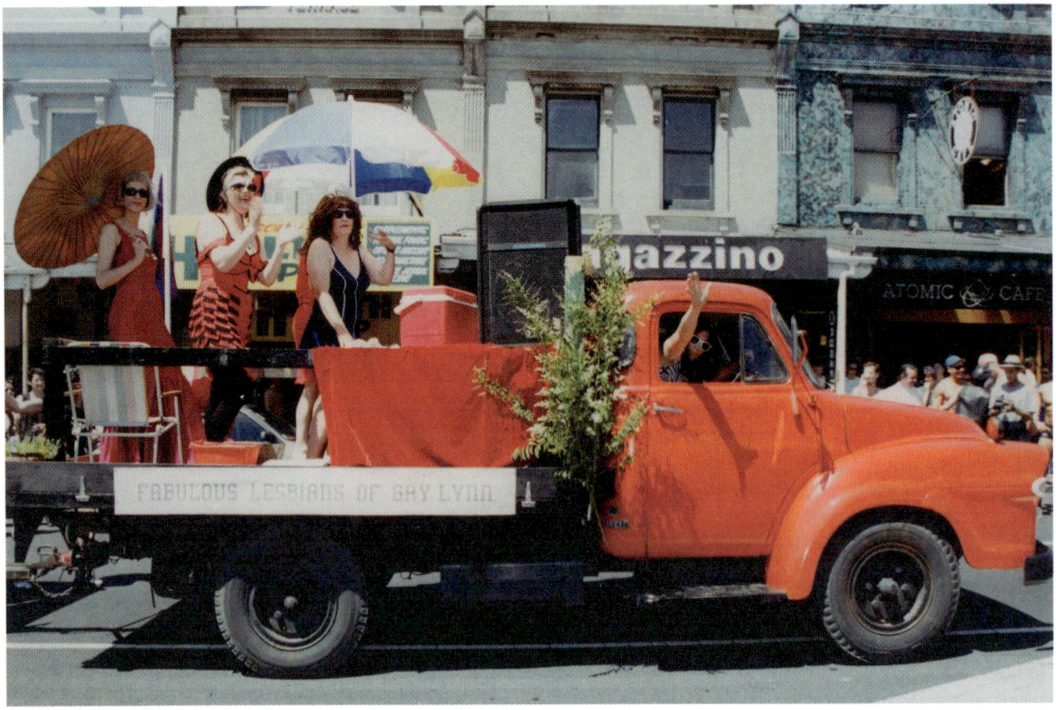
FABULOUS LESBIANS OF GAY LYNN

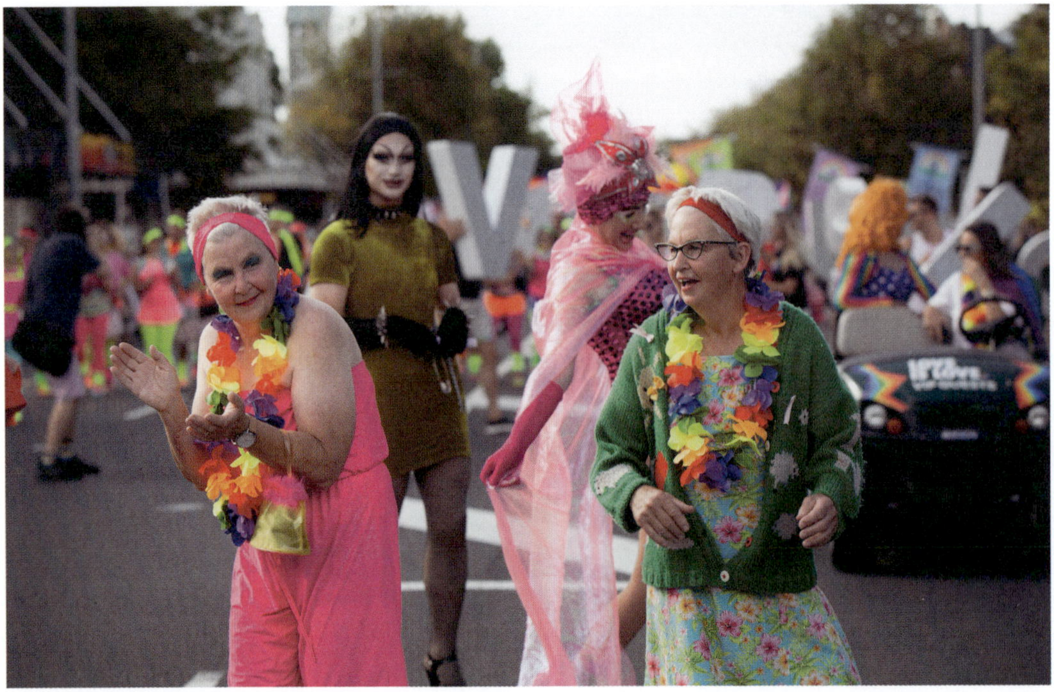

truck and cruised down Ponsonby Road with some of our mates on board.

Initially the parade drew some really big crowds, with more than 100,000 people lining the streets — and at its peak twice that number. But in 2001 the Auckland Council withdrew support for the Hero Parade and it became too expensive to run without their help. Unfortunately, there was also a lot of political infighting. After a 12-year hiatus, the parade was back as part of the Auckland Pride Festival, but it never regained its previous excitement and glamour. It became a daytime event, and much more corporate-looking. For us, the magic of those early Hero Parade days lives on in our memories.

We were like old friends as soon as we met. It was a very sad day when Georgina died in March 2023.

We also felt privileged to lead the walk with Georgina Beyer a few years ago. She had been unwell for a while and it was good to see her out in the gay community again. We had met her in Carterton when she was mayor of that town — the world's first transgender mayor — and she invited us to dinner. We were like old friends as soon as we met. It was a very sad day when Georgina died in March 2023. She was beautiful, funny, smart, fearless and a great inspiration to the young transgender community in our big gay family.

Opposite top: The twins taking part in Auckland's Hero Parade on Ponsonby Road in 1995. Jools is behind the wheel and Lynda (holding the umbrella) is on the flatbed with friends Trudi Green and Annabel Lomas.
ARANI CUTHBERT

Opposite bottom: Camp Mother and Camp Leader at the Auckland Pride Festival in 2020. NEW ZEALAND HERALD

Which brings us to another wonderful event: Big Gay Out. This inclusive festival has been running since 2000. Everyone heads to Point Chevalier for a giant celebratory summer picnic. Outfits are splendid, all types of gayness are supported and welcomed, and for one day in that place we are the majority in a very big straight world.

John Hore Grenell's annual Whitecliffs music festival at his farm in Coalgate, Canterbury, was a whole different vibe. It ran for a few days and was mainly country music, but I remember his kids playing some rock on a night-time stage behind his beautiful big log cabin that he built with his wife Deidre.

> We'd done a bit of shearing work for the neighbours growing up, so we instantly put our hands up — we weren't due on stage till eight o'clock that night.

In 1991 we arrived the day before it began so we got to check out the farm and his stunning Appaloosa horses. We were enjoying a good ol' farm breakfast in the log cabin when a local farmer arrived looking a bit stressed. He told John they had just started shearing a few hundred sheep and there had been an incident. The first sheep out on the boards had ended up being cut, whereupon one of their two young rousies fainted and the other one didn't want to continue.

He'd come down to ask them to put a call out on the main stage to see if anybody at the festival wanted a job throwing out fleeces for the day. We'd done a bit of shearing work for the neighbours growing up, so we instantly put our hands up — we weren't due on stage till eight o'clock that night.

The farmer couldn't believe his luck, and we headed off for a long and interesting day in the shearing shed. As usual there was plenty of good tucker — hot savouries and scones with jam at morning tea, a big roast meal at lunch, and a smorgasbord of home baking for afternoon tea.

It was just like being at home on the farm.

The last sheep of the day were a mob of six big merino rams. As they came into the pens behind the shearers, someone said it was a tradition in the shed for the rousies to bring the first rams on each stand out to the shearer. Of course we hadn't seen the rams yet, so we agreed and off we went to haul them out.

Well, these boys were massive, but luckily Dad had showed us a trick to bend their head to the left so they end up on their bums, unable to move and ready to be slid out to the waiting shearers. If you got it wrong and the ram got its back legs under it, you'd be doing a dance with a six-foot woolly bugger.

So we earned our brownie points that day. They paid us cold, hard cash and we headed back to the festival with one of the shearers, who dropped us at the gate. We were back just in time for dinner and had a couple of hours to rest up before we were due on stage.

Whitecliffs was a really lovely festival and the crowd was ready for a bit of fun with a few yodels, some old Aussie ballads and some new songs. Once we got backstage after our gig, there was the sheep farmer and his wife waiting for us. They'd had no idea during the day who we were or that we'd be performing at the festival — we'd never mentioned it once we got to work that morning.

He started to apologise about making us bring the rams out but we interrupted: 'Hey, that's what country gals do — they know when to rise to the occasion.'

The Topp Twins at the Michigan Womyn's Music Festival in 1993. TONI ARMSTRONG JR.

The Michigan Womyn's Music Festival was something different again.

Michigan is famous for its Great Lakes, but if you're a gal who loves outdoor concerts and camping in the wilderness, then this festival in the 1990s was *the* place to be.

We were invited to play in 1992 on the 'day stage', and were such a big hit we were invited back the following year to perform on the big stage at night.

We loved Michigan. Our first festival, we arrived in Lansing late at night, well after the last bus to the festival in Hart. There was one other woman there who looked to fit the description of 'lesbian searching for festival', so we introduced ourselves. Sarah 'Bear' Westlake had come all the way from England and we became great friends, even travelling together up to New York after the festival. We visited her when we performed in London.

Anyway, the locals let us sleep in the regional airport, where there was an all-American diner in the lounge, so we ate and hunkered down for the night.

Next morning it was like there had been a lesbian invasion in the night. The locals seemed quite amused — they were used to this annual influx at their normally quiet airport. There were 9000 women at that year's festival. As performers we were picked up in a beautiful old bus and driven a couple of hours to the site.

The festival was so exciting — thousands of women all camping out under the stars, with big fire-pits dug into the ground and a team of chefs who fed everyone on site morning, noon and night. Everything had been built or set up by women.

The performers' area was a little city all of its own, with a security team, a musical instrument storage space, massage tents and a catering tent called the Belly Bowl that fed crew, workers and artists. They did early breakfast for early risers, and later breakfast for performers, who never get up early. There was morning

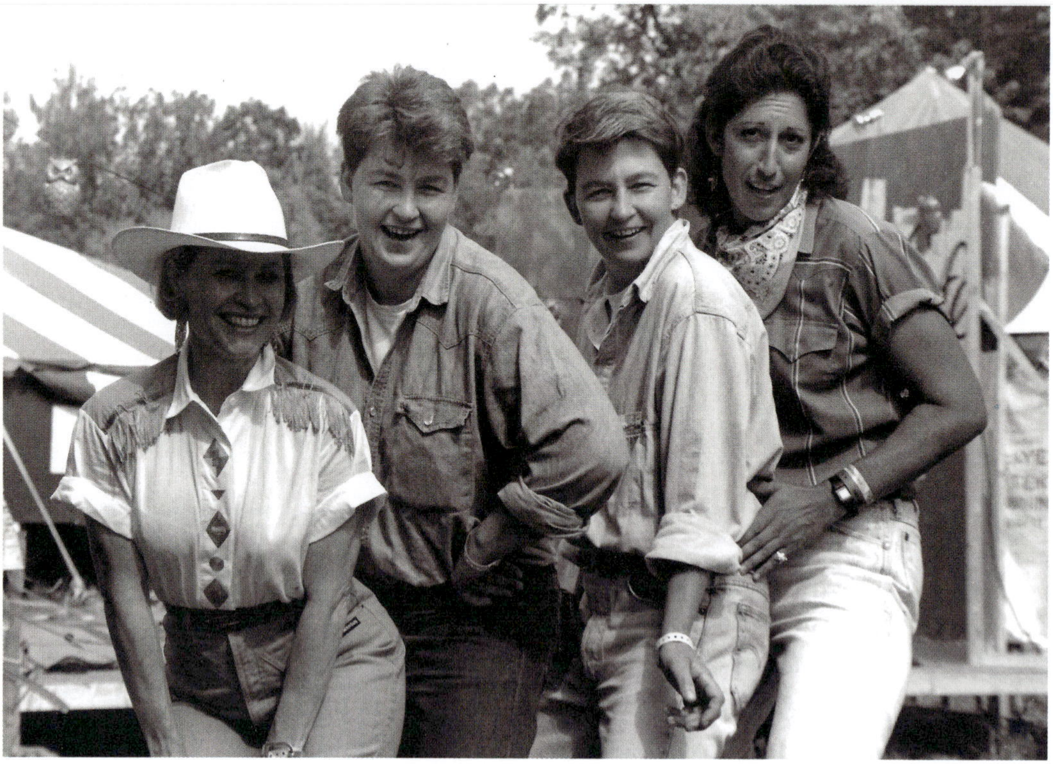

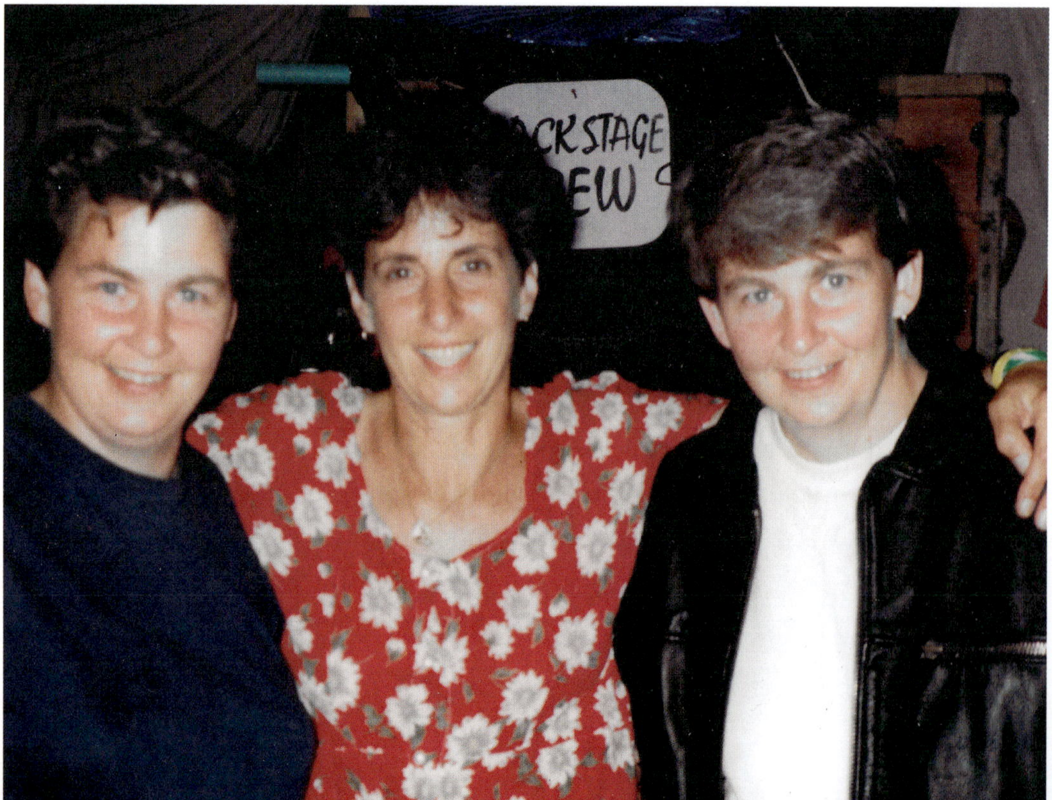

tea, lunch, afternoon tea, dinner and a midnight feast after the late shows.

It ran like clockwork and the women were just so happy to be doing it for themselves.

Our first year we played the comedy stage, and they loved the Ginghams and the yodelling. We got to see some of the amazing acts on the main stage at night — lesbian royalty like Alix Dobkin, Cris Williamson, Ferron, Holly Near, Sweet Honey in the Rock. That's where we met Teresa Trull, a great singer and accomplished horsewoman who eventually came out to live in New Zealand and work with horses on my ranch back home in Helensville.

> The organisers said we were the first performers who had ever volunteered to be on the work crew — it's a Kiwi thing.

We volunteered to stay on after the festival to help pack down the entire site and return the space to its natural state. We ended up on tent crew, helping dismantle a hundred performer tents. The organisers said we were the first performers who had ever volunteered to be on the work crew — it's a Kiwi thing.

The following year we were up on the big stage; we helped MC the show and performed as ourselves. It was a brilliant festival to play at and the women were so supportive.

In 2009 we were invited for one last time to share the magic that was the Michigan Womyn's Music Festival.

Opposite top: The twins with popular country and western dance teachers Marina Hodgini (far left) and Maile Klein on the day stage at the Michigan Womyn's Music Festival in 1992. TONI ARMSTRONG JR.

Opposite bottom: Lynda (left) and Jools with American lesbian icon and singer Alix Dobkin at the same event. ARANI CUTHBERT

Welcome to downtown
LUCKENBACH
EST. 1849
TEXAS
POP. 3
Home of the Ladies Only Chili Bust
Held 1ST WeeKend in October

19

'You Boys Sure Are Funny'

It's always pretty hard to leave the magic of Michigan and re-enter the real world, but the next festival on our itinerary was about as far removed from Michigan — in every way — as you could get. It deserves its own chapter.

Avoca is a small town in Iowa, 150 km west of the state capital, Des Moines. It's in the middle of nowhere but every year thousands of country music fans turn up for the Old Time Country Music Festival. It's a competition festival, meaning the performers compete in different categories over the course of five days, and the judges are hidden in the audience. The main rule is simple: no plug-in instruments allowed; the whole competition is acoustic only.

Jools and I arrived on a Greyhound two days before the start of the 1993 festival. We stepped off the bus and onto the main street of Avoca with a guitar, spoons, a bag each and a tent. A small classic American diner caught our eye and we wandered in with our gear. We were greeted by a middle-aged woman in a classic 1960s pink

Opposite: The twins in Luckenbach, Texas, during one of their tours of the US in the 1990s. MARY MASSARA

diner uniform. She stood behind an oval servery with a pencil behind her ear and a jug of freshly brewed coffee in her hand. 'Take a seat, boys, and I'll be with you in a minute,' she said to us.

We decided not to correct her and sat down where she had pointed. Before we had even looked at the menu she waved her jug of coffee at us and poured two big mugs of the thick dark brew. No milk was offered. Then she plucked her pencil from behind her ear and, in a southern drawl, told us the pancakes were on special. I ordered them straight away, as I thought it was probably not a good idea to mess with this local. Jools asked for eggs and crispy bacon, to which the woman replied, 'Over easy or sunny side up?'

She wandered over to the open kitchen and handed our order to the chef, a big dude in a cap and a striped apron. The food arrived and it was good. Our waitress was chatting to a couple of old guys who looked like farmers, then she headed over and refilled our mugs.

'Where you boys from?' she asked.

'New Zealand,' we replied.

'Wow, you've come a long way.'

She knew all about the festival, and we told her we were performing.

'What's your names?'

'Lynda and Jools,' we answered.

There was a pause while we all looked at one another, then she calmly said, 'My mistake,' and headed off to fetch meals for the two farmers.

As we were paying the bill the waitress pulled out two coffee mugs from under the counter and handed them to us. They had 'Avoca Iowa' written on the side.

'You keep these,' she said, 'to remember your time in Avoca.'

The Pottawattamie County Fairgrounds were overrun with folks setting up small outdoor stages, food tents, and stalls selling everything from musical instruments to folding chairs and clothing. Jools and I set about pitching our tent and found a couple of old logs to sit on and some rocks to make a campfire.

We headed to the registration building and asked if there was anywhere to lock up our gear. 'Just leave it in your tent,' the woman said. 'It'll be safe there.' Wow. So we did. Then we headed back into town and bought ourselves new cowboy shirts and big black cowboy hats at the local farm store for our show.

We ate once again at our diner and headed back to our tent for an early night.

The following morning we unzipped our tent and wondered where the hell we were. We were completely surrounded by *hundreds* of RVs — it was a miracle we hadn't been run over in the night. The two vehicles parked either side of our tent were the biggest we had ever seen, with satellite dishes on the roof and every conceivable item of luxury camping bling on board.

The door of one of them opened and an old bloke stepped out to take in the morning air. He was dressed in OshKosh striped overalls, like the ones American train drivers wear. He tipped his hat at us. Then his wife peered out. She was dressed in a gingham skirt, cowgirl shirt with fringes and a straw hat tied under the chin — the spitting image of one of the Gingham Sisters. Jools and I tried to stifle hysterical laughter. One of the competition categories was Country Comedy and we had ticked that box, so the Gingham Sisters would be performing.

She yelled out to us, 'Morning, boys, and what a fine morning it is. I just thank the good Lord I'm here on account of my heart.' It was quite an opening line. And was everyone here going to think we were twin brothers?

Overleaf: Lynda (left) and Jools as Belle and Belle Gingham in Avoca, Iowa.
ARANI CUTHBERT

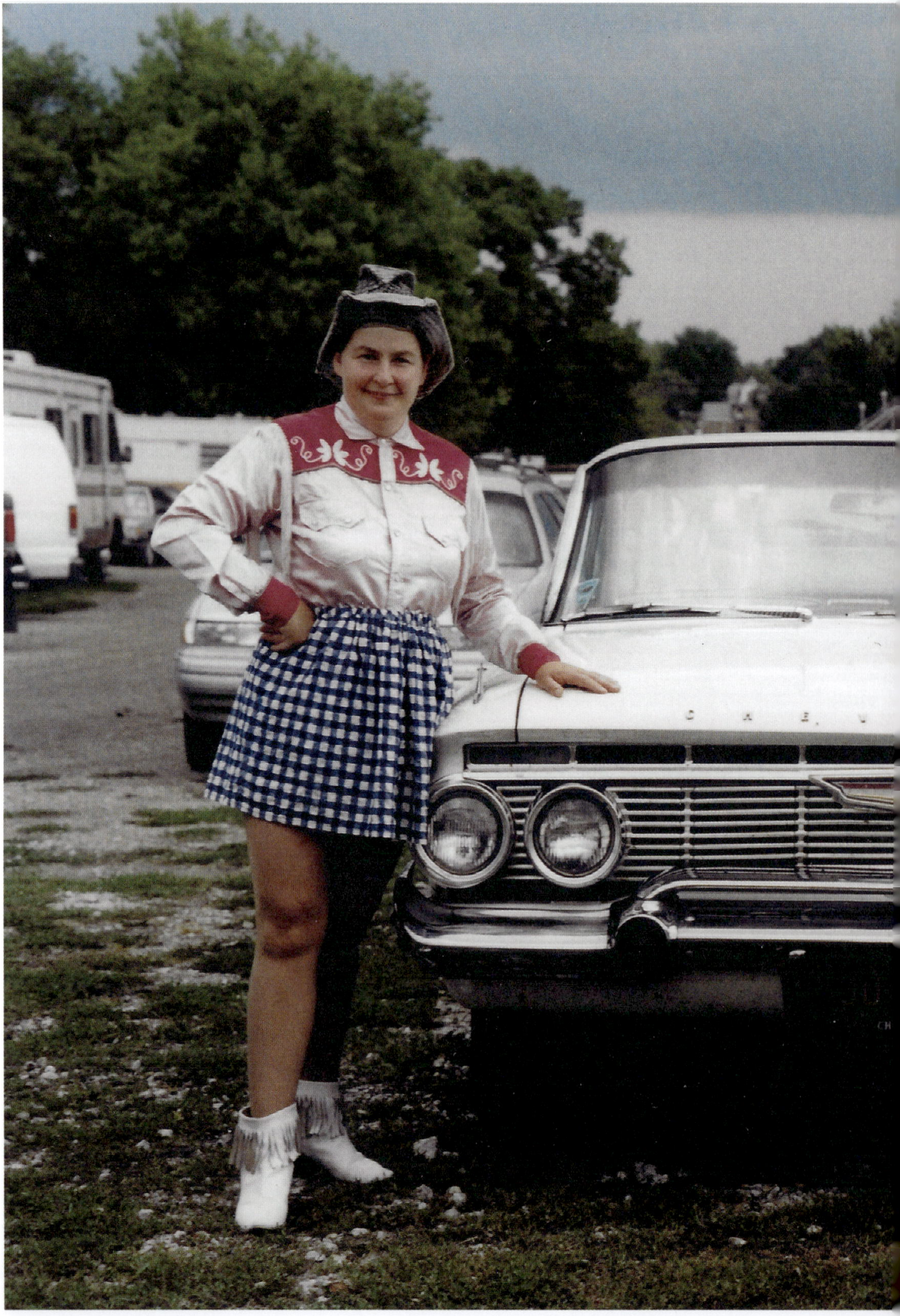

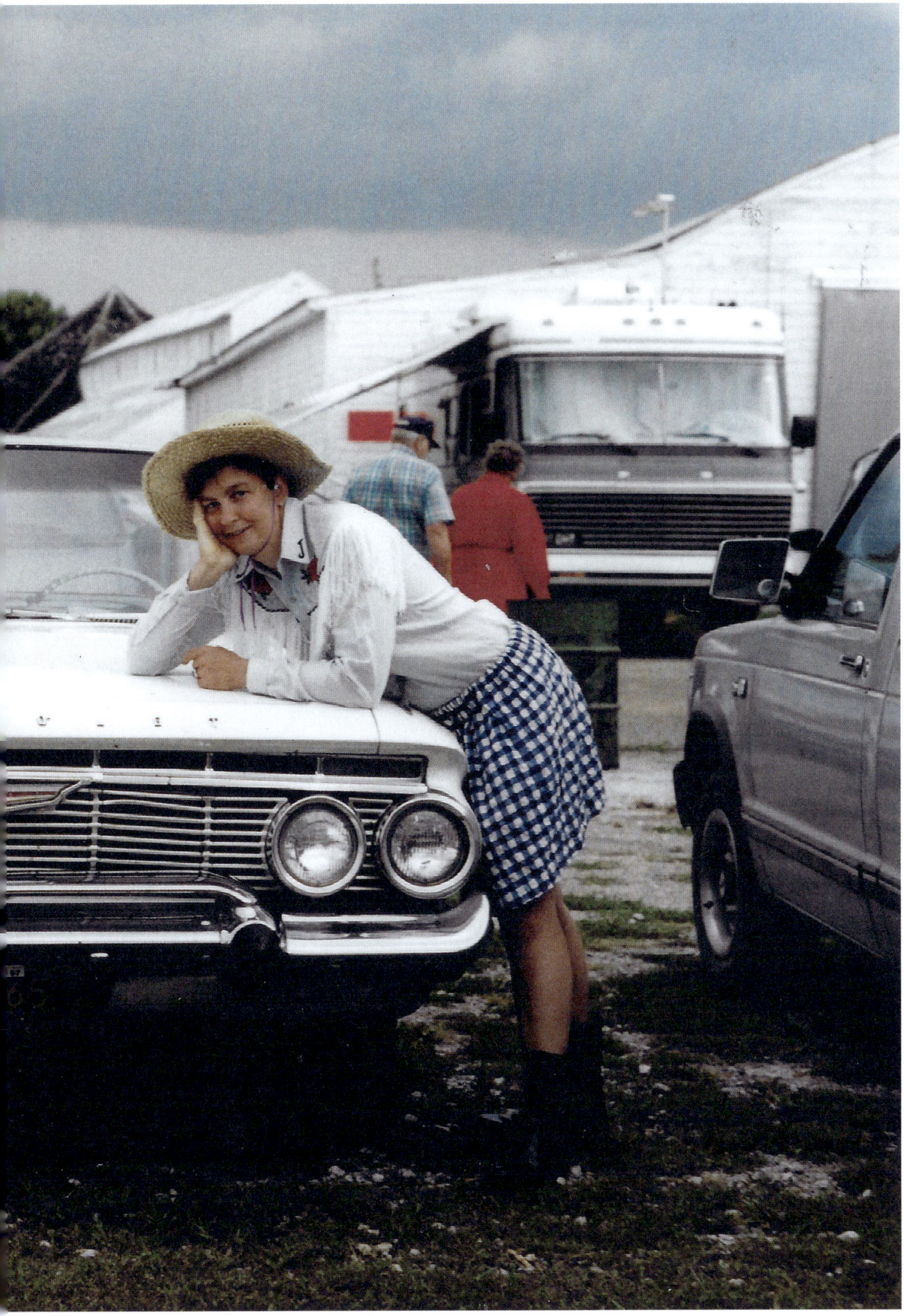

One by one all the folks in their RVs came out to see the morning sun. About 95 per cent of the men were wearing striped overalls, and most of the women were in gingham skirts or dresses in varying shades. We wondered how the Gingham Sisters were going to go down with this crowd . . .

We had a day to kill before the festival started, so we spent the time wandering around the site. We checked out the 'Indian Village', which was full of teepees, with people decked out in full buckskin cooking over fires and making wooden bows and flint arrows. It looked like a scene straight out of the 1800s, except that the whole lot of them were American white folks.

> Most of the women were in gingham skirts or dresses in varying shades. We wondered how the Gingham Sisters were going to go down with this crowd . . .

There were luthiers on site making guitars, banjos and Appalachian dulcimers. Food stalls were pumping out hamburgers, ribs, pizza, fried chicken, slaw, corn on the cob . . . and when you had finished your main course there was pie. Apple, pecan or pumpkin.

Late afternoon we headed back to our tent and got out the guitar for a practice. Within two minutes of starting our first song, people started appearing from their RVs. Many were carrying some kind of instrument and they all joined in. By our third song there would have been over 50 people jamming with us.

And that was what it was like for the next five days. Every night the word would go around that there was a jam happening somewhere, and everybody would flock there. Often there were several jams going on at once in different parts of the site. It was pure joy for a couple of musos from distant New Zealand to hear the talent that was there, performers and audience members alike, who could play the meanest fiddle, the sweetest dulcimer or a virtuoso moment on the spoons or the washboard.

We had entered four competition categories: Country Comedy, Family Harmonies, Jimmie Rodgers Yodelling and Instrumental (harmonica and guitar).

Our first performance was as the Gingham Sisters and we had the audience in stitches. I played the spoons on people's heads, and we performed our pelvic yodel, with me doing my trademark move of pulling out the elastic waistband of my gingham skirt. There were about 15 entries in the Country Comedy section and our main competition, we reckoned, was a woman who did a pretty good rendition of Minnie Pearl, star of the Grand Ole Opry.

As we headed out of the backstage tent, a couple came up and one of them said, 'You boys sure are funny!' So now they thought we were boys dressed up as women . . .

The following day we had no performances so were free to wander around. By now the site was overflowing with more than 20,000 people (and thousands of RVs). We came upon an old guy rigging up 20 miniature horses to a miniature stagecoach. We introduced ourselves and he straight away invited us to go for a ride with him around the festival grounds. It was a great way to see everything, and the old guy was a fount of knowledge about horses and of stories about stagecoaches and the Pony Express.

We visited him every day and became great mates. In fact he and his wife damn near adopted us. He knew straight away we were not boys, just girls who loved horses. They insisted on taking us out to dinner on our last night in Avoca. They picked us up and we headed out of town. There wasn't much out there except farmland and the odd feed and grain store. After about an hour we were quietly wondering if they had decided to kidnap us, but soon enough the old boy pulled into a carpark beside a smokehouse set back off the road.

'We'll order everything — you gals just sit back and relax,' he said. The smells wafting from the chimney were hickory, honey and whisky, which seemed pretty promising. The place was full of country folks in their best clothes all seated around tables covered in red gingham.

We waited a few minutes for a table to come free and then sat down. The old boy headed up to the counter and ordered for us.

Beers arrived first, Budweiser and Busch Light. Then someone set down the biggest platter I have ever seen — stacked with meat. There was every kind of meat a girl could eat — brisket, ribs, pork, chicken and crispy salmon, all smothered in a rich, smoky, sticky sauce, with a side order of Mac & Cheese and Beer & Cheese Hashbrowns. There was not a single green item in sight.

It was the best meal we'd had in a long time, and by the end of it we were smothered in sticky sauce and full of beer. To top off a great night, the old boy picked up the tab.

The clothes we wore that night never recovered from the experience. Every time you popped on that fresh clean shirt you got a whiff of the heady smoky smell, a lasting reminder of one of our many amazing trips overseas.

We also left the Old Time Country Music Festival in Avoca with a clutch of prizes: we won the Country Comedy award and came second in the Jimmie Rodgers Yodelling category, as well as second in Family Harmonies.

20

Camp Mother, Camp Leader and the Kens

We'd been overseas for a while and it was nice to get back home. We were finally making good money, and our last overseas stint had the added bonus of making us American dollars and English pounds.

In 1994, at the ripe old age of 36, we thought we should start planning for our old age, and we decided to buy a house together. We drove around Ponsonby looking for For Sale signs, and went to a few open homes, but everything seemed to be beyond our budget. So we shifted our focus to Grey Lynn, where most houses we saw needed a lot of work.

On one of our searches we turned down Sherwood Avenue and there, halfway down the street in a dip in the road, we spotted a little house for sale. It was neither a villa nor a bungalow: it had a closed-in porch at the front and a beautiful big orange tree to the left as you walked to the front door. Beside that was a farm gate that led to a big overgrown garden out the back.

We rang the number on the For Sale sign and the real estate agent said she would meet us there in half an hour.

Scenes from an early photoshoot for Camp Mother (in the pink) and Camp Leader.
MEL CHURCH

She turned the key to the front door and it was like stepping into a nightmare museum. The first bedroom on the left had purple shagpile carpet, orange wallpaper and one of those velvet paintings of a Tahitian gal on the wall. The bedroom opposite had an archway framing the bed, and full-on floral wallpaper. Down the hallway was a small lounge with the remains of a fireplace that had at some point housed a coal range, and off that was a tiny kitchen. The back wall of the lounge had an old sash window and a back door to the outside porch, with concrete tubs and the toilet.

A set of rickety old steps led down to the massive back yard and the foundations of another bedroom, work on which had obviously come to an abrupt halt a few months earlier — the timber had started warping.

We loved it, and told the agent we'd get back to her.

Then we rang Arani and told her we'd found a house we liked, and she should come and have a look at it. I remember her pulling up, getting out of the car and bursting into tears. She said we deserved something better, but Jools and I honestly thought it was awesome, and God knows we gals love a project.

We paid $149,000 for it and moved in two weeks later.

Camp Mother and Camp Leader came into our lives in 1995. We created them for a summer show at Auckland's Watershed Theatre, a venue that occupied an old warehouse on the waterfront. It was dismantled in 1996 to make way for the Viaduct Basin.

It had been a terrible summer and had rained a lot, so we promised the audience sunshine and warmth at Happy Valley Camping Ground with Camp Mother and Camp Leader, two quintessential Kiwi women. Camp Mother could whip up a batch of

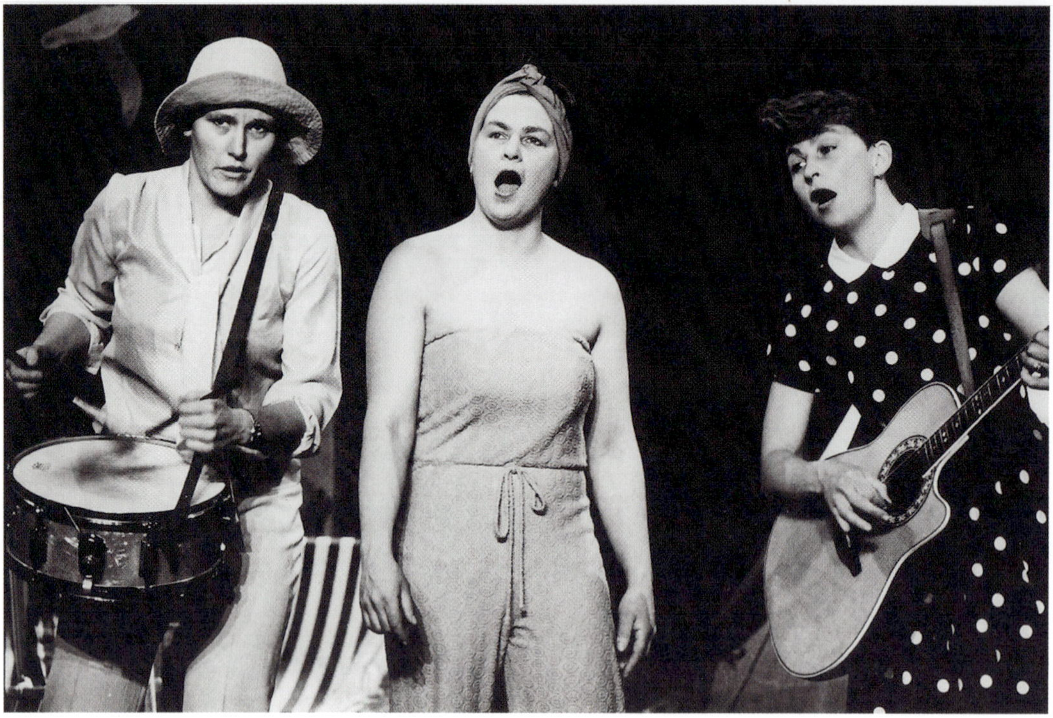

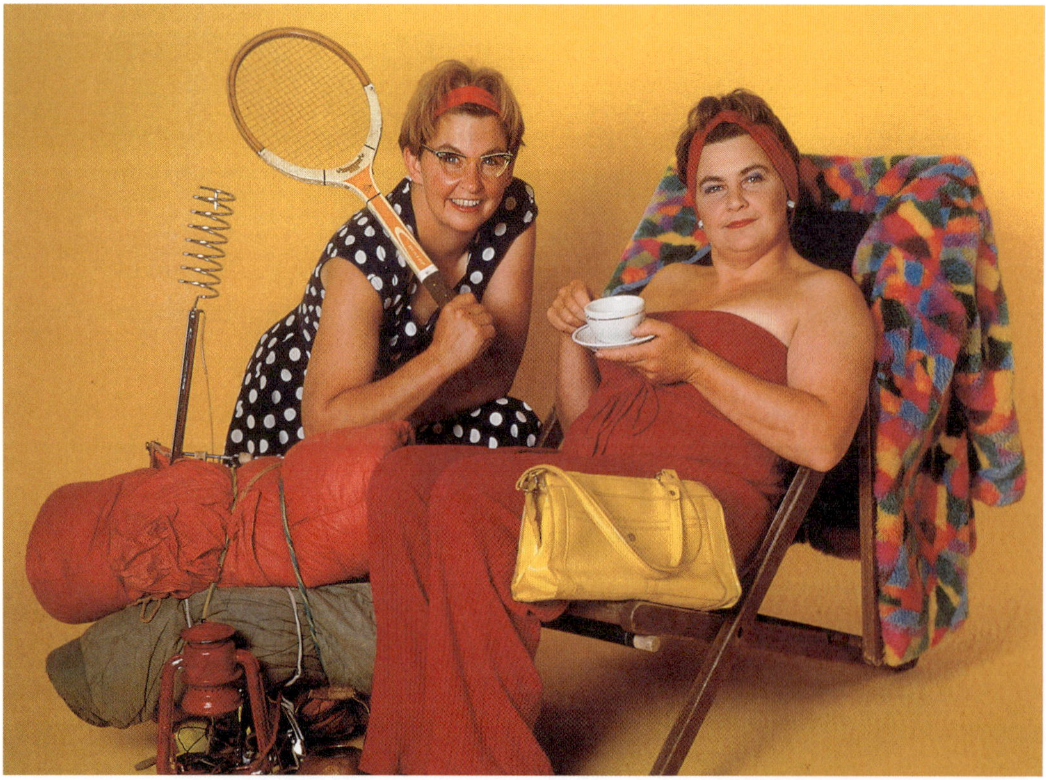

scones, change a truck tyre, then grace the red carpet in her slinky pink jumpsuit anywhere in the world.

Her trusty sidekick, Camp Leader, was a happy nerd, totally unpredictable but loyal to a fault and ready to try her hand at anything. (Well, anything that Camp Mother told her to do.)

The show had a picnic theme and our casting director friend Annabel Lomas had an old pink towelling jumpsuit in the wardrobe that she thought would be perfect for Lynda's character. We also invited our musician friend Nettie Bird to join us on stage, and she played stand-up drums and offered some brilliant harmonies.

The first shows included our little blue Fiat Bambina, which I drove on stage with Nettie in the passenger seat and Camp Mother standing in the back, her head sticking up through the sunroof.

Opening night got off to a terrible start. Camp Mother was waving to the audience while Camp Leader parked the car. As Camp Leader got out she slammed the door shut, managing to trap Camp Mother's fingers in the top of the door.

I could see the blood draining out of Lynda's face and quickly opened the door again. Lynda looked down to see if her fingers were all still there . . . If it had been a heavier car she might well have lost them, but the Bambina was very light and thankfully the old door didn't close very well.

Camp Mother, ever staunch, leapt out of the car and carried on with the show as if nothing had happened.

The second night was full of terrible mishaps of a quite different sort. I had managed to get food poisoning and began to feel violently

Opposite top: Nettie Bird, Lynda and Jools on stage in the first-ever performance of their show *Camping Out* at Auckland's Watershed Theatre, 1992. KYLIE TONAR

Opposite bottom: Camp Mother reclines on a chair while Camp Leader prepares for some tennis. SALLY TAGG

ill as we drove on stage. I let Lynda know I was about to be sick, and luckily we'd stationed a bucket off to the side of the stage just in case. Lynda then proceeded to incorporate my sickness into the show. Everyone thought it was hilarious that a tummy bug was going around our campground.

Nettie played along with the spontaneous change of script, wandering over to me at the side of the stage, bent over my bucket, and calling out to Camp Mother that it was all peas and carrots coming up. It got a huge laugh.

After I puked I ran back on stage to continue with the show. Lynda brought me a chair so I could sit down to play the guitar.

Somehow we made it to the end, and after the show I collapsed backstage and had to lie down in the dressing room for an hour.

The next day a newspaper reviewer said it was a genius idea to script a tummy bug into the show. However, the third night did *not* feature Camp Leader being sick, so anybody who'd read the review was probably confused and possibly even disappointed.

Camp Mother and Camp Leader had not got off to an auspicious start, but we knew they were special characters and we persevered. They have not looked back.

We loved performing live. We loved that people would cram into a local hall or theatre to be part of our audience for one night of entertainment — it was challenging and exciting. No two shows were the same. Every performance was spontaneous and unique — and sometimes bloody scary. But it was such a buzz to work that crowd.

In 1995 when Arani suggested we make a TV series that was *not* a live performance special, we weren't sure it would work for us. How would we get on without any instant audience feedback?

The filming and post-production business can take months, meaning we'd have to film an entire series before we got to read the crowd reaction.

Somehow Arani convinced us to give it a go. She reckoned a show in which we took our characters to real events around New Zealand would work, and she got Caterina De Nave to come on board as executive producer. After the enormous success of our TV special on TVNZ nine years earlier, we found it surprising and disappointing that they had not offered us any other work. We felt that TVNZ had had their chance to work with us, so Arani and Caterina pitched the idea to TV3, the Canadian-owned network, as it was fresh and less risk-averse. Bettina Hollings, TV3's head of programming, supported the idea. Fortuitously, Ruth Harley, our former champion at TVNZ, was now the head of the government agency NZ On Air, which funds homegrown shows. Hey presto, we had our very own TV show: *The Topp Twins: Do Not Adjust Your Twin-set*. It was an alignment of top women that made the show happen, and we will always be immensely grateful to all of them.

The first series of six half-hour episodes was pretty much entirely impromptu, with our characters turning up to public events and getting involved in whatever was going on. This was before the world had heard about Borat! It was spontaneous, riotous and a whole lot of fun to film at many iconic New Zealand events — the Golden Shears in Masterton, the New Zealand Polo Open, an ironman triathlon in Mt Maunganui, the waka regatta at Tūrangawaewae Marae and the Speedway at Western Springs, plus many more. For that first series, we had to learn many new tricks, including how to work a camera — from close-ups and single shots to our favourite, the dirty two-shot — and how to be very patient on set, because everything gets done a number of times. We came to enjoy the collaborative process and were blessed with a wonderful crew.

The Kens (left), Camp Mother and Camp Leader discover their Scottish roots in the Highland Games episode. SALLY TAGG

The show ran for three seasons, 1996–2000, and evolved from being largely impromptu to more scripted, giving us the opportunity to develop our characters more.

We created Ken and Ken especially for the Golden Shears episode. We thought they would be good for hanging out with the shearers, as it's a predominantly male competition.

Lynda felt her new character was a bit of a ladies' man and her Ken ended up being absolutely besotted with Camp Mother, but since Lynda played both characters, Ken would never see his romantic dreams come to fruition.

> Lynda felt her new character was a bit of a ladies' man and her Ken ended up being absolutely besotted with Camp Mother.

At one of our writing meetings with Arani and some of the TV crew I introduced a character I'd been quietly working on, Ken Smythe. At that time I had a beautiful Border collie with a big bushy tail and he allowed me to take snippets of his hair, in both black and white. I had painstakingly laid the dog hairs onto a piece of double-sided tape cut to the shape of a moustache. The mixed colours made for a salt-and-pepper look that matched my hair colour brilliantly.

Just before I entered the meeting I quietly peeled off the backing on the tape and pressed my instant facial hair into place. I was wearing a white shirt and a blue sports coat with a yellow tie and grey trousers.

Everybody completely lost the plot. Ken was gratified at the glorious reaction he garnered from our creative team.

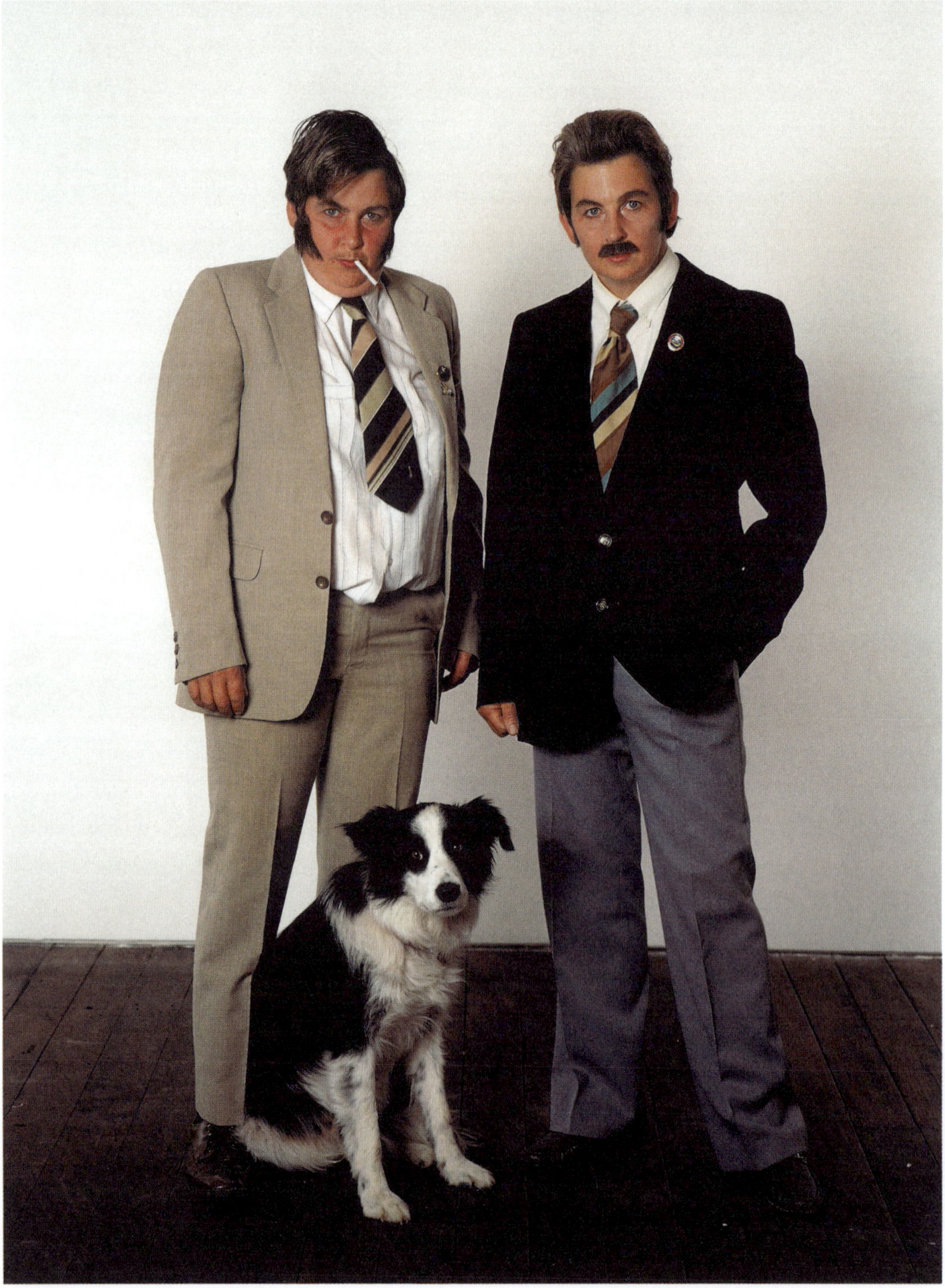

Characters don't really come alive until you've got the costumes and hairstyle and everything in place, so that afternoon Lynda was inspired to find an outfit for her Ken. She had decided she was a light-coloured type of bloke so we set out to find a suit of that colour. We hadn't been looking for long when there, on the rack in a Grey Lynn second-hand store, standing out among the black, blue and brown smoky-smelling old suits, hung an insipid and altogether stunning beige suit.

'Oh, please let it fit,' Lynda said as she wandered over to the changing cubicle. When she emerged from behind the curtain a few minutes later she looked perfect. She reached into the inside jacket pocket and pulled out an old dollar note. 'It's a dead man's jacket,' she said, and she kept that dollar in a little plastic bag in her costume room at home. It's still there.

It was always fun searching for costumes. Nearly all of them came from second-hand stores, and the staff often got excited trying to help us find what we needed. They would call to let us know if they had something they thought might be useful.

Lynda decided her Ken would have big bushy sideburns, so our facial hair was quite different. His hair would be parted on the side and combed over flat.

The Kens were a big hit with the boys at the shearing event, who even invited them to the pub after filming — the ultimate sign of acceptance in rural New Zealand.

They really are a tribute to Kiwi blokes: men who'd give you the shirt off their backs (although Ken never gave his shirt away for

Opposite: Ken and Ken's first publicity shoot, late 1990s. SALLY TAGG

Following spread: A selection of characters the twins have created over the years. Clockwise from top left: The Private Eyes; Vince and Zippy; Brenda and Raelene; General Motors and Private Parts; Hertie and Gertie; the Bowling Ladies. SALLY TAGG

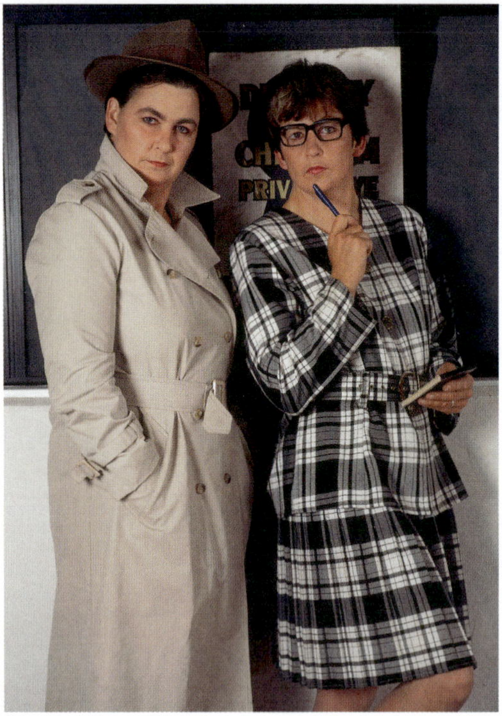
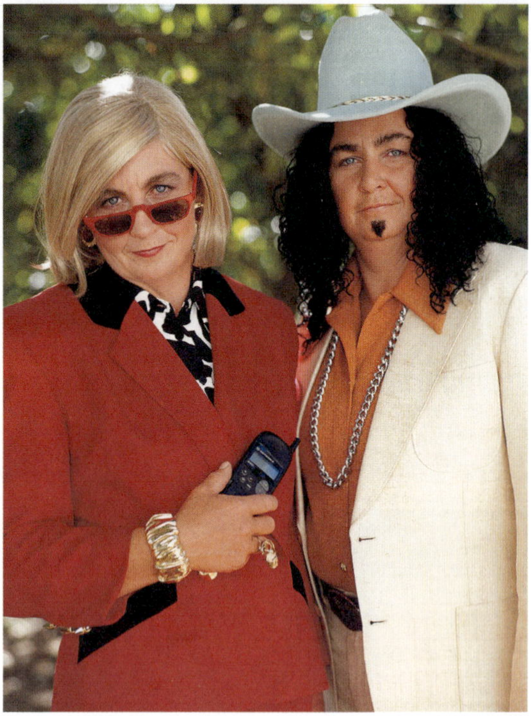
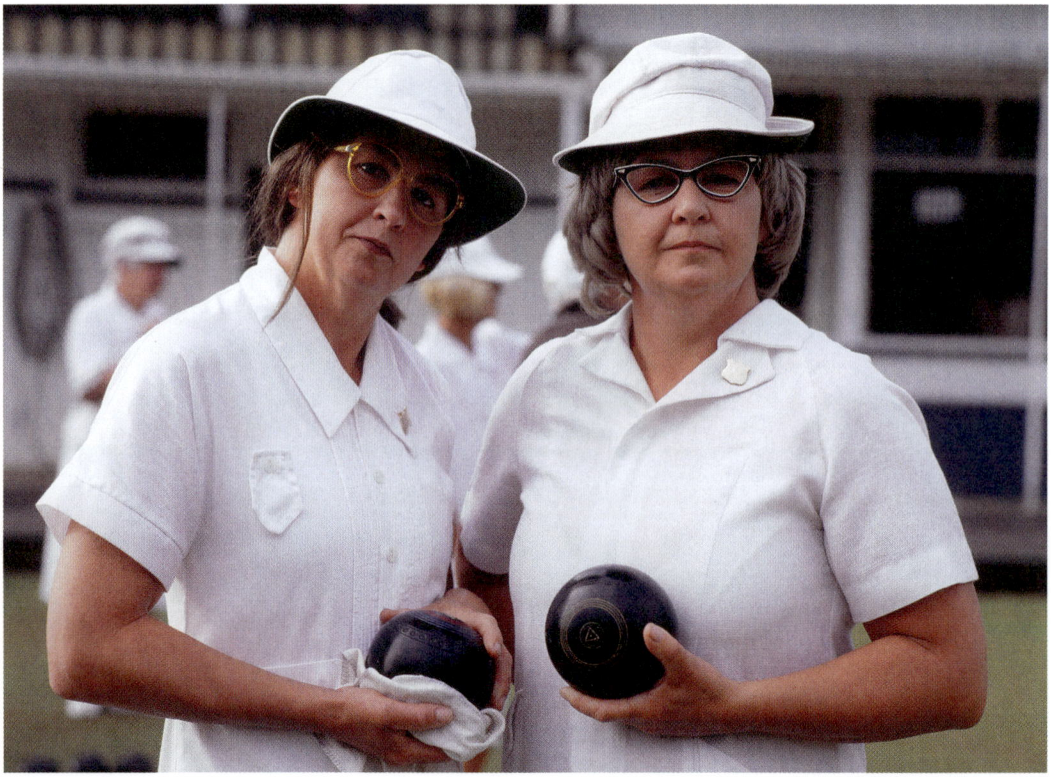

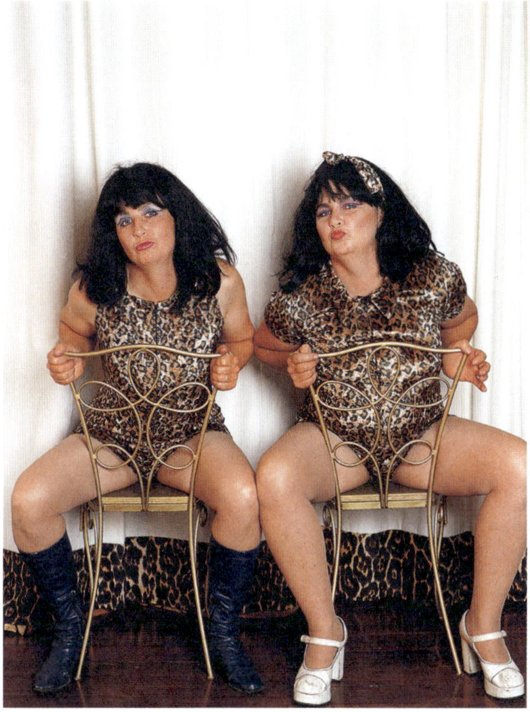

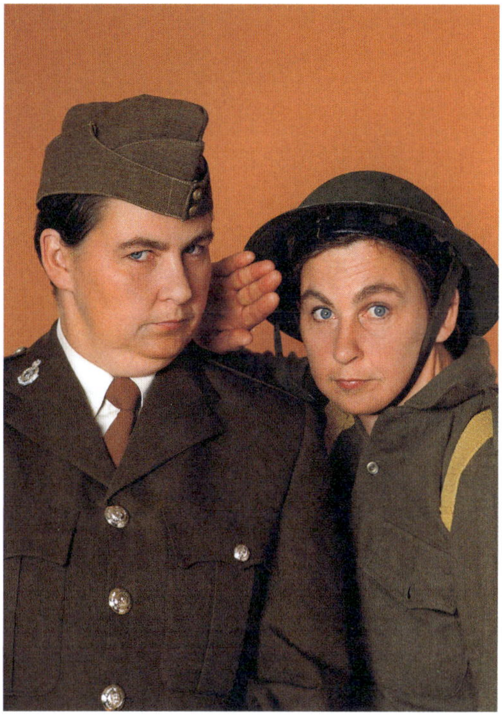

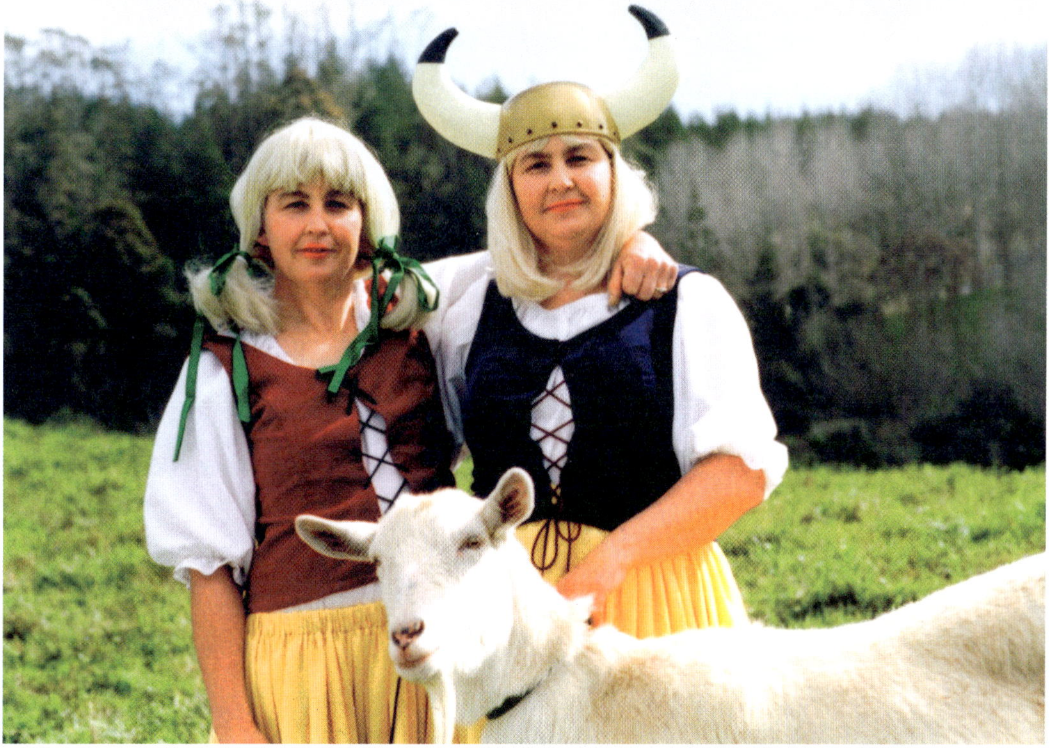

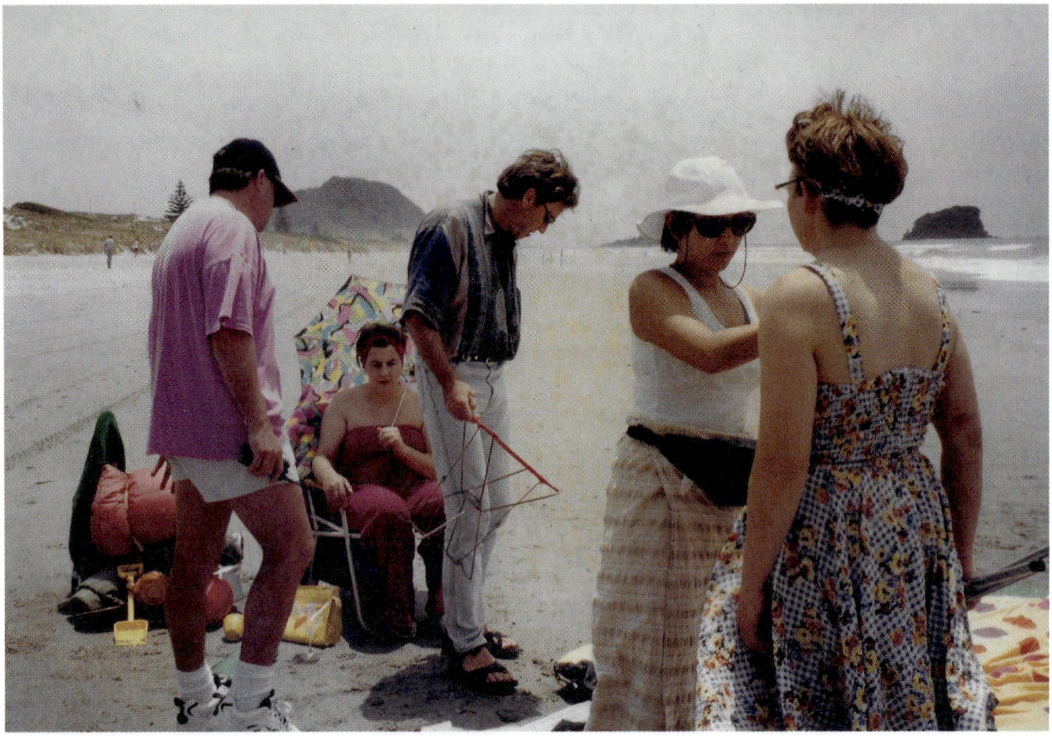

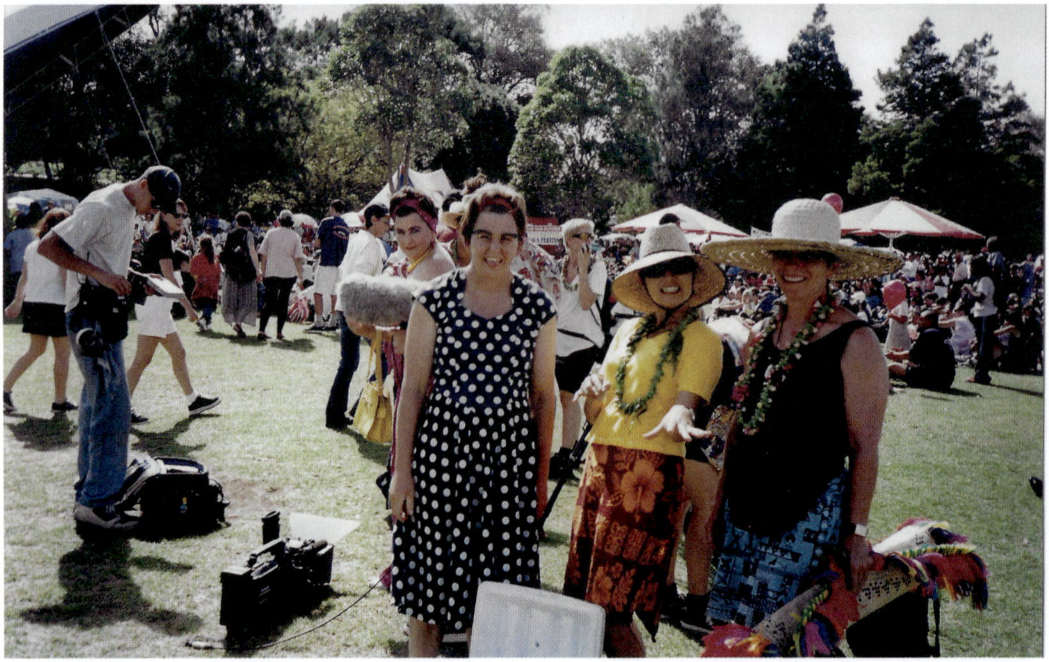

fear of exposing his breasts). The Kens are warm characters and easy to play. We've been sent many photos by fans dressed up as Ken and Ken.

One of the funniest gigs the Kens did was for retail chain Hunting & Fishing New Zealand, which had organised a night out for 400 blokes in Invercargill just before the opening of duck-shooting season. The Kens were happy to oblige. It helped that Lynda is an avid fishing and duck-hunting type of gal who counts the number of sleeps till opening day.

Her duck breast marinated in stewed tamarillos is legendary, as is her duck-breast paté with walnuts, fried mushrooms and port.

―――

Sometimes the events our characters attended only ran for one day so we had a pretty nightmarish filming schedule, with a lot of very quick costume changes. Our crew were amazing and worked like demons.

I remember at the Golden Shears Lynda had been doing a scene as Camp Mother cooking scones in the hall kitchen to feed the shearers. Once that was finished, she shot off to change into Ken, to return and be filmed trying to get a cuppa and a scone from . . . Camp Mother.

After about 40 minutes Ken still hadn't arrived back. Eventually we discovered that the dude collecting the tickets at the door wouldn't let him in without one. Ken was trying to convince him

Opposite from top: Behind the scenes of *The Topp Twins: Do Not Adjust Your Twin-set.* Filming on the beach at Mount Maunganui during season 1 with Nigel Carpenter, Wayne Vinten and Denise Kum (ARANI CUTHBERT); and at Western Springs in Auckland during season 2 with Mark Potter, Denise Kum and Mary Massara (PETER JANES).

that he was actually the woman in pink who had just rushed out, and was coming back to film as a different character.

'Pull the other one,' the dude said, crossing his arms.

A crew member finally vouched for Ken and he made it through.

Getting our characters into people's lounges every week helped make them Kiwi icons, and in 1997 we won Best Performance in an Entertainment Programme in the *TV Guide* Television Awards. But we didn't do it alone.

Lynda and I had never written a script in our lives. Jan Prettejohns worked with us as a script editor for season 1, with friends Di McMillan and Marie Adams helping us with extra ideas. As the series became more scripted, our dear friend Paul Horan joined us for the third season. He's one of the funniest men around and a beautiful writer — he helped give Camp Mother her back-story by describing her as the only woman who had reversed a caravan through the Waikino Gorge. Paul co-founded the NZ International Comedy Festival and the Classic Comedy Club, and has gone on to have a successful TV career in Australia.

Our dear friend Emma Lange also worked on the series with us as Lynda's body double. This would be a challenging role for anyone, but Emma was a natural comedian and did a fantastic job. In one episode Emma had played Camp Mother and Ken in three scenes and one night all the crew sat around watching the rough footage to see if anyone could tell the difference. Nobody could. We had met Emma in Auckland, where she worked on some of the early comedy shows on TV. She was also in *Ultra Super Vixen Women with Really Enormous Tits* with Jaq Tweedie and Michèle A'Court at Downstage in Wellington and the Watershed in Auckland in 1994. She was brilliant and funny to be around; it was a pleasure to have people like Emma who wanted to work with us.

21

The Edinburgh Fringe Festival

We were lucky enough to be invited to perform at the Edinburgh Fringe Festival for the second time in 1997. This was an exciting opportunity in part because Mum's family came from Motherwell, just down the road from Glasgow, and we wanted to trace our ancestors and — most importantly — our family tartan. This was, of course, before the internet made such research so much easier.

Jean Emily NcNeish Dalziel, our mum, was a dab hand at the sword dance and the Highland fling. Whenever she heard the bagpipes, she'd launch into some fabulous dance. Our song 'Jean Emily' was a tribute to Mum — her Scottish roots and her bright red hair.

> My mother is Scotland born but she doesn't live there no more.
> I'll travel the world until I find that old highland town . . .

We flew into Heathrow and stayed with a Kiwi mate, Margie Palmer, who lived in Islington. She flatted with Pip, Kim and Darryl, three of the most gorgeous Poms you could meet, who treated us like long-lost friends.

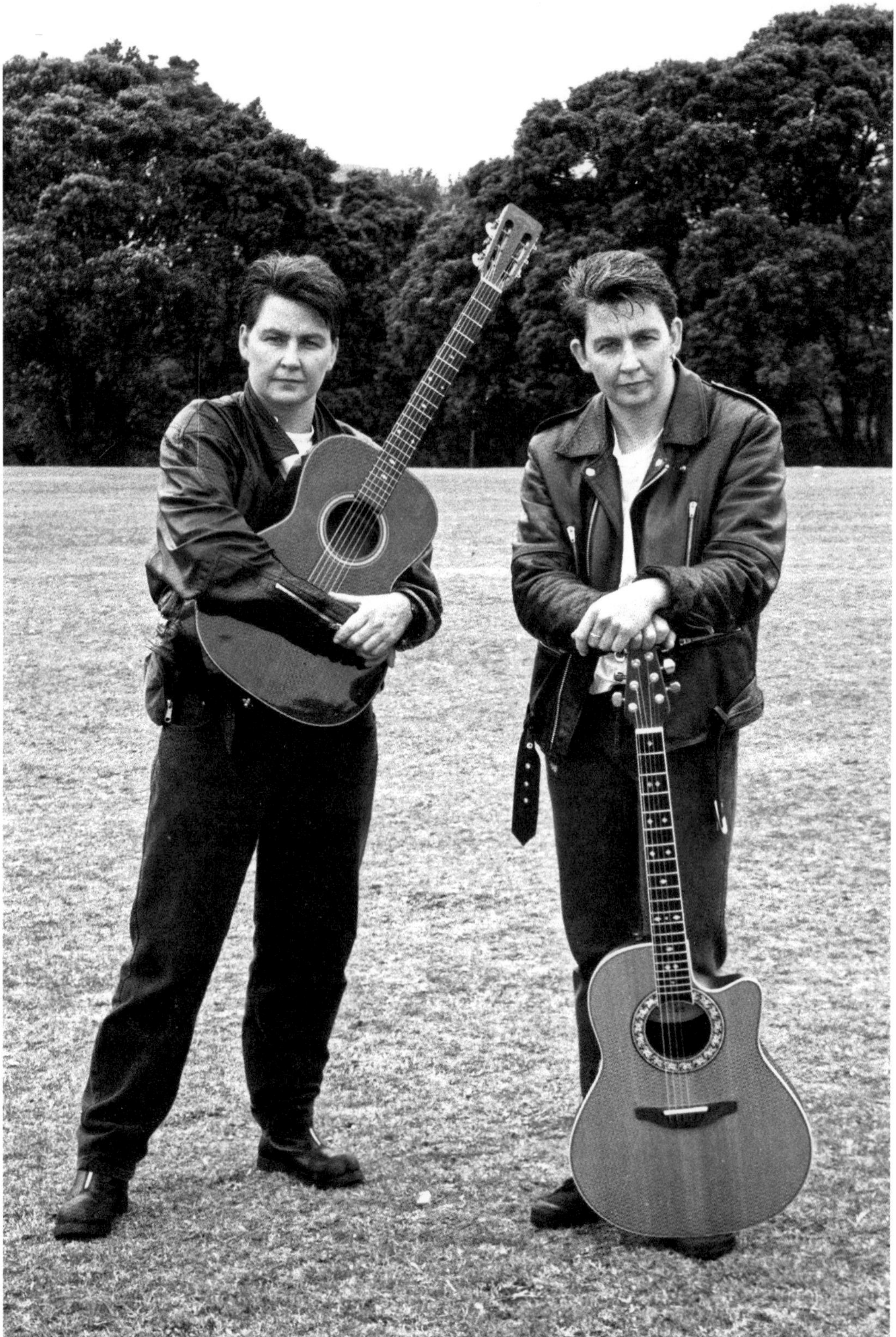

From London we travelled up to Scotland by train, which is a beautiful way to see England. The tracks run alongside canals, where you see canal boats waiting for the locks to fill behind welcoming old pubs where you can get a pint when the train pulls into the station. All along the way are old cottages — some charming, some not so much — with washing out on the line.

As you cross the border into Scotland the English landscape gives way to old stone farm buildings and Highland cattle.

We arrived in Edinburgh late at night, stepping off the train onto a cobblestone street. We looked up to see Edinburgh Castle all lit up on the hill and it took our breath away. It was like time had stood still and history lived on in the present day. There was a lone piper in a kilt blowing a haunting tune on the streets throughout the festival — it was all quite a blast for a couple of country girls from New Zealand.

As I write this, I'm in the oncology waiting room at Auckland Hospital waiting to have two injections, one in each buttock. The needle is 5 centimetres long and it takes three minutes for each of them to be administered. Any faster and the process will tear my muscles.

It's a form of hormone treatment against my cancer.

I will need to do this every month for the rest of my life — or until it stops being effective at reducing my tumours. It's certainly not something I look forward to, but it might keep me going long enough to finish this book.

That was just a reality check for you out there. Now it's back to Scotland.

Opposite: Lynda (left) and Jools on a promo shoot in the Auckland Domain before leaving for the UK, mid-1990s. MEL CHURCH

We were performing our *Camping Out* show, featuring Camp Mother and Camp Leader, at the Assembly Rooms, which is one of the top Fringe Festival venues. We grew to love performing in Edinburgh — the Scots usually got our Kiwi humour, even though we were a long way from home.

Some things got lost in translation, though. One night we sang 'Calf Club Day' and we were trying to explain it to our crowd. They didn't really get it, so I said, in an attempt at a Scottish lilt, 'You have a wee calf . . .' Suddenly an old Scottish guy yelled, 'Oh, you mean a holiday.' We were a bit baffled until we realised he thought I'd said, 'You have a week off . . .' Eventually we managed to convey the crux of the story, and laughter was the order of the day.

Just outside the theatre was a super-quaint short cobblestone street, and in true Scottish form they had closed the road, put a set of glass sliding doors from building to building at either end and turned it into a pub for the festival duration. This is where we were introduced to a beer called Hoegaarden, which was *the* drink at the time. Someone said it was made from coriander so we decided it was healthy.

Those Scots sure know how to throw a party.

We went to our first cèilidh, which is a big old dance party with rugged Scotsmen in kilts and white shirts with long hair and beards playing traditional Scottish musical instruments. It was fabulous.

In Scotland our mum's last name, Dalziel, is pronounced Dee-el — the z and the first l are silent (and we thought English was tricky) . . . Anyway, Mum is a mighty fine cook and makes the best biscuits in the world, which might be because the best bakery in Edinburgh was called Dalziel Bakers. Their advertising catchline

Opposite from top: Jools (left) and Lynda in the mid-1990s at a cemetery in Motherwell, near Glasgow, searching for their ancestors; The twins in the nearby town of Airdrie. ARANI CUTHBERT

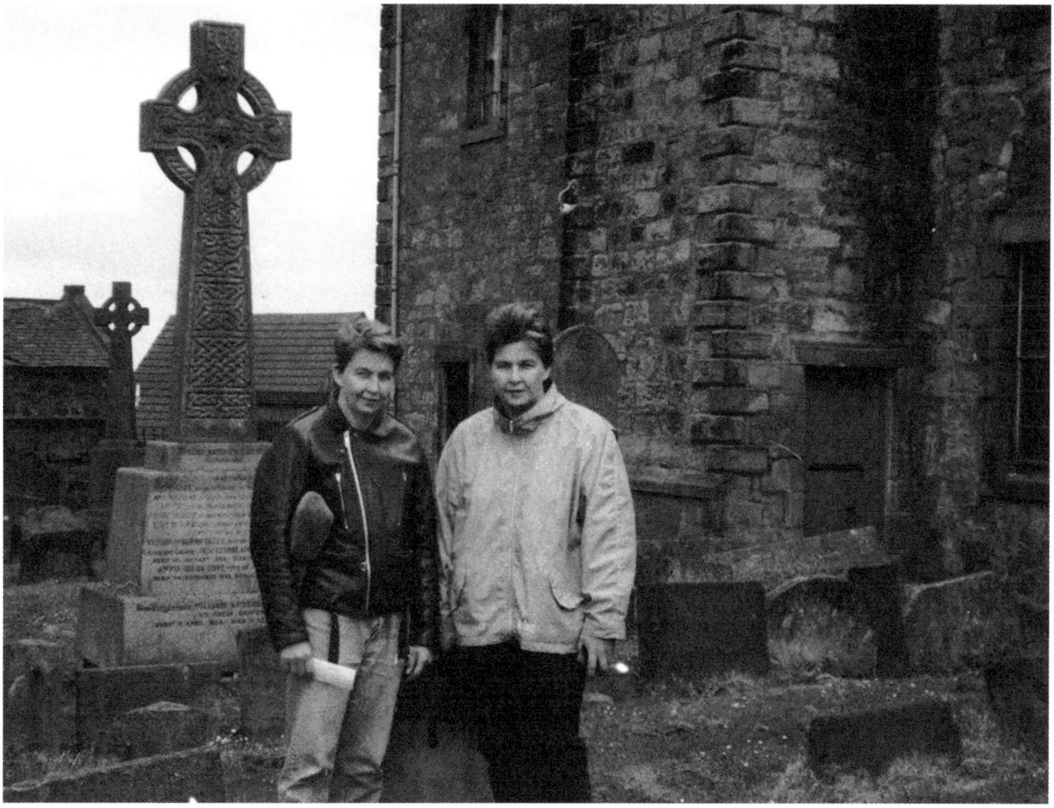

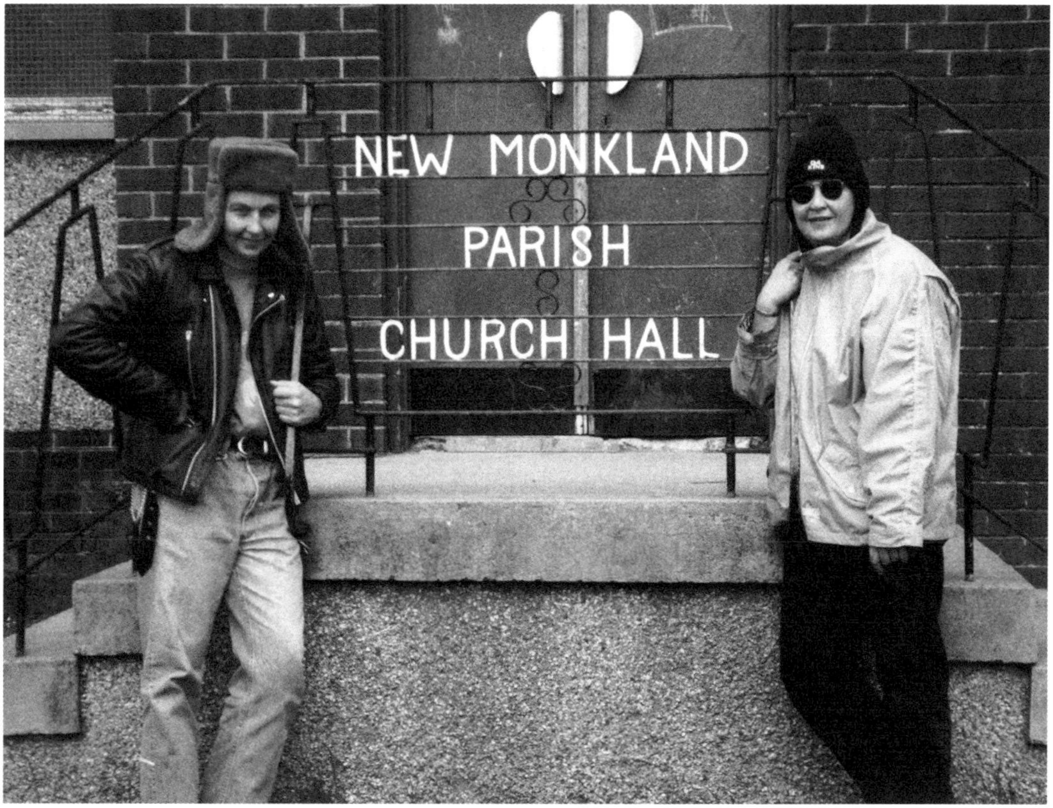
NEW MONKLAND
PARISH
CHURCH HALL

was 'There's nothing like a good roll', so we knew we were related because of their brilliant sense of humour.

Another fabulous food place was the local fish-and-chip shop. They pre-cooked the chips and kept them in a big stainless-steel drum. When you ordered a carton of chips they just heated them up again in the fat and they were all soft and gooey and tasted brilliant. We ordered some every night after our show.

They also made deep-fried pizza, and were said to have been the first to batter and fry a Mars bar. Needless to say, the heart attack rate in Scotland is high.

Most of our time in Edinburgh was about partying, performing, and catching great comedy acts in between our own shows. The Glasgow *Herald* described us as 'New Zealand's finest artistic export since lamb cutlets'. We were happy with that.

Then one morning we woke to the terrible news that Princess Diana had been killed in a car accident. It was 31 August 1997.

The whole place was in shock. It was hard to go on stage and be funny after hearing this, but we did our best. People had paid for tickets, and, as they say in the business, the show must go on.

Then it was time to say goodbye to Scotland, and as we got ready to board the train back to London, two minutes of silence were observed for Diana's passing. At midday everything stood still at the train station, just like everything froze when the little boy in the *Skippy* TV programme threw the boomerang.

Hundreds of people stood motionless and silent — it was a moment we will never forget.

We were exhausted after our busy schedule so the clackity-clack of the train soon lulled us into slumber. Suddenly the train came to a screeching halt. Everyone looked around, startled, then a voice came over the intercom telling us the line was damaged up ahead and we had to vacate the train immediately.

We had bags and guitars and a giant screen in a carry case so we were a bit loaded up, to say the least. The train had stopped just short of the motorway so we had to carry everything up a grassy slope and down to the road. We waited there for buses that took everyone to the next train station, where we transferred back and chugged off again, finally reaching London well after dark.

It was the biggest outpouring of grief and love we had ever seen, and it was remarkable to be there.

We couldn't believe the number of flowers laid by mourners outside Buckingham Palace and in many of the other parks around London as a tribute to Princess Di. In some places they were knee-deep on the pavement and stretched for miles. It was the biggest outpouring of grief and love we had ever seen, and it was remarkable to be there to experience that sad moment in history.

Back in London again, Arani had organised a three-week pre-Christmas theatre run at the Drill Hall Arts Centre in Bloomsbury, just off Tottenham Court Road. It was so cool to hang out with the Islington gang again; there was always a lot going on at the house. Lynda got really excited about cooking for some reason. Every night she would make an early dinner for everyone, then we would catch a tube to the theatre.

We took the same route every time and there was a guy begging on the street who had a real sweet dog that reminded us of our pups back home. He had a routine, just like us, and was always in the same place every night, so we made sure we always gave him some money and some food for his dog. We got to be mates and on our last night at the Drill we said goodbye to him and his pooch and flicked him £100.

There was a great little Italian restaurant just around the corner from the theatre and they would keep the kitchen open for us after the show. A little old mama ran the tables and took the orders — we loved them and the amazing food they cooked up, and they were quite taken by their new Kiwi customers, who came to eat every night for three weeks.

There were a lot of Kiwis living in London and I think just about all of them came to see our show. They'd bring their English mates, who would wind up being Topp Twins fans. One night we were thrilled to spot Sir Ian McKellen laughing in the audience, and he came to see us after the show. On another occasion, the whole London-based staff of Air New Zealand booked the theatre for their Christmas function. They were a great audience — I think they were a bit homesick, so Camp Mother and Camp Leader and the Kens gave them a dose of medicine.

To be honest I think we were a bit homesick ourselves by then. It was in our Islington flat that I wrote 'Milestones', about travelling, about always being on the road, but also about the beautiful and generous friends who made us feel at home when London called us.

22

Mary and Donna

So you've got 800 women on a luxury cruise run by Olivia Travel, an American company that organises cruises and adventure holidays for lesbians and LGBTQ+ women.

Well, somebody has to entertain those gals, don't they? That was us, and it was seven days of a lot of fun.

The passengers were a mix of couples and singles. Some worked in high-powered jobs and hadn't yet come out, and here they could holiday without worrying about being outed. Others were adventurous types who wanted to travel and see the world in a safe environment with other women. Whoever they were, they flocked to these 'Lesbian Love Boats' in the late 1980s and '90s.

We played three cruises, partying in the Caribbean, cruising from Alaska to Vancouver, and dancing on the deck to disco in New York bound for Montréal.

This is where I met my partner of 17 years, Mary Lou Massara, in 1997. Although we are now separated, she is still my soulmate. Born in Nebraska, Mary is a New Zealander now. This is her home and she is part of our family.

We met at the formal introduction for all the performers on the cruise. After the meeting we had a drink and mingled in the lobby

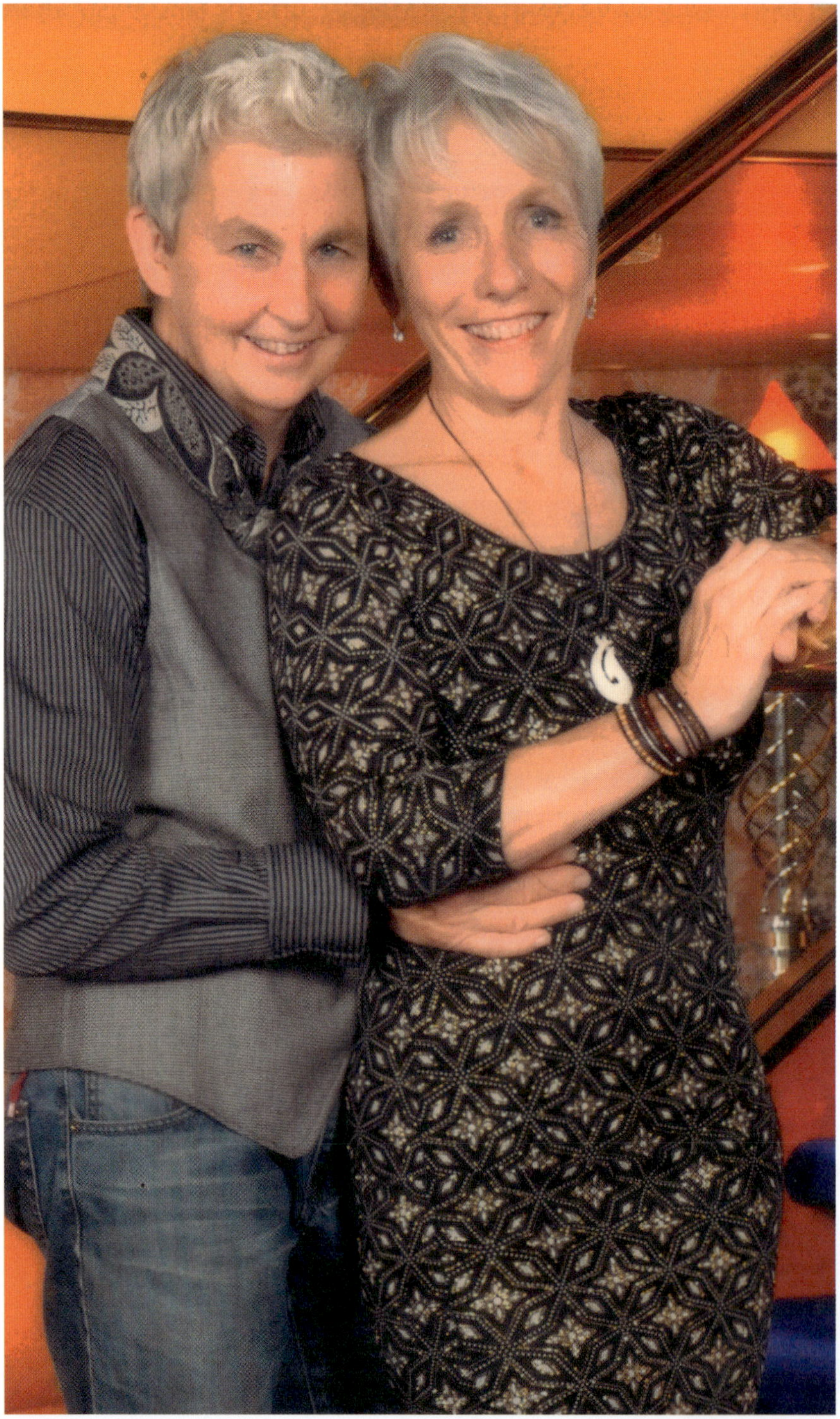

of the hotel we were staying in before boarding the ship. Mary came up to me and gave me her phone number and cabin number.

Wow, I thought to myself, these American girls aren't backward in coming forward! I told Lynda I thought Mary was coming on to me and Lynda pissed herself laughing. She said Mary had given her numbers to *everyone* — it turned out I had missed the part of the briefing mentioning that she was the artist liaison officer for the cruise.

Mary had caught my attention, and if you're going to fall in love it might as well be on the Lesbian Love Boat.

Whatever. Anyway, Mary had caught my attention, and if you're going to fall in love it might as well be on the Lesbian Love Boat.

Especially if you're a lesbian.

I asked her to dance at the midnight parties, bought her cool beers in the hot sun by the giant swimming pool on the top deck, and she dined with all us artists in the spectacular 400-seat restaurant most nights.

We had a fun time getting to know each other and it was clear she liked my company. I definitely enjoyed hers.

By the time we hit Montréal I had made use of the information she had handed me at the beginning of the cruise and knocked on her cabin door. When I left again in the morning I was still in my night clothes and felt a bit conspicuous walking through the upper deck past everyone else in their summer gear or swimwear.

Opposite: Jools and Mary on another cruise in the early 2000s.
TOPP COLLECTION

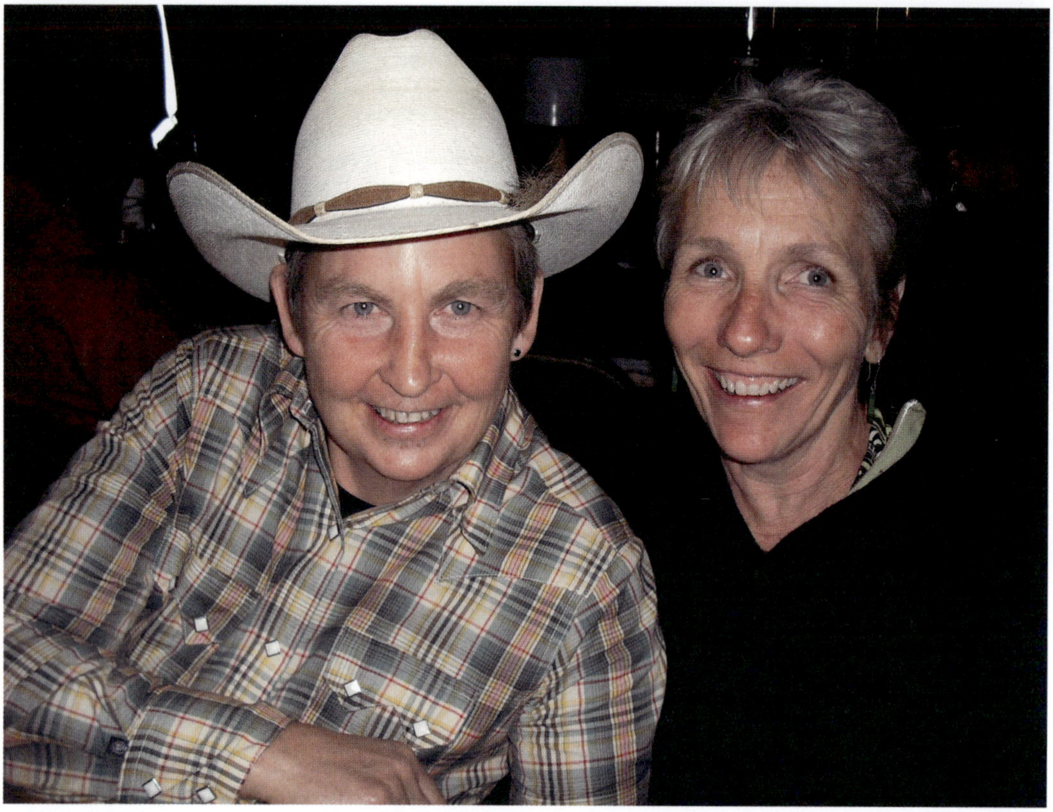

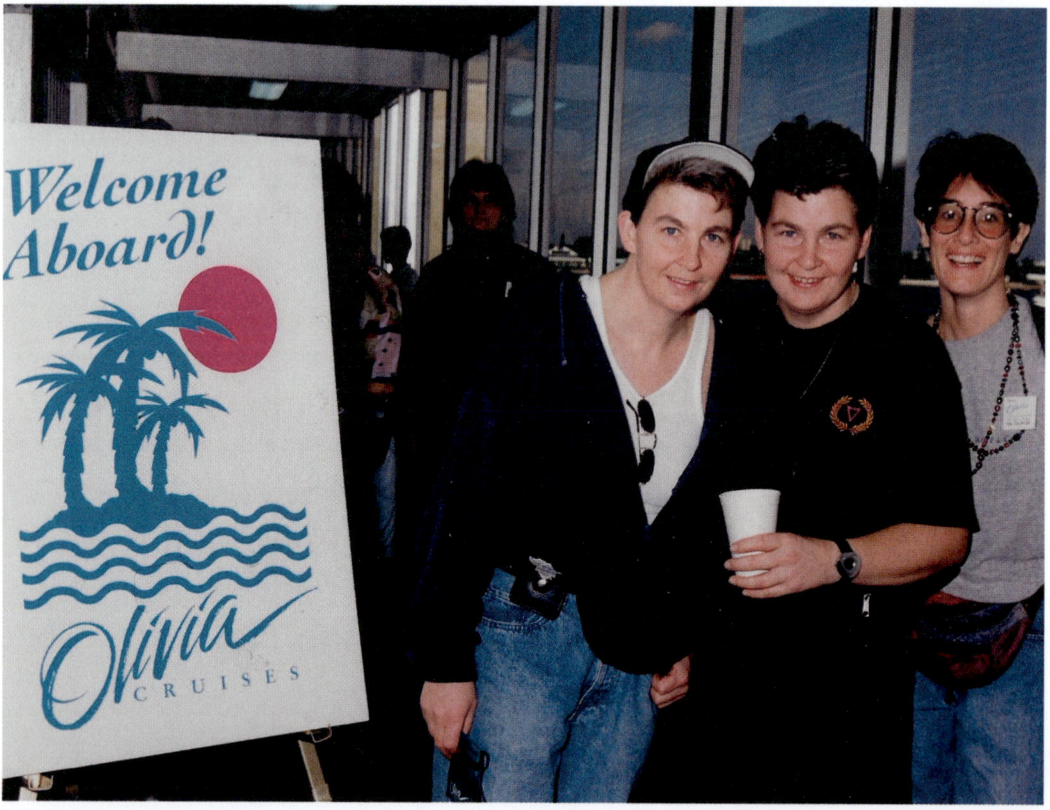
Welcome
Aboard!
Olivia
CRUISES

MARY AND DONNA

We spent our last night in Montréal in a hotel, and then it was time to say goodbye. Mary flew back to Seattle, while Lynda and I flew to London to perform at the Edinburgh Fringe.

For the next year we had a long-distance romance, with Mary joining me for short excursions in London, Edinburgh, Glasgow and Amsterdam. I visited her in Seattle and got to really love that city.

When I returned to New Zealand, life was pretty quiet. Then one evening Mary rang to say she wanted to move to New Zealand.

'Let's do it!' I said.

She lived in our little Grey Lynn house for a while, then Mary and I moved out to Piha on the rugged west coast. Eventually I bought my own house out in Woodhill, near Helensville. Lynda kept the house in Grey Lynn.

> We drifted apart somewhere along the way, after a long time, wanting different things out of life.

Mary and I shared almost two decades together. She was one of my caregivers when I was diagnosed with cancer, and we built a house together.

We drifted apart somewhere along the way, after a long time, wanting different things out of life. I was tired of travelling and always wanted to be at home to ride my horses, while Mary still had the adventure bug. She moved to Napier and made a new life there. I stayed in the Helensville area, ending up in South Head (Auckland's best-kept secret).

Opposite from top: Jools and Mary on the Summer Hoe-down tour more than a decade after that first meeting; The twins and Arani on board the Olivia cruise. TOPP COLLECTION

Although I'd had other partners before Mary, all of whom I remember with great fondness, she was my primary love. We still enjoy each other's company.

I choose to be single now, and I'm okay with that. Remember: I'm a twin, so I'm never really alone.

———

Arani had called and asked us to pop into the office. A few offers of gigs had come in and she needed to know which ones we wanted to do. One of the reasons we have had such a successful working relationship with her is because it has always been a cooperative, not a dictatorship.

We got all sorts of requests — to play corporate functions, private birthdays, festivals and fundraisers. We tried to do as many as we could, but sometimes dates would clash and we couldn't be in two places at once. The Tamworth Country Music Festival wanted us to confirm for 2007, and Arani was also trying to confirm dates and venues for a planned national tour to coincide with our 50th birthday in 2008, called *100 Years of the Topp Twins*.

Then she handed us a letter. 'You might want to read this,' she said. 'There's no money in it but it's a cute story.' It was from a young boy who was organising a fundraiser for Heart Kids New Zealand in Ashburton. His mum was helping him and he went on to say he needed a big act to bring in an audience. Would the Topp Twins like to play?

He explained that he had been diagnosed at birth with a hole in his heart. He was one of the lucky ones who got better, but some of the other children he had met through Heart Kids were not so lucky and had prolonged hospital treatment. He said he would be performing in the show, along with some of his country music friends. It was signed 'Cameron Luxton, 11 years old'.

Jools and I looked at each other, then at Arani. We agreed to confirm Tamworth and both corporate gigs. 'And let's do the gig for the kid,' I said.

Three days before the Heart Kids gig in Ashburton, Jools was diagnosed with breast cancer. When she phoned me, I was driving on the Auckland motorway but somehow managed to do a U-turn and head out to the farm. There, a few tears were shed, and we hugged each other as we sat down in the horse area. I told her I'd be there for her and we'd get through this.

Remembering the Heart Kids gig, I asked if she wanted me to get Arani to cancel it. Jools said no, let's do it, so we rang Arani and broke the news to her. She was of course devastated.

The Luxtons met us at Christchurch Airport, where brothers Cameron and Oliver and their dad Matthew carried our bags to a waiting limo. They had gone all-out to make us feel like superstars. Cameron told us we were staying at the Ashburton Trust Hotel — the best accommodation in town — and that his mum was there organising things for us. She had also been doing last-minute decorations for the show at the Ashburton College hall.

We met Donna, Cam's mother, in the hotel lobby. She was in full cowgirl regalia — red checked shirt, fringed jacket, tight Wranglers and turquoise swirl-patterned Ariat boots. With her curly shoulder-length hair she was as pretty as a heifer in heat, a pocket-rocket organising our dinner while taking phone calls from volunteers helping with the show.

Next day we went down to the venue for sound checks, and I ended up helping out with the lighting, refocusing some of the lamps and helping the school kids programme the lighting board. It was good to be busy; every now and then I would forget that my sister had just been diagnosed with cancer. The show, a matinee, was sold out and the house lights faded at 4 p.m., bang on time. Cameron was first up. He welcomed everyone to the show and then the follow spot picked him up and he blew us all away with his rendition of 'No More Night'.

Damn, the kid could sing. His timing was impeccable, he had perfect pitch and his stage presence was far beyond his 11 years. Watching from backstage, I looked over at his mum, who had tears streaming down her face. You could tell she was so proud. Jools and I slipped in beside her.

'He's good!' we both whispered to her.

> Damn, the kid could sing. His timing was impeccable, he had perfect pitch and his stage presence was far beyond his 11 years.

All the other kids who performed were great as well and we discovered that most of them had competed in the Gore Country Music Festival.

Jools and I were last up, by which time the crowd were having a ball with all the talent that had gone before us. We invited all the kids back on stage for a grand finale, and then we called Donna up on stage to thank her for organising such an awesome gig.

She was a little reluctant, but Cam beckoned to her and she finally took a small bow.

The after-show party was a huge success as well — performers, mums, dads, grandparents and friends sang and partied into the night.

I was sitting with Donna when she said, 'Why don't you two stay on for a couple of days and take a break?' It would have been nice,

Opposite: Lynda and Donna on holiday in Bali in 2012. SALLY TAGG / USED WITH PERMISSION OF ARE MEDIA

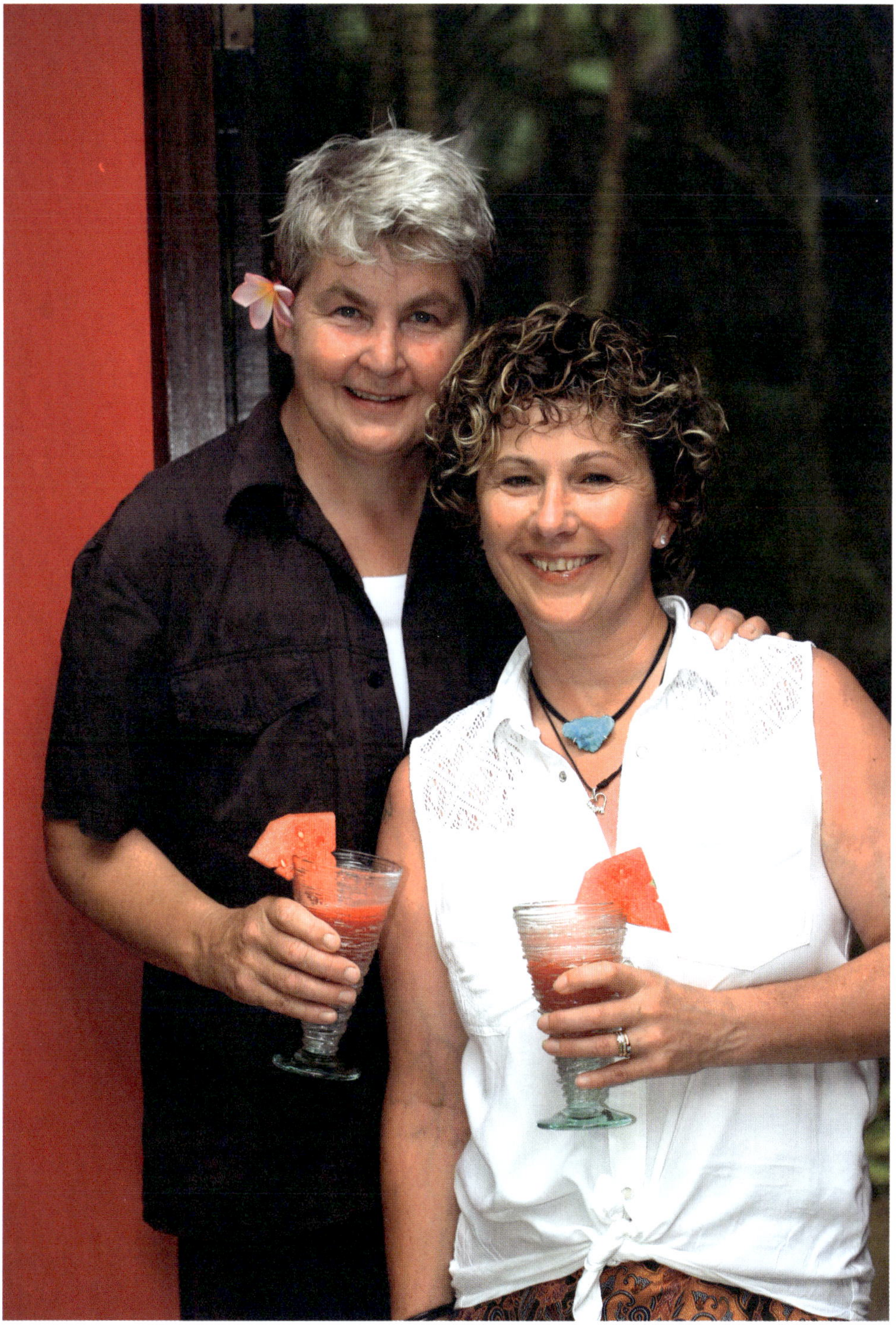

but I told her we had to get back up to Auckland. She said, 'What could be more important than having a couple of days off?'

I don't know why, but I told her. It felt like we'd known each other for more than the two days we'd been there. 'Jools has just been diagnosed with breast cancer and has an appointment at Auckland Hospital on Monday,' I said.

She was the first person I had told besides Arani, and it felt like a weight had lifted off my shoulders. It's okay to talk about it, I thought.

Next day the whole darned Luxton family drove us back to the airport, and big hugs were the order of the day as we headed into the departure lounge. Donna whispered into my ear, 'I'm here if you need to talk,' and it seemed like her hug lingered a little longer than you'd expect from someone you'd just met.

23

When Cancer Comes Calling

When cancer comes calling, a girl needs a mum who has a few words of advice, and a hug as big as a bear.

In 2006 that's what happened to me — I was diagnosed with breast cancer that had already spread to my lymph nodes. Cancer likes to travel — it has its very own highway and if it decides to go on a road trip it can stop off anywhere it wants: maybe a sightseeing tour of your sternum, or a picnic behind your tenth rib, or perhaps a sleepover by your collarbone with a campfire on the right side of your throat.

This is a road map of the cancer that now nestles in my body.

It wasn't that bad at the beginning.

After our gig in Ashburton my surgeon recommended a mastectomy of the affected breast. Lynda called me the one-tit wonder and I settled in for six months of chemotherapy. It's a shitty treatment and there's no guarantee it will work. My understanding is that the chemo kills fast-growing cells, which cancer cells usually are, but other, healthy fast-growing cells in your body are also dealt to by the poison and left to die by the side of the road.

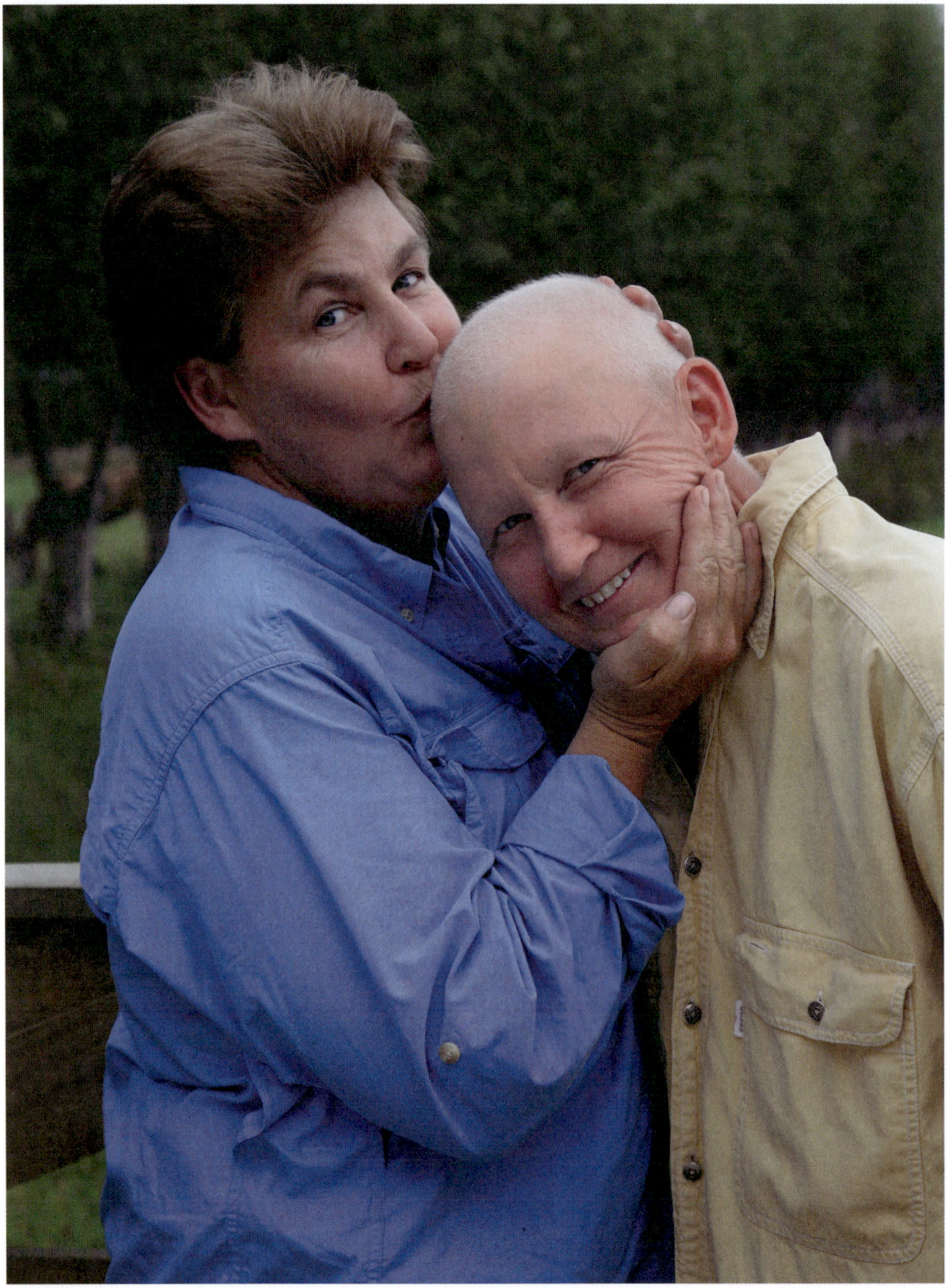

Being a positive little bunny, I knew I could grow these cells back. If I ever cut myself while working out on the farm I knew that a wash and a plaster would see the skin neatly join up again in no time, and it would be hard to see where it had been damaged. I had been growing new cells all my life, because our bodies are amazing, and I was counting on mine to help me out in this time of need.

By January 2007 I was well enough to go to our confirmed gig in Tamworth. I was as bald as a badger but I could wear my cowboy hat the whole time. We had invited Cam Luxton to be our guest, so we didn't have to do such a long performance.

> I had been growing new cells all my life, because our bodies are amazing, and I was counting on mine to help me out in this time of need.

It was good to catch up with Cam, Oliver, Donna and Matthew — and we felt the kid had the potential to be a star.

There was more chemo once I got home but, as an avid Greenpeace supporter, I just couldn't allow them to use radiation on me — that prospect scared the hell out of me.

Jools and I would head into oncology every month for her chemo hit. The February dose was not as bad as the one before. Each one took her about a week to get over, then she had a couple of weeks of getting better before she had to do it all over again. The next one was scheduled for late March.

Lynda and Jools at Liberty Circle Ranch in 2006. SALLY TAGG / USED WITH PERMISSION OF ARE MEDIA

I had planned a fishing trip a year earlier with my fishing buddies from America and they were arriving early March. I'd met Sally in America and she'd given me a couple of fly-fishing lessons. A year later she rang out of the blue and asked if I could organise a fishing trip in New Zealand for her and her friend Teresa. I did, and now they were coming back for their second visit.

Jools was feeling pretty good and insisted I go, so I loaded up the caravan and drove south. I picked the gals up at Christchurch Airport and we headed towards Nelson to start fishing.

Arani rang the following day to say the Mussel Festival in Havelock had asked if we could perform, and did I want to do it since I was already down that way? She'd already spoken to Jools, who was keen, so we confirmed.

My American friends were pretty stoked as they had never seen us play. We fished around the Nelson area for a while, then headed over to Havelock. Jools was flying in and the festival organisers were picking her up. We were all booked into a beautiful little cottage in town.

Another phone call — this time from Donna, Cam's mum, to say she and the family were thinking of heading up to the Mussel Festival. I said, 'Great, tell the boy to bring his guitar and we'll give him a set in our show.'

We all had a ball at the festival. Jools was well and in good spirits, Sally and Teresa got to see us perform, and Cam wowed the crowd once again. Donna's parents, Ken and Lynn, also had a great time — we had managed to get everyone backstage passes and the sun was shining all day long.

The following day my friends and I were packing up the caravan to head off for more fishing. Ken was admiring our 1960s Concord caravan and mentioned that he could give it a sand down and a spray-paint if I wanted. Hell yes, a free upgrade of our beloved caravan would be awesome! It was arranged that I would drop the

Top: Lynda fly-fishing with American buddies Sally Stoner (left) and Teresa Le Blanc in the South Island. TOPP COLLECTION

Bottom: The Kens and Cameron perform together at the Matariki Gourmet Hāngi, a few years after Jools' initial diagnosis. The event raised funds for the Raukatauri Music Therapy Trust. PHOTOGRAPHER UNKNOWN

others off in Christchurch after the fishing finished, then whip down to Methven to drop the caravan at Donna's place for its spruce-up.

The Luxtons lived in an old farmhouse just out of Methven. I dropped the caravan off as arranged, then headed to Fairlie for another couple of days' fishing. When I came back for the caravan I could see that Ken had done a brilliant job. She looked glorious. Donna and the kids had helped with the sanding, I was told.

I stayed the night and prepared for the long haul back up to Auckland. The next morning I said my farewells and thank yous and jumped into the old Pajero. The whole family were standing there to wave me off, and then Donna calmly walked to the truck, opened the passenger door and said, 'Do you want some company on the trip back?' She climbed aboard before I could answer. I remember looking in the rear-vision mirror as we drove out the gate at Cam, Oliver and Matthew waving goodbye.

It took us four days to drive to Auckland, but only two for me to fall madly in love with Donna. She stayed with me at Jools' and Mary's place for a week, then flew home to her family to figure out what she was going to do.

Jools had two more months of chemo so I stayed on and continued to take her into the hospital. There were many phone calls to Donna, but the one I specifically remember is the one in which she asked me to come down and move in with her and the two boys.

I packed up the caravan again, and this time my old mate Jack the dog was coming too. I said goodbye to Jools and Mary, and off I went on a new adventure. I was excited, and also slightly apprehensive. I couldn't wait to see Donna, but the prospect of being a stepmother to two young boys was something very new.

Jools (left) and Lynda preparing for The Recovery Tour in 2007. SALLY TAGG

In October 2007, a year after being diagnosed with cancer, my hair had grown back and I felt great. I'd promised Lynda that if I got through it, we'd go back out on the road and sing our hearts out, so in late 2007 we headed off on The Recovery Tour. I'd made Lynda promise to sing 'My Pinto Pony' every night of the tour. It was my favourite yodel of hers — a slow yodel that's quite hard to sing, and every night she threw her heart and soul into that sweet tune just to please me.

Cam was on that tour with us. He'd reached the grand old age of 12 and we thought the rest of New Zealand should get a chance to hear this talented young man. It was good to catch up with Donna again — she was great to have on the road and ended up selling the merchandise for us after the gigs. And it was great to see Lynda so happy.

We donated around $20,000 to the Breast Cancer Foundation NZ at the end of that tour, to help other women going through the same struggle. Through our association with the Breast Cancer Foundation NZ we had the joy of meeting Rosie Horton and we became friends. She was a powerhouse philanthropist and an absolute darling to us. We performed at a few of her charity events and at her husband Michael's 60th birthday party. At one event at their beautiful home in Remuera, we mixed and mingled with guests as Prue and Dilly, and many people thought we were just guests — even when we took paying tours to look through Rosie's wardrobe in her bedroom. Rosie thought it was a hoot. She raised millions for Auckland's Starship Children's Hospital and for breast cancer. She was a true dame.

24

Untouchable Girls

By 2008 Arani had been our manager for 15 years, a trusted friend who's always prepared to take risks to help build our careers. But when she came up with the idea of booking the Aotea Centre for a one-off gig we thought she had lost her mind.

The Kiri Te Kanawa Theatre seats just over 2000, and Arani's idea was for a double bill of the Topp Twins' two Kens and Bob Downe, the creation of Australian comedian Mark Trevorrow. Arani reckoned the show could sell out.

We were not nearly so sure but, undeterred, Arani booked Mark Trevorrow, booked the venue, produced a massive poster of Bob and the Kens, and arranged everything. She proudly reported to us just before we went on stage on 9 May 2008 that the show was in fact sold out.

She now wanted another big project. What do you do next when you feel like you've done pretty much everything? Well, you make a movie of course. A documentary, to be precise, about our lives, our career, our story. Arani was instrumental in getting this project off the ground, and we spent most of the rest of 2008 researching, writing and filming.

Prue and Dilly at Rosie Horton's house for a promo shoot ahead of the Topp Twins' concert with the Auckland Philharmonia Orchestra. SALLY TAGG / USED WITH PERMISSION OF ARE MEDIA

Leanne Pooley, the film's director, poured her heart and soul into making it happen and making it good, as did the editor, Tim Woodhouse. It would be based around a live concert featuring our original songs, with interviews with Jools and me and lots of other people woven through it, and segueing into all the protests we'd been involved in and other things we had done.

We insisted that all our characters be interviewed about the Topp Twins, which was pretty entertaining.

A review of *The Topp Twins: Untouchable Girls*, as it came to be called, described it as the history of New Zealand in the time of the Topp Twins. We also insisted that all our characters be interviewed about the Topp Twins, which was pretty entertaining.

The movie was released in New Zealand in 2009 and broke all records for opening day and opening weekend for a New Zealand documentary. After just four weeks it had made over $1 million. For the next seven years our film was the highest grossing New Zealand documentary of all time. It was finally bumped by *Chasing Great*, which told Richie McCaw's story. Classic Kiwi film history: our two top documentary films being about a couple of lesbians and an All Black.

After the New Zealand release Arani set about getting *Untouchable Girls* into film festivals around the world. We were invited to tour the American festivals and speak after the movie had shown. We were amazed at how much the film resonated with international audiences, and gay and lesbian communities in Canada, the US, Australia and Germany who came in their droves to see it on the big screen.

The film itself won 21 awards worldwide. In 2009 at the Toronto International Film Festival (TIFF) it won the Cadillac People's Choice Award, beating the famous documentary-filmmaker Michael Moore. I bet he was googling the Topp Twins to find out who the hell we were.

It was great to reconnect with Brian Sweeney when he flew up from New York to be at our Toronto premiere. We were thrilled that his and Jane's investment in our film had paid off. The film went on to win Best Feature Film (Budget under $1 Million) and Best Original Music in a Feature Film at the Qantas Film and Television Awards in New Zealand in 2009. It became a box office hit and is still one of New Zealand's top 10 films.

While we were in Toronto we did dozens of press interviews, and the City of Toronto paid us to perform a free outdoor concert to help promote the festival — not that it needed it. TIFF is considered one of the most prestigious film festivals in the world, and it was gratifying to see queues of people lined up around the block to see our film.

One of the most exciting accolades we received was an email from North Korea. Someone had managed to smuggle a DVD of *Untouchable Girls* into the country and they wanted to let us know we were big stars in the gay and lesbian community there.

Not bad for a couple of girls from Huntly, eh.

It's always fun to set out on a new singing adventure and in 2010 we headed off on the Topp Twins Summer Winery Tour with Don McGlashan — five shows in the North Island with Don and his band, The Seven Sisters.

Don is a brilliant songwriter and could have easily filled a show by himself but the combination of two Kiwi acts seemed to be a winner.

From top: The twins enjoying Cadillac limousine rides at the 2009 Toronto International Film Festival; (From left) Lynda, Donna, Jools and Mary in Brooklyn in 2010. ARANI CUTHBERT

We'd spent a good number of days beforehand recording *Honky Tonk Angel* at Neil Finn's stunning Roundhead Studios with Don as producer. It was a lot of fun and he was so easy to work with — he's a musical genius and the softest man we know (I mean that in a good way).

That all seemed to lead naturally to a joint tour. We started the show with the Ginghams, and Don performed some of his most famous songs to finish the first half, then we were all on stage to showcase the songs from *Honky Tonk Angel*.

When asked by media what it was like to work with the Topp Twins, Don replied:

The Topp Twins are a couple of hard-living, shooting, horse-wrangling women. Getting them to show their sensitive side was a dangerous job but somebody had to give it a crack. This is one of the most enjoyable records I've ever worked on. I'm sure it will connect with the Topp Twins' legions of fans and I hope it wins them some new ones too.

Honky Tonk Angel was our biggest-selling album, and Don McGlashan gained the respect he deserves as one of New Zealand's finest from a couple of country gals when he accepted the offer to work with us.

We'd got a taste for working with other musicians so it was a blast to put another big show together the following year. The Topp Twins Summer Hoe-down 2011 was a biggie that went the length of New Zealand, featuring some of the finest country music artists in the country.

When we were little we used to watch a programme on TV called *Country Touch*, which was introduced by the legendary Tex Morton. Stars of that show were the Hamilton County Bluegrass Band — the only New Zealand group to ever play the Grand Ole Opry in Tennessee. In 2011 these guys were still performing, so we asked them to join the Hoe-down tour. They had formed in 1966, telling a local newspaper their origins were in the green grass of Waikato but their inspiration came from the blue grass of Kentucky.

Added to the lineup was the fabulous Tami Neilson, who was new on the country scene then, having arrived in New Zealand from Canada after marrying a Kiwi bloke.

Marian Burns, everybody's favourite Kiwi fiddle player, set the Hoe-down scene and Cam Luxton, Lynda's handsome young stepson, joined the oldies for a taste of life on the road. We partied and sang our way along the highway on a bus, and that was the best bit for Lynda and me — we just loved being on the road.

The Summer Hoe-down lineup was such a success that the WOMAD festival booked the show in its entirety and we were included in the official entertainment programme for the 2011 Rugby World Cup.

You know you've made the big time when your manager rings to say you've got a gig with the Auckland Philharmonia Orchestra.

To be honest, we were terrified to be playing publicly with 75 other professional musicians. We couldn't read a line of music if our lives depended on it, so when the conductor said we had to count four bars before we came in, it was a moment of truth. Lynda said the only bar we knew served drinks, and he'd have to tell us when to sweep into the song in a different way. Luckily the conductor was

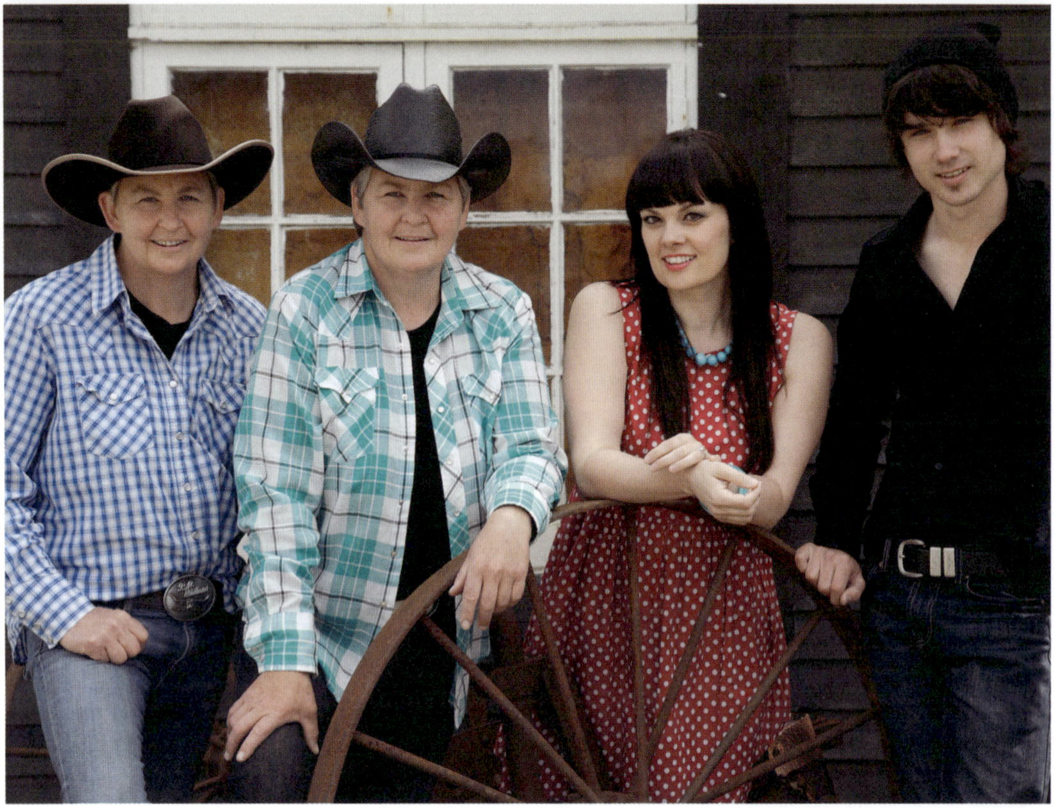

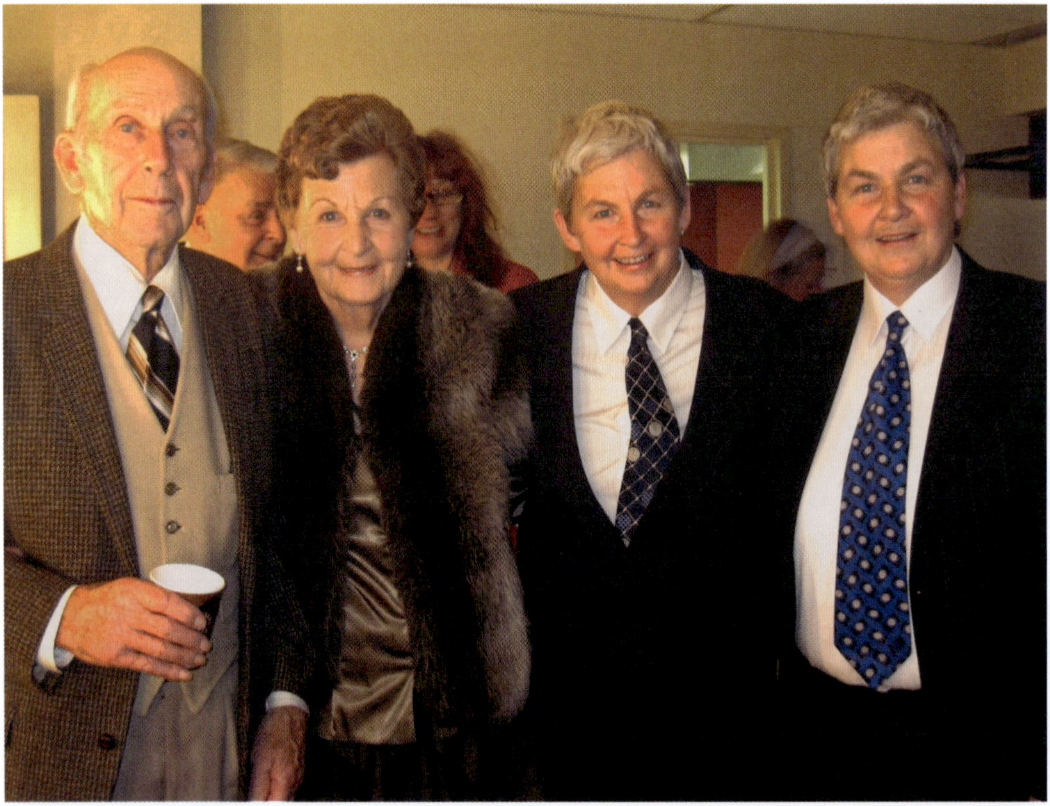

the charming, talented Ken Young, who was completely unfazed by this. In fact he made the whole gig feel like a walk in the park — and a fun one too.

It was exciting hearing an orchestra playing our original songs. Usually we give a strum on the guitar and away we go, but the orchestral arrangements by Penny Dodd were outstanding. There were wonderful intros with long sweeping violin passages, and dramatic and moving sounds from everything from tubas to cellos. It was a dream come true for us to be up there listening to our songs being honoured in such a way. It was something we never thought we'd hear in our lifetime.

It certainly was a different audience at this APO concert, the diehard classical music lovers rubbing shoulders with spiky-haired dykes, but it was a magical night. Mum and Dad and Bruce and his partner Richard came along; they were all so proud of us.

'Palomino Moon' and 'Calf Club Day' made a shiver run up my spine, but what really made the night for us was the fact that the orchestra were ready to have a bit of fun with our characters.

The William Tell Overture with Camp Mother on the spoons and Camp Leader on a pair of Morris Minor hubcaps was something else. The Kens sang a classy rendition of 'Holy Cow' (cue tubas), and they got to thank the conductor (a third Ken), leading to a joke about The Three Kenners.

The last song of the night was 'Untouchable Girls' and, like all good classical divas, we went with the full sparkly evening gown look, with high heels and a diamond or two.

Mum never looked happier than in that moment.

Opposite top: Jools, Lynda, Tami Neilson and Cam Luxton on the Summer Hoe-Down tour in 2011. SALLY TAGG

Opposite bottom: The twins and their parents at the after-party for the APO concert. TOPP COLLECTION

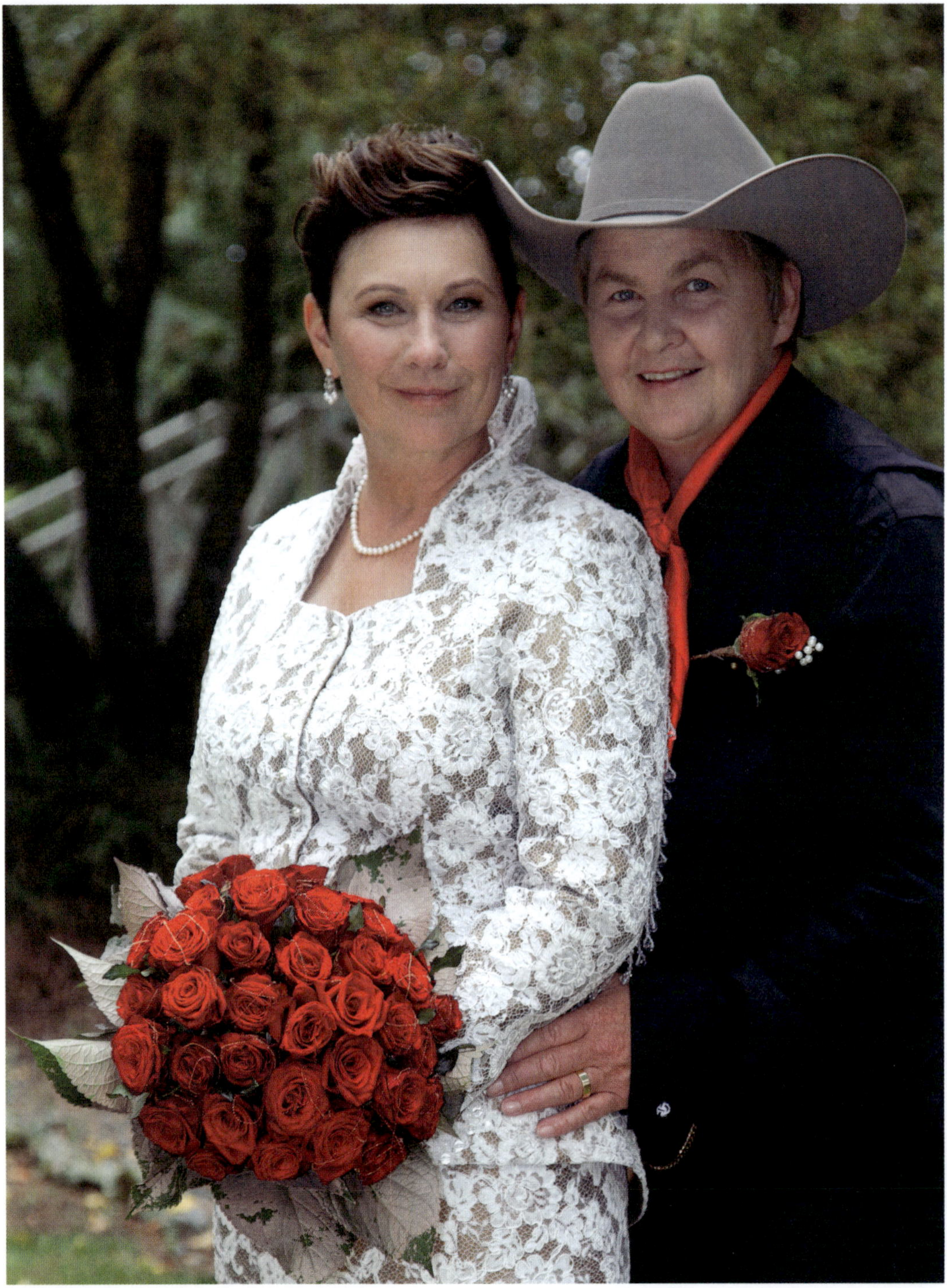

25

Wedding Belles

It was December 2011 and we'd had a great year. To top it off, on Christmas morning I asked Donna to marry me. We'd been together for six years and I had decided she was my soulmate, the one I wanted to see out my twilight years with.

I made her breakfast in bed, with poached eggs and bacon and a lavender garnish from the garden. I carried it in to her on a tray, along with a small black box.

Donna knew straight away and cried like a baby. The boys came in and were sitting on the bed when Donna said yes, and then I cried.

Same-sex partners were still not permitted to get married in New Zealand but I refused to have a 'civil union'. I said we were getting married right from the get-go.

And so on 9 March 2013, the marriage of Lynda Bethridge Topp to Donna Fae Luxton took place on the lawn of our home, Topp Lodge, at Staveley. *Woman's Day* had exclusive media rights, both Donna's and my parents were there to give us away, and Oliver and Cameron walked their mother down the aisle.

Opposite: The wedding of Lynda Bethridge Topp and Donna Fae Luxton.
SALLY TAGG / USED WITH PERMISSION OF ARE MEDIA

Shani, her best mate from school, was Donna's bridesmaid, Jools was my bestgal, and my friends Linden, Nic and Emma were my groomsgals. Our celebrant was Marilyn Holmes, who had let us use her old gramophone to learn to yodel back in our teenage years. Brother Bruce and his gay friends did the flowers and decorated the hall, and the local Mayfield Lions did the catering for the reception at the nearby Staveley hall.

What a party it was. We had a hundred friends and family with us for the wedding feast, and invited another hundred locals to join us for the dance and supper.

Meanwhile, in the hallowed halls of Parliament, Louisa Wall, Ngāti Tūwharetoa, Ngāti Hineuru, Waikato and Ngāti Kuri, was waving the rainbow flag, fighting to legalise same-sex marriage through a private member's bill.

The gallery was packed and the atmosphere was tense. When the outcome of the vote was announced the crowd erupted.

On 25 March our wedding made the front cover of *Woman's Day*, three weeks before the final vote on Louisa Wall's bill. Donna and I were invited to sit in the gallery of Parliament on 17 April for the final reading. The gallery was packed and the atmosphere was tense. When the outcome of the vote was announced the crowd erupted: the bill had passed by 77 votes to 44. We all stood and clapped to acknowledge Louisa for all her hard work, then we all sang 'Pokarekare Ana'. It was an emotional and uplifting moment for the gay community, and the new law came into force on 19 August 2013.

I like to think the publicity around our marriage helped the process along in some way, and on 29 October that same year Donna and I signed a legal document to say we were married. I always insist on celebrating our marriage on 9 March, as I refuse to let a government rule our lives; Donna on the other hand celebrates both days — she loves an excuse for a party.

Not only had I been Donna's partner for six years, but also I had been a stepmother to Cameron and Oliver — the hardest and most rewarding role I had ever played. The pride I felt every time Cam performed with us was beyond expression; he could bring tears to my eyes. Oliver is the most supportive brother in the world, even though at times he must have felt left out with all the accolades falling on Cam.

There were times when I thought I wasn't cut out to be a mum, but I did my best. Some things I learnt early on, like never to get between a lioness and her cubs. My role was to try to help them grow up to be good men, to make sure they had everything they needed, and to give them boundaries. As a step-parent I don't think you can ever replace the parent who is not there. There were times when things went pear-shaped, but there were also plenty of good times.

When Oliver announced that he wanted to be a chef, and that he had enrolled at polytech in Timaru, we were all gobsmacked. The only thing he had ever cooked at home was store-bought pizza. After he graduated I rang Peter Gordon, one of New Zealand's finest chefs, and told him my son had just graduated from chef school and needed a job. Peter said send him up to Auckland for the weekend — I'll put him through a few tests and see how he goes.

Two months later Oliver was off to London to work in Peter's restaurant, The Providores. He now lives in Sydney with his beautiful girlfriend Christina and works in a five-star French restaurant. He still sends me a Father's Day card every year.

Cam and I were close — after all, it was he who had brought us all together with his letter. We went hunting together, me guiding him to start with, then him taking me hunting as my guide, but my idea of boundaries did not sit well with him. I could hear my father in my 'requests' to him: 'Bring the firewood in, do the dishes.'

I tried to teach him how to use a tool correctly, as Dad had done with us, and offered advice on the entertainment world, but we kept clashing and for a while we drifted apart. He stopped singing and that broke my heart because he is so talented. But he was there for me as soon as he found out I was sick. He works in forestry now and is married to the lovely Amelia with two beautiful daughters, Lyric and Willow. I guess that makes me a grandma. It was Donna who taught me to never give up on your kids. Oliver and Cameron will always be my sons — I am deeply proud of them both, and they have grown up to be good men.

After all the excitement of the wedding and honeymoon it was back to work, and Jools and I started planning a new theatre show called *The Grand Ole Toppry*. We hit the road in October 2013. Of course it was loosely based on the Grand Ole Opry in Nashville, Tennessee, outlining the history of country music. The tour was a family affair with Jools, Lynda and Cameron performing, Donna on merchandise and Oliver as backstage crew.

A fun new character I played was Tammy WireNetting, who told the story of the famous venue that has showcased the biggest names in country music. She also sang an emotional version of 'Stand by Your Man' with Lynda's Ken to start the show.

Tami Neilson joined us again, with her three-piece band. With a voice closely resembling Patsy Cline, she paid tribute to the superstar singer who was killed in a plane crash early in her short but

Top: Tammy WireNetting and her admirer Ken at the Dunedin Town Hall. ARANI CUTHBERT

Bottom: Donna and Lynda on their wedding day at Topp Lodge in Staveley with Oliver (left) and Cameron. SALLY TAGG / USED WITH PERMISSION OF ARE MEDIA

memorable career. We knew Tami was a star the moment we heard her sing, and she has gone on to win numerous New Zealand country music awards with her own songs. She even had Willie Nelson sing on one of her albums.

We had a fantastic array of talent on show in *The Grand Ole Toppry*. No country show is complete without a fiddle player, so Marian Burns also joined us for most of the tour. The Johnnys were an all-girl band from Nelson who sang the hits of Johnny Cash, and country guitar legend Phil Doublet played some hot licks and joined Cam Luxton for some beautiful man-duets. Phil also led the group jam at the end of the show.

The tour sold out and it was a blast. Sadly, soon after this tour The Johnnys' lead singer, Suzi Fray, was diagnosed with an incurable form of cancer. She passed away four years later. We'd like to say that she was the best female Johnny Cash in the world.

26

Topp Country

We'd been on the road a lot, and we thought it would be good to see if we could get back on TV to help cement our local audience. Arani spent a few months sending proposals to networks and the funding agencies. The ideas were varied: comedy shows featuring all our characters, a country music show titled *Show Ponies* with up-and-coming artists, and a live theatre show filmed for TV. All were rejected.

In desperation we said to Arani, 'Send in a proposal for a Topp Twins cooking show — they seem to be flavour of the month,' (no pun intended). So you can imagine our dismay when TVNZ came back with a yes.

We obviously had not thought this through — we were entertainers, not chefs. So we brainstormed and came up with the concept of the Topp Twins visiting people all around New Zealand who were cooking, growing and producing amazing food. This became the theme, and in 2014 *Topp Country* was born.

Playing ourselves was certainly a lot easier and less time-consuming than playing all the characters, and a small segment featuring our characters was recorded for each episode. Camp

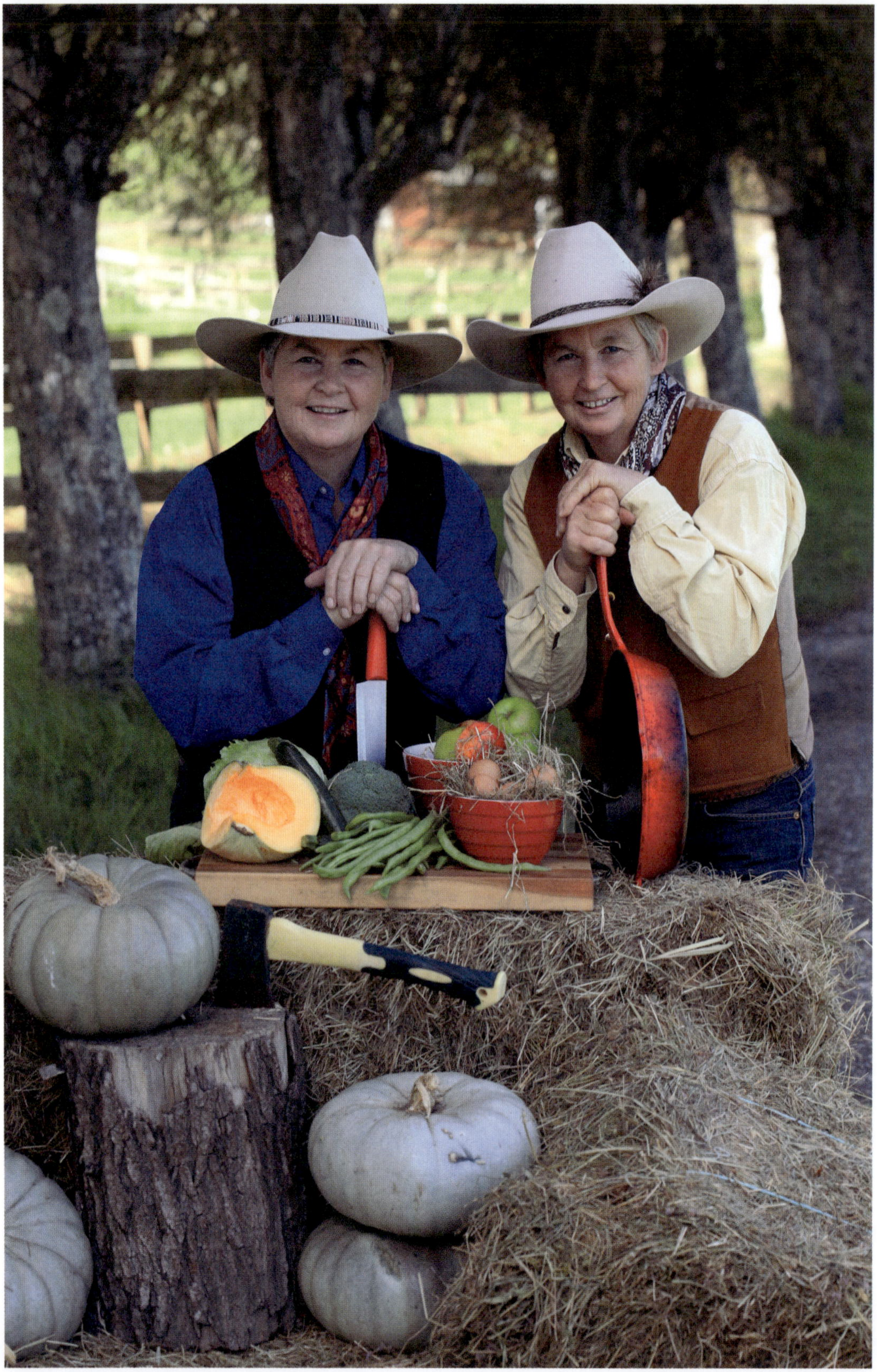

Mother and Camp Leader made sauces, Prue and Dilly prepared finger food for charity fundraisers, and the Bowling Ladies 'brought a plate'. We also wrote food-themed poems for Ken and Ken to end each episode.

The real stars of the show were the Kiwis who were passionate about the food they grew, cooked or produced. Our job was to make them feel at home and capture their story.

> **Playing ourselves was certainly a lot easier and less time-consuming than playing all the characters.**

We had a fantastic crew. Felicity Morgan-Rhind won an award for Best Director: Documentary Factual and Best Lifestyle Programme for *Topp Country* at the Television Awards 2018. We formed a lasting friendship with Felicity through that series. Her energy and commitment were inspiring.

The series producer was our own Arani Cuthbert, who did all the legwork of finding the money, getting the show off the ground and making sure it went to plan, along with wrangling cast and crew. Our amazing camera crew, Clayton Carpinter and Richard Harling, with the unflappable and delightful Lizzie Koroivulaono assisting, made the series look beautiful. Our soundman Nigel Gordon-Crosby was great to work with and we didn't mind him getting up close and personal as he fitted our mics. The gorgeous Michelle Duff worked with Arani in the office for around 10 years and became her right-hand woman, as well as our dear friend. She helped organise the

Opposite: Lynda (left) and Jools promoting *Topp Country*. SALLY TAGG

many logistics and keep everyone happy. And, although we didn't work with him directly ourselves, we wish to thank the legendary editor Wayne Cook for helping craft the series.

After three successful seasons of *Topp Country* we all thought we had a winner and were in the throes of developing another lifestyle series for TVNZ when they pulled the plug. We all felt devastated after all the hard work of establishing a show that had collected awards for best presenters, best director and best lifestyle programme. We were convinced *Topp Country* was an amazing brand.

> We were in the throes of developing another lifestyle series for TVNZ when they pulled the plug.

Instead of letting this get us down, we opened Topp Country Café in Methven, which is still going today. Donna and Lynda are the main team behind the café and I am a silent partner, although according to Lynda sometimes not silent enough . . . Donna had worked in hospitality as maître d' of Noahs Hotel in Christchurch and is a trained barista, so she makes the coffee as well as being café manager.

Lynda was put in charge of the menu and was also chief cook and bottle washer for the first six months, which was pretty impressive when she had no training whatsoever. I flew down to Methven for the grand opening and was given the responsibility of clearing tables and washing dishes.

I thought there should be something on the menu that was created by me, and Lynda suggested I use up all the leftover ham, spinach, cheese and tomatoes mixed with eggs and cream to make individual frittatas in big Texas muffin cups. I got to work and an

Top: Jools (left) and Lynda with Kerry Harmer of Castleridge Station in Canterbury, one of the locations featured on *Topp Country* in 2015. TOPP COLLECTION

Bottom: Arani and Felicity at the NZ Television Awards in 2018. LYNDA TOPP

hour later I proudly carried a tray of six out to the food cabinet, naming them Jools' Frittatas. Lynda thought they were a bit fiddly to make and probably wouldn't make it onto the permanent menu, but were fine as a special for our opening.

What a weekend it was, with locals and a bunch of Topp Twins fans stopping by to check out the new café. My frittatas sold out on the first day and I was quite pleased with myself. I headed home on the Monday, leaving Donna and Lynda to carry on. Lynda rang me on the Tuesday to say a group of women had arrived for lunch and were very disappointed that there were none of my frittatas in the cabinet, so she'd had to make a quick batch. I'm proud to say they have now been added to the menu, in *three* flavours.

When Covid came along the café was hit hard by lockdowns and restrictions, but Topp Country Café survived and is now in its sixth year, with a staff of six and a brilliant chef, Karma, who has been with us for four years.

The moral of this story: if you've got a good idea, or a good brand, no matter how many times you get knocked back, rise up, believe in yourself and make it happen.

On 20 May 2017 an exhibition about the Topp Twins opened at the Te Manawa Museum in Palmerston North. It was developed by the museum's wonderful chief executive at the time, Andy Lowe, who had the vision and tenacity to make it happen and to ensure a successful tour.

During the planning phase, museum curator Siân Torrington rifled through about a million photos, posters, flyers, fan letters and pieces of memorabilia that Arani had deposited at the Alexander Turnbull Library. Then she met with us to talk about other interesting items from our own collections that could go on display.

Among many other things, the exhibition featured the original costumes from Camp Mother, Camp Leader and the Kens, and several videos of our live shows and TV programmes that could be played on demand.

One of the coolest interactive parts was a set of costumes of all our characters made by design students in Wellington. Each one tied on like an apron, and visitors who wanted to partake were given script cards allowing them to re-enact scenes. People had a lot of fun with these.

Te Papa Tongarewa invited us to dress up as Camp Mother and Camp Leader and wander through the building being 'Living Treasures' for the day.

Another exhibition at Te Manawa Museum at the time showcased New Zealand's rugby history, something of a contrast to ours. Museums often feature displays from the distant past so it was great to be part of a show celebrating history that is still happening.

I remember many years ago Te Papa Tongarewa in Wellington, trying to change the way people viewed museums, had invited us to dress up as Camp Mother and Camp Leader and wander through the building being 'Living Treasures' for the day. We had a great time having cups of tea and chatting to the people.

The Te Manawa exhibition ran for five months and then went on tour, opening in the National Library in Wellington on 20 March 2018. It was a grand affair as the exhibition was to be opened by a former and a present prime minister. Helen Clark and Jacinda Ardern both did the honours and we felt very honoured.

Also on display at the National Library is the 1893 Women's Suffrage Petition, which helped make New Zealand the first country

Top: Filming *Topp Country* while on horseback. ARANI CUTHBERT

Bottom: Flanked by former PM Helen Clark and then-PM Jacinda Ardern at the opening of the Topp Twins exhibition. MARK BEATTY / NATIONAL LIBRARY OF NEW ZEALAND

in the world to allow women to vote. We were very excited to see Charlotte Elizabeth Topp on the list. Clearly, protest is in our genes.

Another project we've been associated with since about 2015 is a series of children's sing-along stories published by Scholastic New Zealand.

It was an opportunity to lend a hand helping kids learn to read in New Zealand, and we were all-in. Scholastic would pick an old traditional song, usually something the parents would know and could sing along to, and we would come into the studio for a day and record our version of it.

Then the fabulous Jenny Cooper, an award-winning illustrator from Christchurch, would produce artwork to the words and hey presto — a beautifully illustrated book and CD were ready to help kids all over New Zealand fall in love with books.

The Topp Twins Treasury of Sing-along Stories so far includes *Dingle-Dangle Scarecrow*, *There's a Hole in My Bucket*, *Do Your Ears Hang Low?*, *She'll Be Coming Round the Mountain* and *The Farmer in the Dell*.

We got a funny letter from a parent once that said they were moving from Auckland to Dunedin, and to keep the kids entertained on the long car journey they played one of our books on the car stereo, while the kids read along and sang their hearts out. They said it kept the kids happy for much of the distance, and they were grateful for that, but they *never* wanted to hear that CD again.

It's been a real pleasure to be associated with this project and we hope we've helped a few little ones learn to love reading along the way.

Jools and her horse Intrigue at Liberty Circle Ranch. TESSA CHRISP / NZ LIFE & LEISURE

27

Horses are My Life

While Lynda and Donna worked away at the café, I spent time on my lifestyle block up in the Kaipara, named Liberty Circle Ranch.

Horses have been a constant in my life. Riding and caring for horses is one of the only things that makes me forget I have cancer.

In order to work a horse you have to be in the moment. There's no time to worry about the future or dwell on your past: you must be completely present to tune in to how the horse is feeling and work with him.

Dad was a great teacher and instilled in both of us confidence around horses, cattle and dogs. But in my early thirties I was lucky enough to learn a traditional style of horsemanship that I have practised ever since. It's called vaquero, and came from the Spanish who colonised Mexico in the 16th century. As California was once part of Mexico, the old style of horsemanship was kept alive in the US and is now practised all over the world.

While travelling overseas I have squeezed in some amazing clinics with Ray Hunt and Buck Brannaman, two of the leading lights in vaquero. Then Buck started travelling to New Zealand to run three-day clinics, and for 16 years I never missed one.

Trouble was, he only came every two years so it was a long time between lessons, so I kept attending clinics in the US also. When I was diagnosed with cancer I booked a three-day at a clinic in Chico, California, starting a young horse (we don't call it 'breaking in') with Buck. An American woman I befriended at the Michigan Womyn's Music Festival, Teresa Trull, had acquired a wild mustang and she offered to let me start him.

> The mustang had not been ridden before. I'd be lying if I said I wasn't nervous putting my foot in the stirrup for the first time.

Teresa and her partner Michaela Evans, a New Zealander who could ride like the wind, were also attending the clinic.

The mustang had been handled and taught to have a halter but had not been ridden before. I'd be lying if I said I wasn't nervous putting my foot in the stirrup for the first time, but Buck was a great teacher and instilled confidence in all the people and the horses who were at the clinic.

Michaela was starting a young Welsh mare, and Teresa was riding and taking horsemanship lessons in the afternoons. We all stayed in a big caravan on the ranch.

Vaquero is a style of natural horsemanship aimed at taking the time needed to educate the horse gently and efficiently, using cooperation rather than force. It relies on building a strong relationship of trust between horse and rider. I adored every minute of

Opposite top: The twins' dad Peter was a natural with horses. TOPP COLLECTION

Opposite bottom: Jools with horses Floyd (front) and Intrigue. DEB FILLER

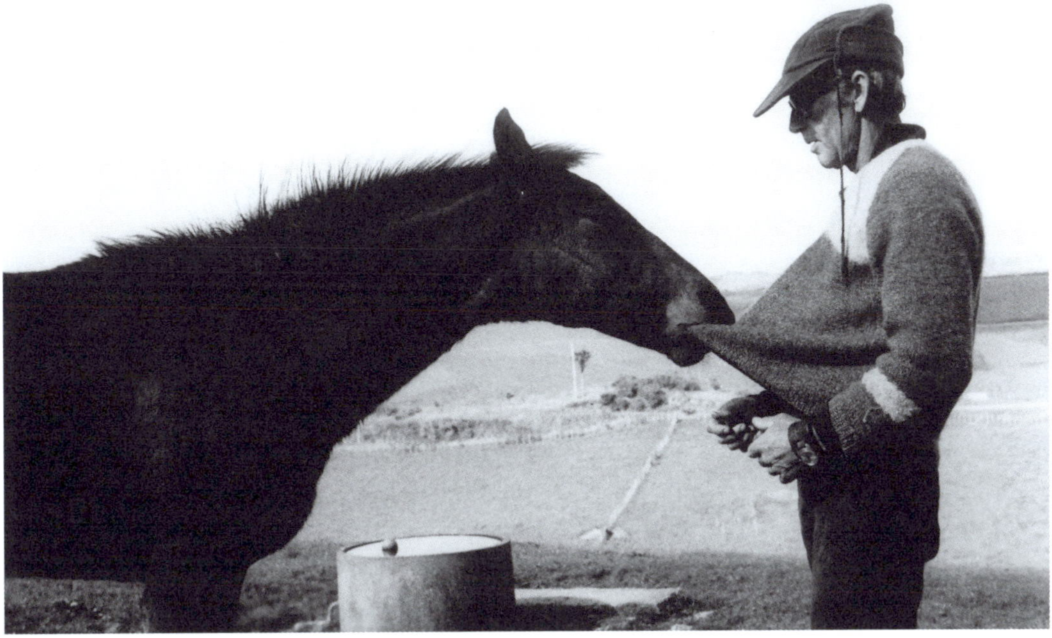

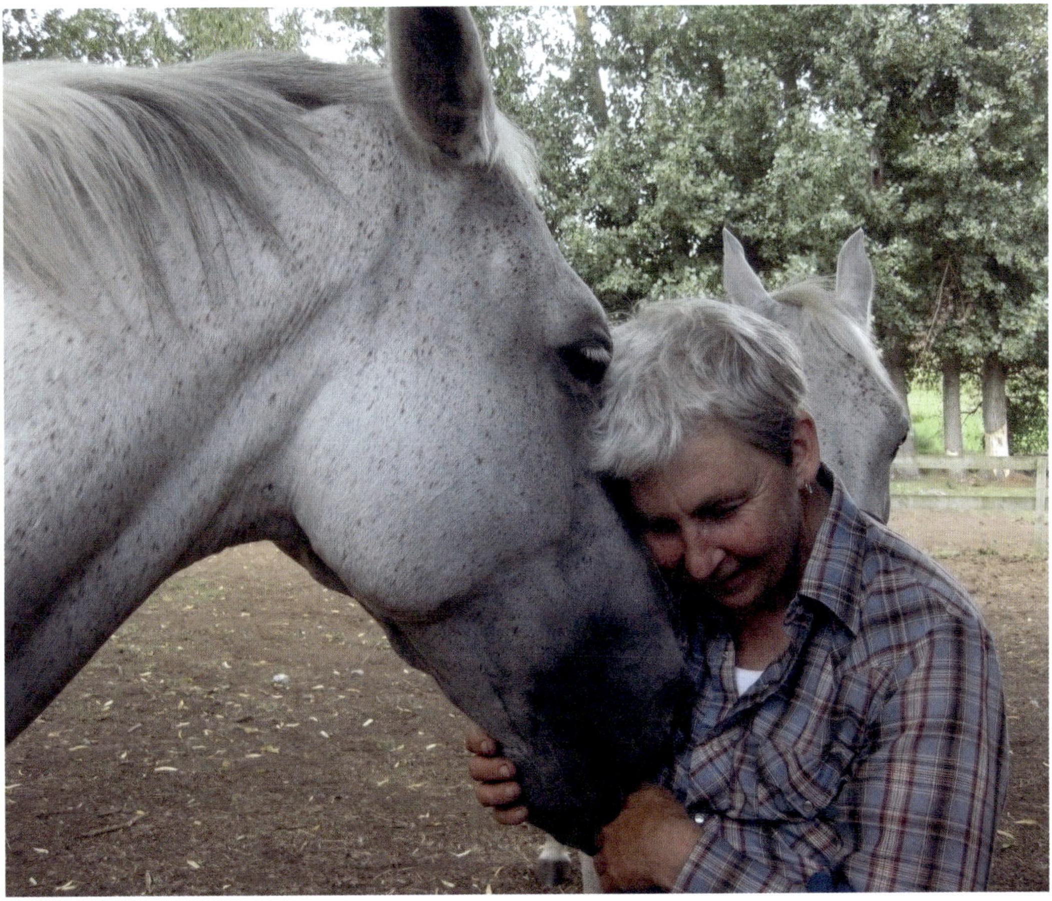

the clinic and came back from that trip with renewed confidence and a desire to be a better rider.

I was thrilled when Michaela and Teresa moved to New Zealand not long after. Teresa set up New Zealand Horse Help, training horses and riders at Liberty Circle Ranch.

Ray Hunt used to say that riding a horse was a privilege, not a right; and that the horse was the teacher. I didn't quite understand at first but now I know how right he was. Unconditional love for the animal is the key to being a good horsewoman. It's a dance, and that moment when a horse decides to go with you, to work with you: that's the moment when you promise never to let the horse down. You commit to supporting him and caring for him so you feel like part of his herd.

I have two beautiful riding horses at the moment: a gelding called Texas, who is a Gypsy/Welsh cross; and a beautiful little Arab mare called Tijuana Rose. The horse that taught me the most, though, was a talented grey Arab named Intrigue. He was the first horse I started and I had him for 23 years. I cried a bucket of tears the day that horse died, and he is forever in my heart.

I'm so lucky to have my own little 8-hectare ranch, with a beautiful mud-brick house with a tiled floor, a big veranda and a 180-degree view of the Kaipara Harbour. I ride my horse and gaze out at the sea . . . The locals say my place used to be called The Birds Nest because it has a beautiful little valley below a steep hill that would make a cool place to lay a few eggs and raise a family of chicks.

Sometimes at night when the moon is out and the stars fill the entire sky, I go out and sit with my horses, then I lie on my back and just stare at those stars. With almost no artificial light, the night sky is a thing of beauty.

The horses wander over and stare at me, and the dogs probably wonder what I'm staring at but they just sit quietly next to me. The moon puts a glow on the sea and in that light within the darkness my horses look amazing.

Horses are my life — they fill me with such great joy. It's 80 per cent hard work and 20 per cent fun but I love every minute of it.

Feeding out hay, picking up shit, grooming, cleaning saddles, trimming feet — you name it, I'm up for it. And when you finally have the time to put your foot in the stirrup and ride out in the forest or play in the arena, the worries of the world disappear. You're at one with another sentient being, and there is peace in the valley.

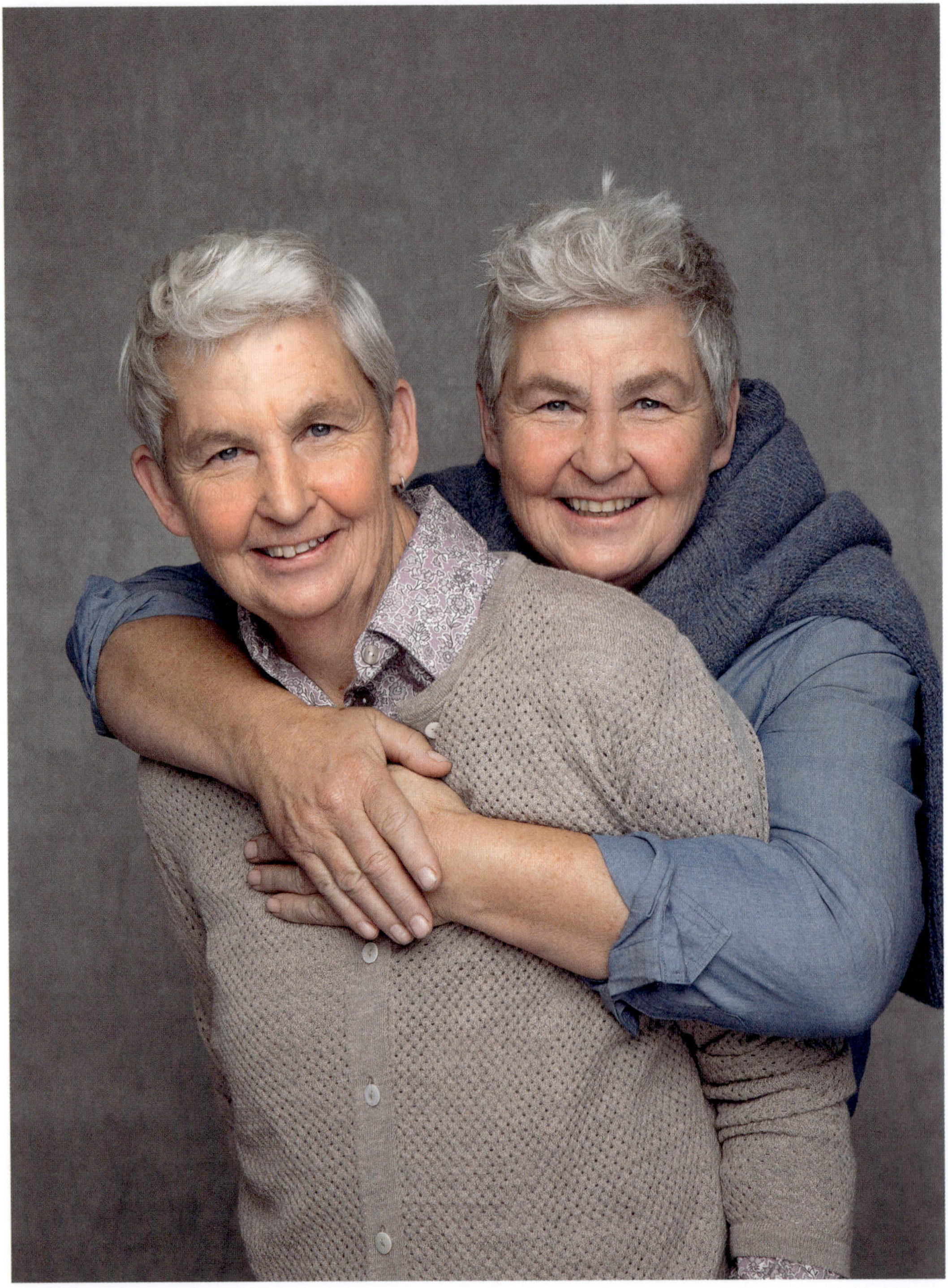

28

Two Dames Lose their Beloved Dad

Donna and I had been out for a drive in the country and were heading back to Topp Lodge. I pulled in by the mailbox and hauled out a couple of bills, a local paper called the *Snowfed*, and a letter with a crown stamped on the front, addressed to me. I handed the other mail to Donna and opened the envelope. Next thing, I had a bloody big grin on my face — I couldn't believe what I was reading.

Donna was intrigued. 'What does it say?'

'They want to make us Dames,' I said. 'The Topp Twins have been included in the Queen's Birthday Honours list, and they want to know if we'll accept!' I grabbed my phone and dialled Jools. 'Gidday, did you get a certain letter in your mailbox today?'

'Yeah, what a hoot, eh? "Dame Companions of the New Zealand Order of Merit".'

'Do you think we should accept?'

'Hell yes,' she said. 'Let's do it.'

Opposite: Jools (left) and Lynda celebrating 100 years of women's suffrage on a cover shoot for MiNDFOOD magazine. KRISTIAN FRIRES / MINDFOOD

We were so gobsmacked it was hard not telling anybody about it until the Honours list was released to the media, which seemed like ages. The day before the ceremony, Lynda and I sat Mum and Dad down, and our brother too, and told them why we'd asked them to travel to Auckland.

Dad thought we were joking at first. Mum had a smile on her face like a gash in a watermelon and Bruce was so proud. His partner Richard attended the ceremony with him, and Donna, Arani and Felicity came too. It was so good to have whānau there to enjoy the occasion with us.

> Dad thought we were joking at first.
> Mum had a smile on her face like a gash
> in a watermelon and Bruce was so proud.

Governor-General Patsy Reddy pinned the medals on us. Men receiving a knighthood are touched by the sword on each shoulder, but women (and priests) were not allowed to bear arms back in the day, so they are not included in the sword ceremony. A korowai (Māori cloak) is placed around the shoulders of women recipients. As there were two of us, I gather another korowai was hurriedly made so we didn't have to share. The korowai had to be handed back to be used again. Those korowai will have some big-time mana as the list of recipients grows.

We felt it appropriate to sing, so burst into a waiata for guests at the distinguished event. The media were all over us and, asked for a comment, I said, 'The rebels finally got their medals.'

We spent a whole hour doing interviews and missed the lunch and drinks — when we finally arrived at the catering tent on the lawns of Government House the staff were clearing the tables. But good old Dame Patsy stepped in, and a few beers and a plate of freshly made sandwiches soon arrived.

Even though this was a momentous occasion, at the end of the day a dame still needs a beer and a feed.

A dame also needs her dad. You're never prepared when you lose your dad — it hits you like a bullet.

Our father was always there for us, always teaching us things, making sure we had the skills to make it on our own. His belief in us made us who we are — strong, independent women. He never doubted us, always supported us, even though at times it must have been hard for him: living in rural New Zealand and having three gay children can't have been an easy road. But I reckon he just loved us all so much it didn't matter to him who we might fall in love with.

> **Dad's belief in us made us who we are — strong, independent women. He always supported us, even though at times it must have been hard.**

One of the things I fondly remember is the way he taught us things as kids. Like the time Jools and I asked if we could have homing pigeons. We thought we had put up a pretty good argument: that we could use the pigeons to send a message to Mum to bring us a thermos of tea and biscuits if we were working out on the farm, or we could send a message to the neighbours if we needed a hand.

Dad thought about our request for a while, and one evening after we had finished milking the cows he produced a small glass from

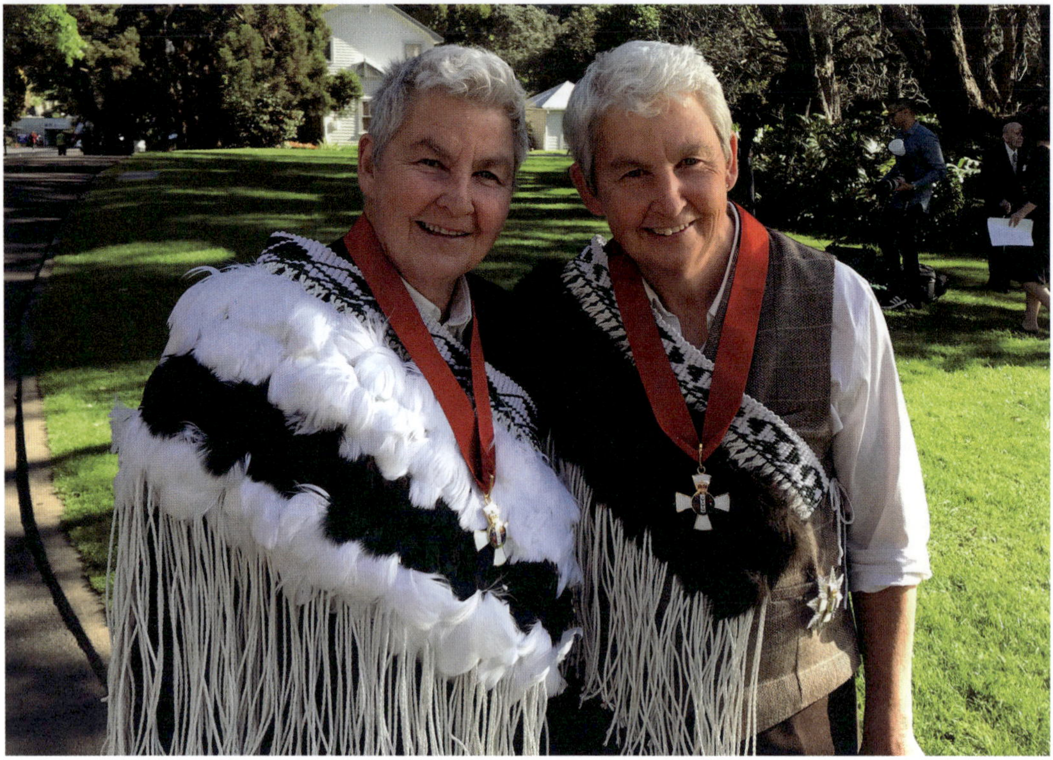

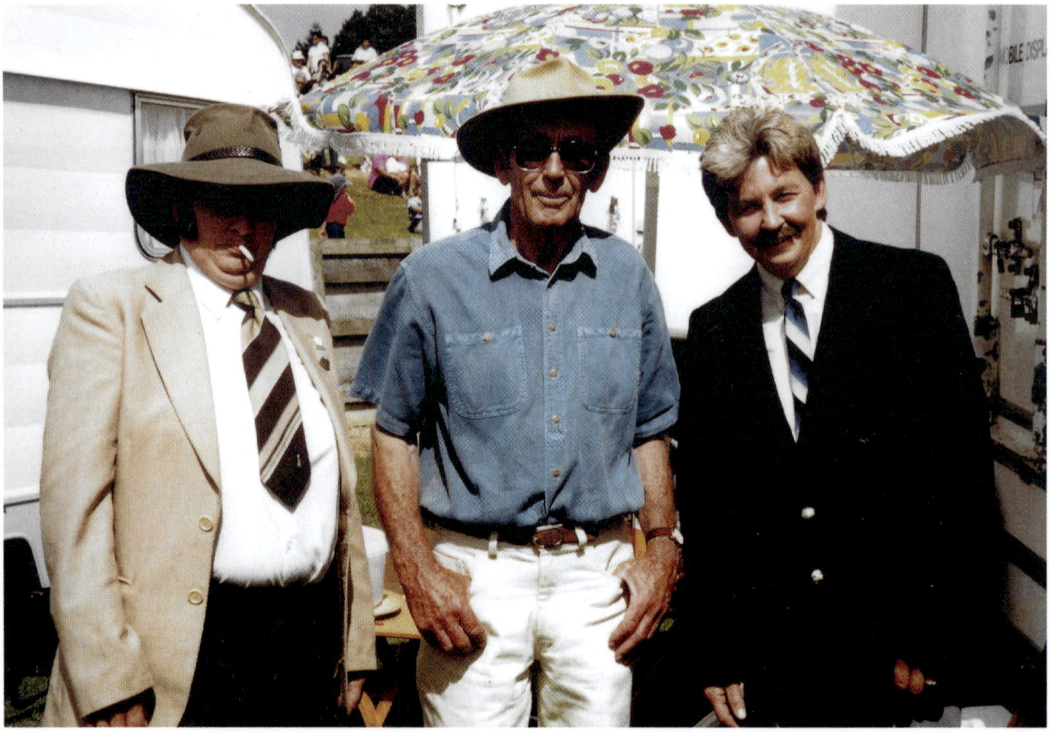

his pocket. Jools and I were sent on a mission to fill it with the biggest, ugliest chook poo we could find in the chook run.

We thought Dad had flipped his lid but took off to complete his request. We think it must have been the rooster that produced the poop we retrieved, as it was the biggest, gnarliest one we'd ever seen. We scraped it into the glass and handed it to Dad, feeling pleased with ourselves.

Dad went to the sink and filled the poop glass with cold water, then slapped it down on the bench. 'Now, which one of you girls is going to drink that?' We were both horrified. Had the old man really just asked us to drink a glassful of birdshit? We shook our heads vigorously. 'No way, Dad!'

He calmly poured the contents of the glass into the rubbish bin and said, 'There'll be no more talk of pigeons then, eh.' He explained that we collected our drinking water from the roof of our house, and pigeons roosting up there would have contaminated it.

He had turned a lesson into an adventure for us, and it worked. We never spoke of pigeons again.

Dad taught us to ride horses — not just to jump on and take off, but to have a soft feel on the horse's mouth, a good seat and an understanding of where your balance should be, so that at a walk, trot or canter there was a harmony between rider and horse.

He was there when Jools came out of hospital after her mastectomy with the wise words: 'Don't worry until you have to, and do you have Trackside on the TV?'

He stood alongside Mum, proud as punch, at our investiture as we received our damehoods, and he spoke lovingly of having another daughter in his life at my wedding to Donna.

Opposite top: The rebels show off their medals. ARANI CUTHBERT

Opposite bottom: Dad gained two more sons with the Kens. TOPP COLLECTION

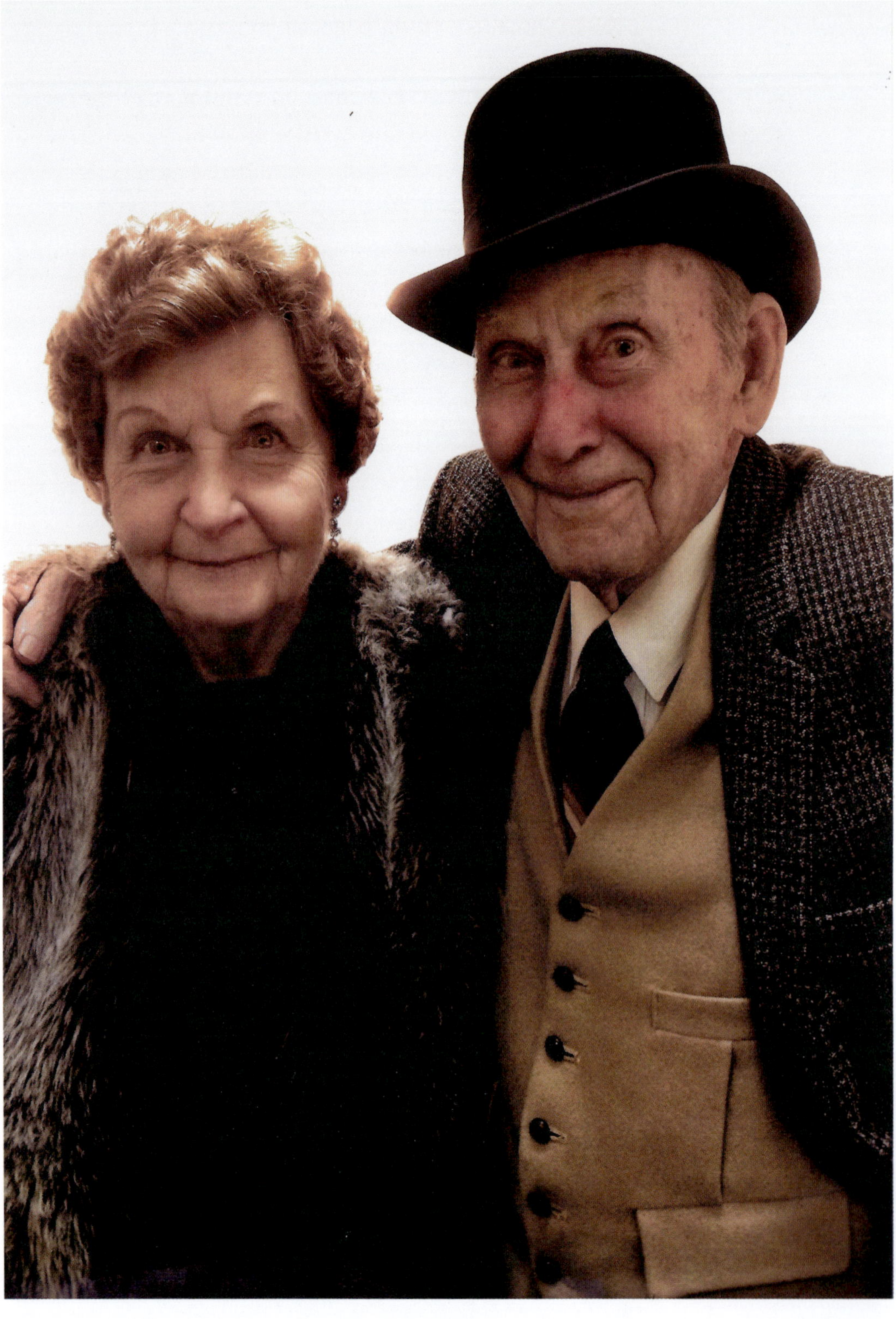

He was kind, soft and funny, and we did everything in our power to make him proud of us. But in the end it was we who were so proud of him. His love and acceptance of us showed what kind of man he was: the greatest dad on Earth.

Our last days with him were sad but also special. We all sat with him and reminisced about old times. Jools and I were not with him when he passed — I think he chose to head off without too much fuss — so we spent time with him at the funeral parlour, telling him how amazing he'd been.

We filled his coffin with his favourite things: a couple of Mum's gingernuts tucked into his old weathered hand; a newspaper — he had read one every day of his 91 years; some money — he always had coins in his pocket; and a tiny piece of horseshit pressed onto the sole of his shoe. Dad always said the smell of horses was the best smell a man could ever know.

That year was rounded out by a Lifetime Achievement Award at the *NEXT* Woman of the Year Awards. We were running out of room on the mantelpiece, but that one sits proudly in the centre to remind us of our beautiful dad.

We miss him every single day.

Opposite: The twins' parents Jean and Peter dressed to the nines for a special occasion. TOPP COLLECTION

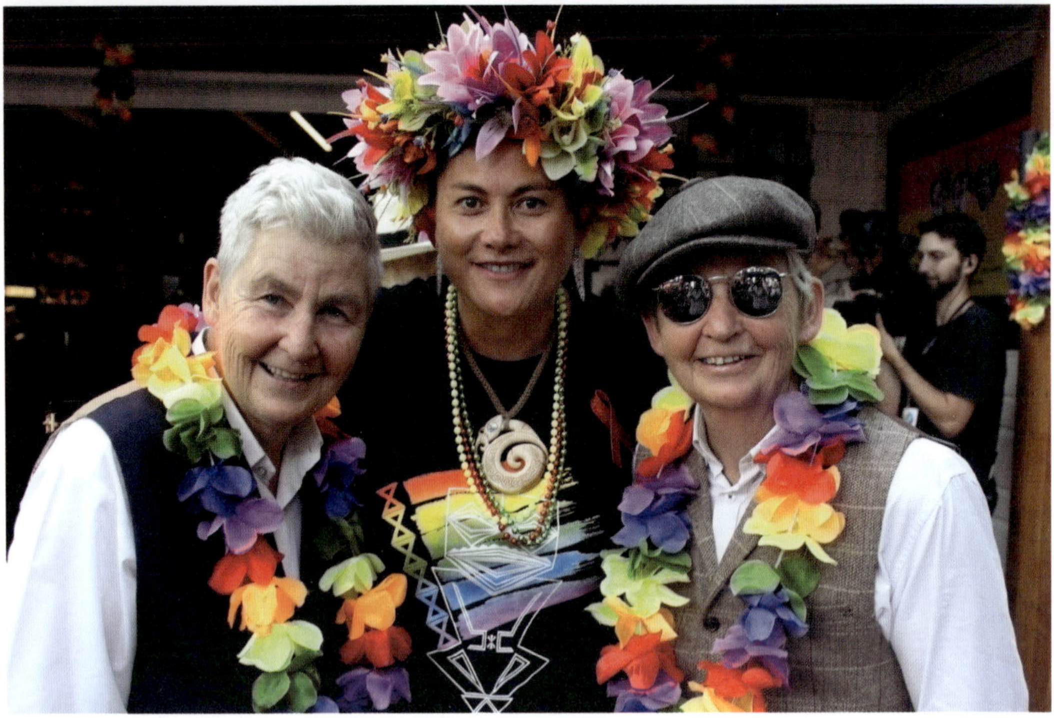

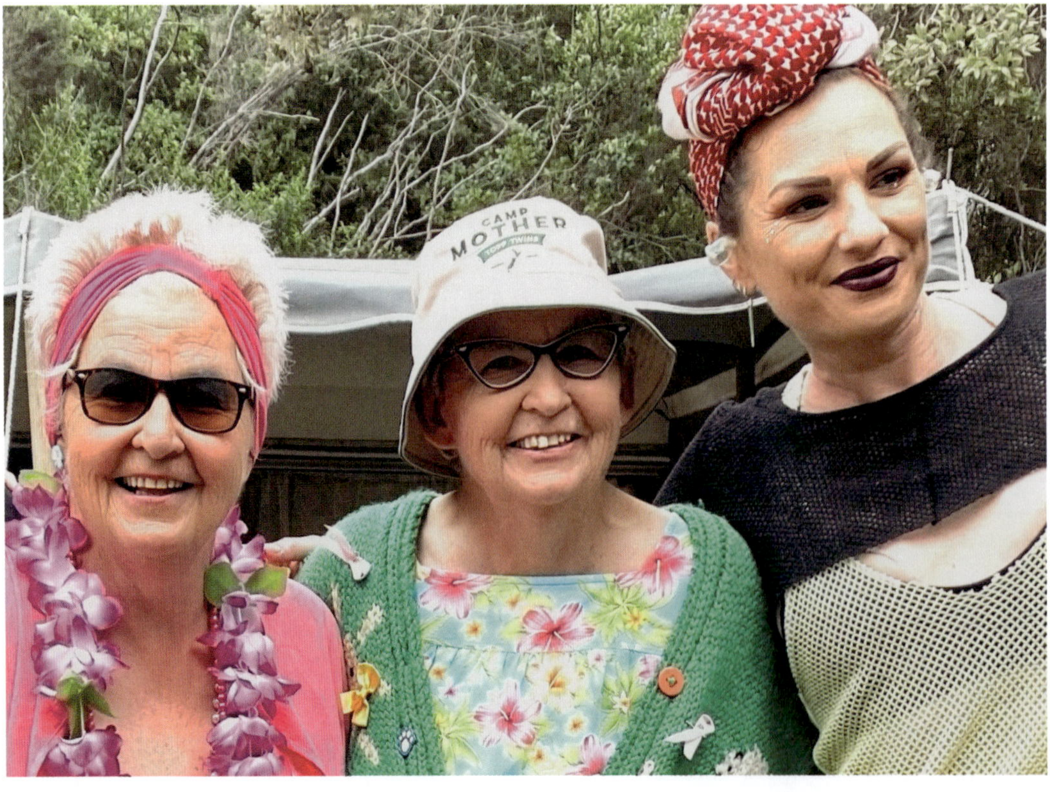
CAMP
MOTHER

29

Lockdown

The year 2020 was shaping up to be a busy one, starting with the Pride Party in February, a joyous occasion in Ponsonby. Then on 23 March at 1.30 p.m. Prime Minister Jacinda Ardern announced that New Zealand was going into lockdown for Covid-19.

We lost a whole year's worth of gigs with that one announcement. Covid effectively crushed our career, and then later in the year cancer kicked it right out of the ballpark.

I immediately landed a new job — a very important one. The day before lockdown kicked in, I raced down to Morrinsville to get Mum. At 90 she was in the high-risk group for Covid and would have been on her own through the lockdown otherwise.

I loved every minute of caring for her. We laughed, we cried. I cooked her meals she'd never tried before — I snuck garlic into

Opposite top: Lynda (left) and Jools with Labour MP and rainbow advocate Louisa Wall at the Auckland Pride Festival in February 2020, just weeks before the first Covid lockdown. ARANI CUTHBERT

Opposite bottom: Camp Mother and Camp Leader backstage at Splore 2021 with singer Hollie Smith. ARANI CUTHBERT

her evening meals and made her scrambled eggs from my free-range chickens.

When we were a bit short on food she'd say 'We'll make do', and reminded me about the food shortages her family went through during the war. She talked about her childhood, and growing up in the 1930s and '40s, and how everyone got dressed up to go to the dances at the local hall. I finally had a moment to reconnect with my beautiful mum.

My guitar sat in the corner of the lounge and I lost interest in playing it.

Lynda seemed a long way away in the South Island and we had no idea when we would see each other again.

It was weird not performing. Lockdown hit the entertainment industry hard, and when restrictions first eased and people could go back to work there were still no mass public events allowed — no gatherings of more than 10 people. Even when that number increased to 100 it wasn't much help. There's no way to make a living singing to audiences of that size.

My guitar sat in the corner of the lounge and I lost interest in playing it. I planted a beautiful vegetable garden and designed a plant protector so the chooks wouldn't eat it all.

Lockdown for Donna and me was a family affair. Oliver, our oldest boy, raced down from Christchurch and stayed with us right through lockdown. There was lots of Monopoly, experimenting with new recipes and watching movies.

LOCKDOWN

We headed into Methven once a week to stock up on groceries and it was weird driving down the main street and seeing no one. On our way home one day a couple of people waved to us from their window and that gave me the idea for 'drive-by music'. The following Saturday I rigged up our little PA and a small generator on the back of my truck, plugged my phone in the socket and off we went. Donna was in charge of choosing the music while I drove up and down every little street in Methven with loud music blaring.

The first time we did it, locals came to their windows to see where the music was coming from. The following Saturday, people were texting us to ask if we were coming with the music. By the third time, people were sitting outside on deckchairs with chilly bins, in their little bubbles. It was awesome — people loved it because it made them feel less isolated.

TV3 turned up on the fourth Saturday and did a story. I was a little worried in case we were breaking Covid rules, but we figured we were just taking the long way around to the 4 Square to get our weekly groceries, so it was all good.

In January and February of 2021 New Zealand was up and down like a yoyo with Covid alert levels changing. Then in March Auckland dropped back to Level 1, which meant that the Splore festival could go ahead at Ōrere Point.

The theme for 2021 was Mother, and the organisers thought Camp Mother and Camp Leader would fit the bill perfectly. We had never done Splore — it was mainly dance parties and DJs and big acts from overseas — but because of Covid in 2021 it was an all-Kiwi lineup. Jools and I headed to the festival site in her old horse-truck, complete with beds, a kitchen and space for costumes and guitars.

The vibe was amazing. Festival-goers were excited to be out and about enjoying live music, and every performer was relieved to be back working. The site was idyllic, overlooking the ocean, with amazing food vendors, beer tents, dance parties till 4 a.m. and an atmosphere of peace, love and happiness. Life seemed to be good again.

By August, the whole country was back in lockdown.

October 2021 rolled around. I hadn't seen Jools since the Splore festival back in March, and it was the longest we'd been apart — seven months and counting. I missed her and our time together performing around New Zealand. The South Island had dropped down a few levels but Auckland stayed at Level 3, so we were still unable to visit each other.

I decided to organise a fishing trip. Jools had her horses; my passion was fly-fishing for trout, and it was still my go-to activity. I had been asked to be a trustee for Hunters for Conservation and I was looking forward to getting involved with the new venture.

Then I got a text from the breast cancer screening programme. Could I come in for a checkup? Due to the Covid lockdown I had missed the mobile screening bus that passed through Ashburton.

'No worries,' I replied. I'd been on the programme for 10 years by that point and every screen had come back clear. So I raced up to Rolleston for my appointment in late October, having booked my fishing trip for 23–24 November.

Five days out from the trip I was recalled for a biopsy. All good, I thought, when the procedure was done and dusted by 1 p.m. The

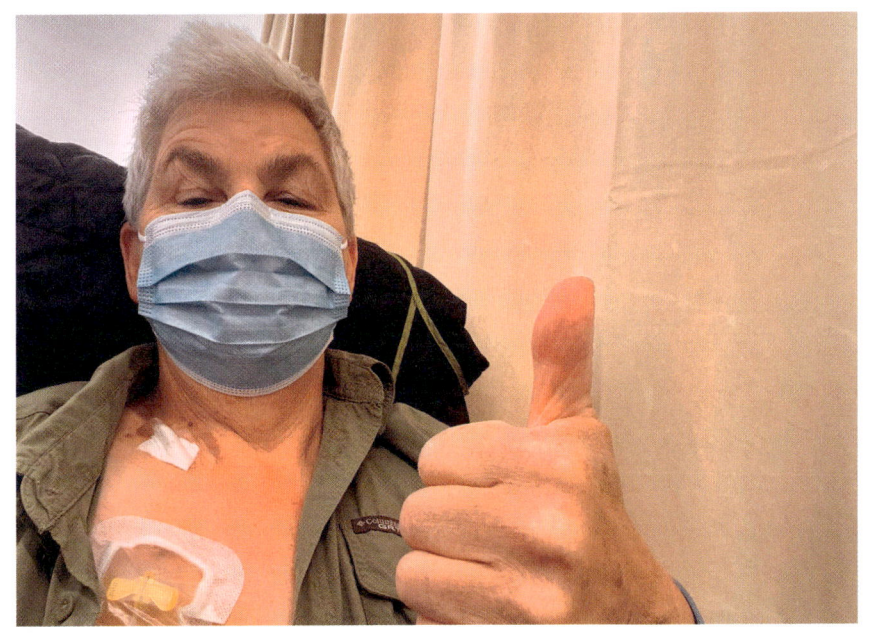

Top: Lynda with her big brown trout, just one day before her cancer diagnosis in 2021. KEVIN PAYNE / BACK COUNTRY TROUT

Bottom: Lynda giving the thumbs-up during her first chemo treatment. TOPP COLLECTION

doctor said she'd have the results on 25 November, and I breathed a sigh of relief: I could go on the fishing trip.

And what a trip it was. I met up with my mate Darcy, a keen fisherman, and my favourite fishing guide, Kevin from Back Country Trout. We had two glorious days of fishing in the Mackenzie district.

I almost forgot about my early morning appointment with the doctor on the 25th, as I was still thinking about the beautiful eight-pound brown trout I'd caught and released. The first thing my doctor asked was, 'Did you catch any fish?' I proudly pulled out my phone and showed her the big brown.

Maybe she was trying to soften the blow, because the next thing she said to me was, 'You've got grade 4 invasive breast cancer.'

I was riding my horse when I got the call from Lynda to say she had been diagnosed with breast cancer. I think I cried for a whole hour.

Auckland was still at Level 3 so I couldn't even get on a plane and go to her. It was a nightmare. Finally, on 21 December 2021, Mum and I were able to travel to see her in Christchurch Hospital. I remember saying to her, the day after her double mastectomy, 'Goodbye Camp Mother, hello Ken.' She managed a smile.

The hospital was still under Covid rules and would only let in one visitor at a time so as I spoke to Lynda, Mum was left crying in the waiting room. It was so hard not to be all together. I came out to let Mum see Lynda and then it was my turn to blubber in the waiting room. Afterwards, Mum and I headed to Methven to be with Donna.

When Lynda arrived home three days later it was a great celebration — many friends arrived to comfort her. She did amazingly well, healing from her surgery, but her scars looked like a giant shark bite, going from one side of her chest to the other.

We all had Christmas together and it was nice to feel like a family again.

30

Sneaky Little Creep

Back in Auckland I struggled to understand: why us? Why did we get cancer? In the years since my initial diagnosis in 2006, my cancer had been on the move, and in year 14 (2020) a CT scan had revealed six new tumours growing in my chest wall. They found another one in my neck a few months later. The cancer had metastasised. My doctor prescribed letrozole to help reduce oestrogen, which is what the cancer feeds on. The letrozole did the job for a while before the cancer outsmarted it — a blood test showed the medication had stopped working. It's a sneaky little creep, cancer.

In February 2022, three months after Lynda's diagnosis, there was another development. I was out with my workmate Pieta, trimming the hooves on a neighbour's horses, when a pain in my back floored me so badly that I had to lie down immediately. Pieta calmly put down her tools and rang an ambulance.

At the hospital, a scan showed that I had a large new tumour in my back, between my ninth and tenth ribs. I had been getting a sharp pain in that area every time I bent over or trimmed a horse's hoof — I didn't know it at the time, but I'd been squishing the tumour between my bones.

Jools (left) and Lynda, both living with cancer. KRISTIAN FRIRES / MINDFOOD

The emergency doctor who was telling me the bad news also said the tumour was a sitter for a zap of radiation. It would be a very straight forward procedure over seven days.

I took a deep breath . . . and said yes.

First they used a machine to find the exact location of the tumour, and tattooed a dot on my chest to guide the radiologist. I told Mum I'd got a tattoo and she had a meltdown.

I had seven days of radiation treatment, and another scan a few months later showed the tumour had reduced in size by at least 4 mm. It doesn't sound like a lot but it was enough to take the pressure off my ribs and stop the pain completely.

Splore 2021 was the last gig we did before Covid and then cancer put an end to our performances. It was a great one to go out on, but by the end of February 2022 we had not performed for close to a year. It was quite an adjustment because prior to that we had been on the road for 40 years without a break. We certainly hadn't played every day, but we'd always had another performance just around the corner. One scary bit about all of this was that we suddenly had no income.

As the Covid restrictions eased, we knew people would be expecting to see us again and we needed to let them know that we would not be performing for a while longer because now Lynda had invasive breast cancer, and mine had flared up again.

We decided to get one media outlet to break the news, so we wouldn't have to deal with a lot of media attention while we were both quite unwell. Miriama Kamo from TVNZ's *Sunday* was our reporter of choice. We have always admired Miriama, and certainly appreciated her integrity and support.

The piece aired on 26 March 2022 at 7 p.m. and we released a statement that was picked up by national media the next morning.

It was probably the hardest interview we'd ever done. We couldn't be together for it and had to be filmed in separate locations. And normally when we talked with the media it was about something positive, like a new recording or another national tour or an award — something that made us happy. So how were we to handle this? It felt like we'd lost our identity — we were no longer entertainers but twins who both had breast cancer.

It sucked big time.

But the outpouring of love and support from New Zealanders was immediate and heartwarming. My darling Mary helped set up a Givealittle page and we had incredible support from that. Fans donated money and sent messages of support and told us they loved us. It made a huge difference.

> It was probably the hardest interview we'd ever done . . . but the outpouring of love and support from New Zealanders was immediate and heartwarming.

We both got on with our respective treatments. I had my seven days of radiation on the new tumour between my ribs, and Lynda continued with the chemotherapy that had started earlier in February. Covid restrictions meant I couldn't be there for her the way she'd cared for me when I had given her the same news 16 years before. She went through her entire chemo treatment alone, which was especially hard for Donna.

Lynda had three months of monthly chemo, then switched to a weekly regimen with a different type of chemo that required her to take steroids as well. She had a pretty tough time of it, as most people do. Chemotherapy makes you feel like shit. We helpfully told her she looked like Uncle Fester from the Addams Family when she lost all her hair.

As Covid restrictions began to ease, and although Lynda was at risk if she caught Covid because her immune system was compromised by the chemo, we made the call to be together for our 64th birthday in May 2022.

Oh, what a reunion it was. It was so good to be able to hug and hold each other again. We spent four beautiful days together with Arani, Felicity, Cody and our mate Linden, who was now living in Australia and flew across. We all stayed in units at Musterer's Acommodation Fairlie. We had the big unit, which is an old renovated woolshed. We had a roaring fire, an outside hot tub, and we ate famous Fairlie pies for lunch. Life almost felt like normal again.

I travelled home and Donna rang to say Lynda had Covid, which meant they had to suspend her chemo treatment. I got Covid five days later.

I was pretty crook by now after three and a half months of chemo and a dose of Covid, and Donna was exhausted, as she had been holding the fort at the café and trying to be my caregiver as well. Our friends Nick and Selina from Mt Somers stepped in and gave Donna a break for a few days. The boys from the local Methven fire brigade turned up with Ross the local cop to do the lawns, and a whole gang from the Alford Forest fire brigade — which I am a member of — came and re-metalled our driveway. Ladies from around the district dropped off pre-cooked meals for us. I cried every time in the face of this kindness. They are all such good-hearted people.

Left: A photo of Lynda the twins shared on social media in March 2022. TOPP COLLECTION

Below: Jools and Lynda, reunited in 2022 for their 64th birthday. FELICITY MORGAN-RHIND

I started my weekly treatments again, but with still a month to go I developed chemo-induced peripheral neuropathy. This is when the nerve endings in your feet or hands get damaged, and it can be permanent.

Oncology recommended that Lynda should stop the chemo immediately. This was just such disappointing news after she had come so far. There is no known cure for peripheral neuropathy, and it is painful and persistent. For the first three weeks after her diagnosis Lynda was using walking sticks to get around and was prescribed pain-relief drugs that gave her horrible side-effects. She stopped taking them and I went on a mission and found a plant-based treatment out of America. But whereas the drugs were free, the plant-based treatment was not.

I was offered a new cancer treatment, involving hormone tablets and painful injections in both buttocks every month for the rest of my life. Who the hell comes up with stuff?

Mum used to say you can't kill a weed, and Lynda has got better on this new treatment but still can't feel her toes and gets bad pain in the soles of her feet.

Later in 2022 I was offered a new cancer treatment, involving hormone tablets and painful injections in both buttocks every month for the rest of my life. Who the hell comes up with stuff? I walked out with a firm *no*.

The possible side-effects didn't excite me much either: mouth ulcers, lung damage and infection at the injection site. But what if it was going to reduce the tumours?

I returned to the hospital a couple of weeks later with my old mate Cody, who is a district nurse, to talk to the oncologist once more. I was over it all by this stage and became quite tearful. It was all too much.

Cody suggested we grab a cuppa and she'd explain it all so I could get my head around it. I thought she was going to talk me through all the medical jargon, but as I sipped my trusty cup of Earl Grey she just said, 'It's a no-brainer, Jools. It might save your life. Just do it.'

And so I did.

31

Topp Class: The Topp Twins Tribute Show

Lynda's hair finally grew back after the chemo, and I seemed to be handling my injections okay, so when Arani rang to ask whether we thought we were up to performing a couple of songs in the Topp Twins tribute show planned for November 2022, we jumped at the chance. Oh, to be back on the boards again . . .

We felt like Covid and cancer had killed our careers, and Arani was out of work now as well. The tribute show was her idea. *Topp Class*, featuring some of New Zealand's best entertainers, would be filmed in front of a live audience at Auckland's iconic Civic Theatre and would help raise money for us while we both went through cancer treatment and were unable to work. The show also celebrated our 40th anniversary as performers.

All our old mates came together to help make this spectacular event happen and everyone gave generously of their time. *Topp Class* was a reunion of the best in New Zealand showbiz. Mike Mizrahi and Marie Adams, our dear friends from Watershed Theatre days, jumped on board as event directors extraordinaire. Musical

From top: Three dames on stage together as Jools and Lynda perform with Dame Hinewehi Mohi; the grand finale of *Topp Class*. NORRIE MONTGOMERY / DIVA PRODUCTIONS

director Don McGlashan did the most incredible job, creating scores to our songs and rehearsing with all the New Zealand musicians over many months from his home in Vancouver, where he now lives for half the year. Jo Kilgour, now one of New Zealand's top lighting directors, got her first break working with us on tour in the early 1990s and learnt a lot about lighting from Lynda. She pulled together the most awesome technical crew for *Topp Class* and managed much of the live show's production. Meanwhile Carol Harding, legendary stage manager, helped wrangle a cast and crew of more than a hundred people.

Many of New Zealand's top performers stepped up when we needed them the most: singer/songwriters Tami Neilson, Anika Moa, Dame Hinewehi Mohi, Troy Kingi, Ria Hall, Hollie Smith, Jackie Clarke, Annie Crummer, Bella Kalolo, Don McGlashan, Sam Ford and Trudi Green, and Jenny Mitchell and her twin sisters, Maegan and Nicola, who are young rising country music stars. We loved hearing our songs sung by these incredible artists, along with new songs like 'Find a River', which Tami and the Mitchell twins wrote — it's about us having cancer and connecting through the river and the sea.

Some of Aotearoa's best comedians joined the lineup: comedy duo Front Lawn (our old mates Don McGlashan and Harry Sinclair) re-formed after 31 years for our special night; Tom Sainsbury and Chris Parker paid tribute to Camp Mother and Camp Leader; Michèle A'Court and fellow Huntly-arian Te Radar were there; and Australia's king of beige Bob Downe flew in from Sydney. The very talented Karen O'Leary was the MC for the evening. Karen had been my on-screen daughter in the TV series *Wellington Paranormal*.

Don had brought on board some of the country's finest musical groups as well. The live stage band consisted of Chet O'Connell, Tom Broome and Chip Matthews. The Blackbird Ensemble, Viva Voce choir, North Shore Brass and the cute-as kids' ukulele ensemble Kiwileles all featured, as well as Jess Hindin on fiddle.

Top: The ticket design for the *Topp Class* show.
HELEN CISOWSKI / DIVA PRODUCTIONS

Bottom: Chris Parker as Camp Mother (left) and Tom Sainsbury as Camp Leader. NORRIE MONTGOMERY / DIVA PRODUCTIONS

As if all that wasn't enough, the fabulous Buckwheat and spectacular drag artistes Nikita Iman, Vanessa LaRoux, Shavorn Aborealis, Medulla Oblongata and Hugo Grrrl performed a special remix of a Topp Twins classic, 'Friday Night Get Up'.

> **It was an extraordinary show and the most joyous occasion. Thinking about it brings tears to our eyes.**

What a night! From the spine-tingling opening by Ngāti Whātua's Te Whare Karioi to the finale of 'Untouchable Girls' with everyone — including us — on the stage, it was an extraordinary show and the most joyous occasion. Thinking about it brings tears to our eyes. So much love poured out that night. We were blown away and felt incredibly supported.

The live show sold out, with more than 2,000 tickets snapped up. It was filmed and aired by Prime TV, which jumped at the chance after TVNZ turned it down, and the wonderful team at NZ On Air agreed to fund it. It's so great that this special show was captured on film for posterity.

Soon after, in early 2023, we played at the Lake Hayes A&P show just outside Queenstown. We said yes when Arani told us about the invitation, hoping we'd be well enough to perform. It was a few months away, and gave us something to aim for. We had played that show once before and loved it. This time they organised a golf cart for us to get around on, and it was such a blast to be back on stage again.

I hadn't played guitar for about two years so all the callouses on the ends of my fingers had worn off, and practising was a bit painful until they hardened up again.

The biggest problem I faced was that since my double mastectomy there was nothing there to hold up Camp Mother's iconic pink jumpsuit. I tried it on and the bloody thing fell down around my ankles. I rang Dawn, my English friend in Methven who has done costumes for Aerosmith, Boyzone, Meat Loaf and Metallica, just to name a few. She said, 'Don't worry, I'll be around to your place tomorrow.' She made me a beautiful and decent-sized pair of breasts out of an old bra and some padding, and as she headed off out the door she yelled, 'Can I put "Making Camp Mother's Boobies" on my CV?'

Jools said they looked like the tail-lights on a 1950s Cadillac but they did the job. Camp Mother's jumpsuit stayed up all day. It was good to be playing the old gal again.

Epilogue

So here we are. A scan in February 2023 showed that after four months of my new treatment all my tumours had decreased in size. My lymph nodes flare up now and again and make me cough, but hey, I'm still here, I'm still excited about my life, and although I can't ride the day after my injections, my horse doesn't mind waiting.

In 2023 Mum is still here for us with a hug and always some new weird and whacky saying. She's 92 now and is a mighty fine inspiration.

As of May 2023 I have been drug-free for six months. I'm not too sure where my cancer's at — I'm hoping it's gone away — but I have a few options. The doctors want to put me on drugs for the next few years. My feet hurt, but right now I'm just happy, so happy, that my sister is still here after 17 years of cancer. She's a good role model for me: she eats healthy and does the things she loves. So, I'll plant my vege garden and head upstream to one of our pristine South Island rivers and go fly-fishing, and if I catch a trout I will kiss it and release it back into the wild.

Our new motto: go hard or go to bed.

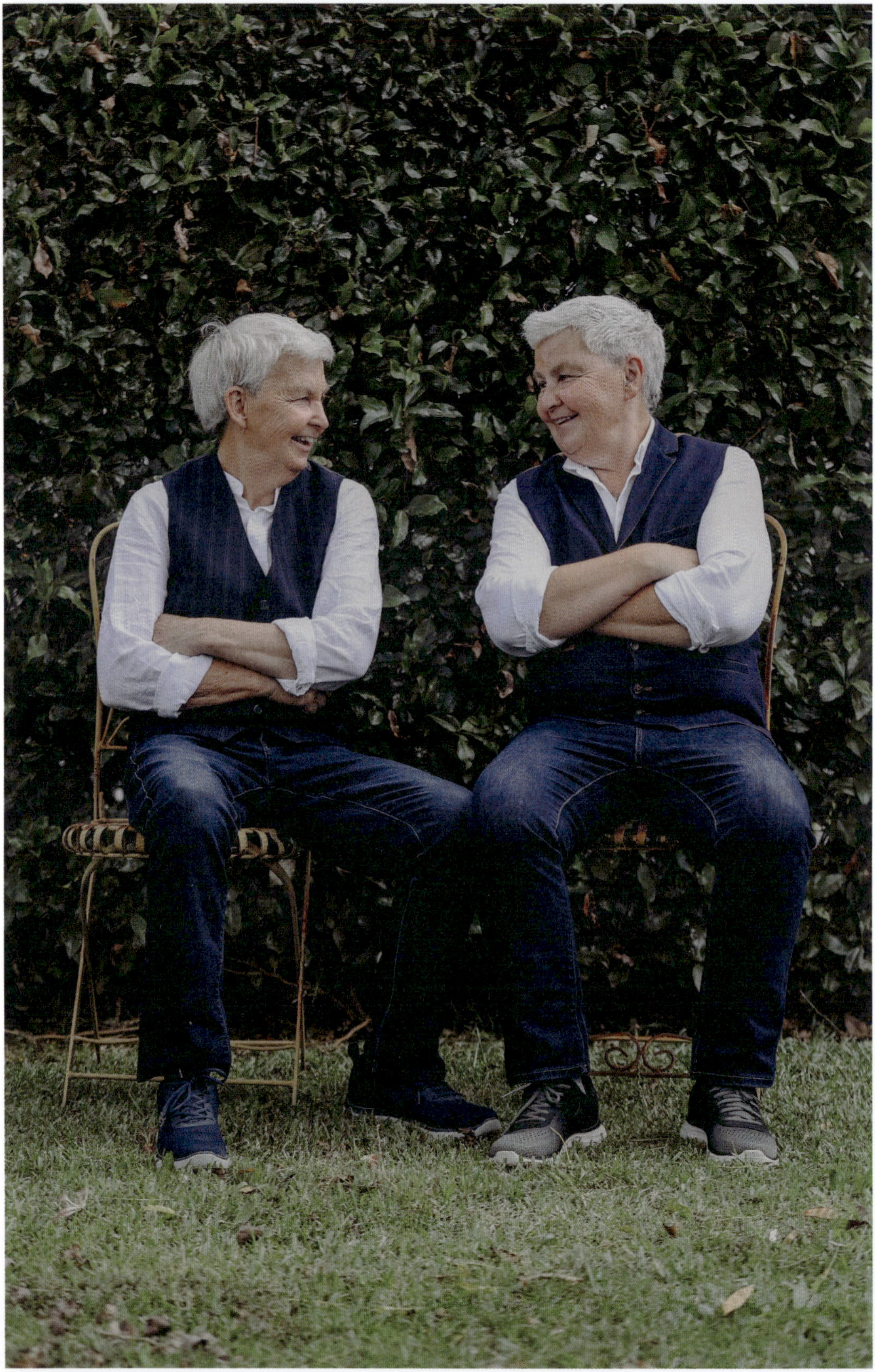

EPILOGUE

We're at the end of this book — we hope you have enjoyed the ride.

Where to from here? Be kind, like Jacinda said. Don't be afraid to give up power in order to gain power, stand up for what you believe in, be nice to the planet, stop judging people, and start loving our diversity.

We're going to need one another to survive in this crazy world, which is getting crazier.

Start sharing your knowledge, turn off your phone for a while, make a meal for someone, be generous with your time, do something in the community without pay, ask for help if you need it, tell your mama you love her, sing a song even if you can't sing, hug your dog, lend an ear to a mate, don't try to solve all the problems of the world in one day — and just sit and listen to others for a while.

Dames Jools and Lynda
The Topp Twins

P.S. Musical duo for hire
Very experienced
Very professional and self-sufficient
Available for weddings, birthdays and bar mitzvahs
(Can help with the dishes and stack chairs.)

Opposite: Dame Jools (left) and Dame Lynda after being announced as finalists for the 2023 Kiwibank New Zealander of the Year Award.
COURTESY OF KIWIBANK NEW ZEALANDER OF THE YEAR AWARDS NGĀ TOHU POU KŌHURE O AOTEAROA

Left: The twins make their mark on the Celebrity Walk of Fame at Auckland's Victoria Park Market. PHOTOGRAPHER UNKNOWN

Below: Lynda (left) and Jools celebrate being awarded honorary doctorates from the University of Waikato in 2011. STEPHEN BARKER / UNIVERSITY OF WAIKATO

Topp Twins Awards and Honours

1987	*Listener* Film and Television Awards. Best Entertainer: Topp Twins
1987	*Listener* Film and Television Awards. Best Entertainment Programme: *Topp Twins Special*
1987	*Listener* Film and Television Awards. Best Original Music: *Topp Twins Special*
1997	*TV Guide* Television Awards. Best Performance in an Entertainment Programme: Topp Twins, *Do Not Adjust Your Twin-set*, episode 2
2001	New Zealand Music Awards. Best Country Album: *Grass Highway*
2004	New Zealand Order of Merit for Services to Entertainment
2005	New Zealand Music Awards. Best Country Album: *Flowergirls and Cowgirls*
2006	New Zealand Music Awards. Best Country Song: 'Tamworth'
2008	Inducted into the New Zealand Music Hall of Fame
2009	Melbourne International Film Festival. Audience Award for Best Documentary: *The Topp Twins: Untouchable Girls*
2009	Qantas Film and Television Awards. Best Feature Film — Under $1 Million: *The Topp Twins: Untouchable Girls*
2009	Qantas Film and Television Awards. Original Music: *The Topp Twins: Untouchable Girls*
2009	Toronto International Film Festival. Audience Award for Best Documentary: *The Topp Twins: Untouchable Girls*

2009	National Country Music Awards. Country Music Group/Duo Award
2010	Brattleboro Film Festival (US). Best of Festival Award: *The Topp Twins: Untouchable Girls*
2010	Outfest Film Festival (US). Special Programming Award for Freedom: *The Topp Twins: Untouchable Girls*
2010	RiverRun Film Festival (US). Audience Award for Best Documentary: *The Topp Twins: Untouchable Girls*
2010	Nashville Film Festival. Audience Award for Best Documentary: *The Topp Twins: Untouchable Girls*; Best GLBT Film: *The Topp Twins: Untouchable Girls*
2010	Florida Film Festival. Audience Award for Best International Feature Film: *The Topp Twins: Untouchable Girls*
2010	Göteborg Film Festival (Sweden). Audience Dragon Award for Best Feature: *The Topp Twins: Untouchable Girls*
2010	Seattle International Film Festival. Lena Sharpe Women in Cinema Award: *The Topp Twins: Untouchable Girls*
2010	FIFO Oceanian International Documentary Film Festival (Tahiti). Special Jury Award: *The Topp Twins: Untouchable Girls*
2010	Portland International Film Festival. Best Feature Documentary: *The Topp Twins: Untouchable Girls*
2010	Mendocino Film Festival. Best Documentary: *The Topp Twins: Untouchable Girls*
2010	Reeling: 29th Chicago Lesbian and Gay International Film Festival. Best Documentary Feature: *The Topp Twins: Untouchable Girls*
2010	Inside Out Film Festival (Canada). Best Documentary: *The Topp Twins: Untouchable Girls*
2010	NewFest Film Festival (US). Best Documentary Film: *The Topp Twins: Untouchable Girls*
2010	Rocky Mountain Women's Film Festival. Madelyn's Choice Award: *The Topp Twins: Untouchable Girls*
2010	21st Hamburg International Queer Film Festival. Best Documentary: *The Topp Twins: Untouchable Girls*

TOPP TWINS AWARDS AND HONOURS

2010   Miami Gay and Lesbian Film Festival. Best Documentary: *The Topp Twins: Untouchable Girls*

2010   Palm Springs International Film Festival. Best of the Fest Program: *The Topp Twins: Untouchable Girls*

2010   Qantas Film and Television Awards. Best Entertainment Programme: *The Topp Twins and the APO*

2010   Wintec (Waikato Institute of Technology): Honorary Masters of Arts (Music)

2011   University of Waikato: Honorary Doctorates in the Arts

2014   Gore Country Music Hands of Fame

2017   New Zealand Television Awards. Best Presenter — Entertainment: *Topp Country*, season 2

2018   Dame Companions of the New Zealand Order of Merit for services to entertainment

2019   *NEXT* Woman of the Year Awards: Lifetime Achievement Award

2023   Kiwibank New Zealander of the Year Awards: Finalists

From top: Lynda (left) and Jools at Auckland Zoo in 2010, supporting the Save the Kiwi organisation; The twins with their darling mum. TOPP COLLECTION

Acknowledgements

Our heartfelt thanks go out to the people who made this book happen: our wonderful publisher Jenny Hellen and the hard-working team at Allen & Unwin, including Leanne McGregor, whose patience and perseverance helped us get over the finish line; our insightful editor Rachel Scott, who instilled confidence in us as new writers; our diligent proofreaders Teresa McIntyre and Mike Wagg; and our very patient designer Katrina Duncan. We wish to thank all the wonderful photographers who have given permission for their photos to be included, especially Bruce Connew, Gil Hanly, John Miller, Mark Wilson, Kristian Frires, Mel Church, Toni Armstrong Jr., Romi Curl, Anne Crozier, the late Peter Molloy, the late Jocelyn Carlin and our friend Sally Tagg, who has photographed us and our characters for 30 years. And huge thanks of course to our manager, Arani, who continues to move mountains for us.

We would also like to give a shout-out to two organisations who are fighting the good fight against breast cancer. The annual Terrier Race Against Time fundraising event was set up by six local women to provide support for all women diagnosed with breast cancer in the Gisborne/Tairāwhiti region. It's all about women helping women with cancer in their own communities. To Pam Hamilton and all the Gisborne gals and volunteers who help run the most amazing event: we have had such joyous moments supporting you on the day and it is one of our favourite gigs. Long may it last — our hats go off to you.

Casting for Recovery New Zealand aims to enhance the lives of women with breast cancer by connecting them to each other and to nature through the therapeutic sport of fly-fishing. To Sherrie Feickert-Carty, who had the vision to launch the New Zealand branch, and to all the amazing volunteers, guides and members of the trout-fishing community: thank you for what you do. I had the best time with you all when I came on one of the retreats; your dedication is inspiring.

Finally, to every single person who has supported the Topp Twins or has come to see our live shows: you're amazing. Your dedication, love and support has kept us going for more than 40 years.

Arohanui
Lynda and Jools

topptwins.com
ondemand.topptwins.com
facebook.com/topptwins